D1254005

NATHAN BOONE AND THE AMERICAN FRONTIER

Missouri Biography Series
William E. Foley, Editor

Nathan Boone. *Archives & Manuscripts Division of the Oklahoma Historical Society.*

NATHAN BOONE AND THE AMERICAN FRONTIER

R. DOUGLAS HURT

UNIVERSITY OF MISSOURI PRESS
COLUMBIA AND LONDON

Library of Congress Cataloging-in-Publication Data

Hurt, R. Douglas.
    Nathan Boone and the American frontier / R. Douglas Hurt.
      p.   cm.
    Includes bibliographical references (p.   ) and index.
    ISBN 0-8262-1159-3 (alk. paper)
    1. Boone, Nathan, 1781–1856.   2. Pioneers—Missouri—Biography.
3. Frontier and pioneer life—Missouri.   4. Missouri—Biography.
I. Title.
F466.B68H87   1998
977.8'03'092—dc21
    [B]   97-40306
                                                              CIP

∞™ This paper meets the requirements of the
American National Standard for Permanence of Paper
for Printed Library Materials, Z39.48, 1984.

Designer: Stephanie Foley
Typesetter: BOOKCOMP
Printer and binder: Thomson-Shore, Inc.
Typefaces: Galliard and ITC Cancione

FOR
MARY ELLEN, ADLAI, AND AUSTIN

CONTENTS

PREFACE

THIS PROJECT began many years ago when William E. Foley at Central Missouri State University conceived the idea for a biography series that would emphasize the people who had made contributions to the history of Missouri and to the nation. I was present for the initial meeting about this series with the University of Missouri Press in 1989. At that time an invited committee of historians agreed that a Missouri biography series should appeal to general readers who were interested in history as well as to professional historians. Over time, Bill Foley and Beverly Jarrett, Director of the University of Missouri Press, invited scholars to contribute to the series. I am particularly honored to have been asked to write a biography of Nathan Boone, who remains the most recognized child of Daniel Boone, although only by a few historians who are interested in the American frontier. I accepted the challenge, however, with a good deal of trepidation, because Nathan spent most of his time hunting and trapping or riding with the Missouri Rangers and U.S. Army Dragoons rather than writing letters, keeping a diary, or saving his personal papers. Consequently, his life had to be reconstructed primarily through the papers of others as well as government documents, especially those that pertain to the military. Despite a dearth of personal papers, however, Boone left footprints on the American frontier that can still be seen today in the form of buildings and place names. He also left a legacy of service that helped the army execute both military and Indian policy and contributed to the settlement of the frontier. Without men like Nathan Boone, the army on the frontier could not have met the needs of Congress, the War Department, or the American public.

This book has been made possible only by the help of many people, and I want to thank them for their invaluable assistance. At the State Historical Society of Missouri, James W. Goodrich, Laurel Boeckman, Ara Kaye, Fae Sotham, and Lucille Malone, as well as Sharon Fleming, Randy Roberts, and Sue McCubbin at the Western Historical Manuscript Collection at the University of Missouri–Columbia, once again proved that knowledge of the collections and courtesy need not be separate characteristics for professionals who aid historians with their scholarly research. I am also indebted for the generosity and help that I received from Martha Clevenger, Dennis Northcott, Barbara Stole, Dorothy Woods, and Edna Smith at the Missouri Historical Society in St. Louis. Carolyn Collings and Patsy Luebbert at the Missouri State Archives also provided crucial aid. Walter Schroeder and Adrianne Nold in the Department of Geography at the University of Missouri–Columbia prepared the maps, for which I am grateful. At the State Historical Society of Iowa, Ellen Sulser graciously assisted my research. Bob Blackburn at the Oklahoma Historical Society also gave essential assistance.

John K. Hulston extended many courtesies and much information about Nathan Boone when I visited Springfield and Ash Grove during the course of my research. Ted Belue at Murray State University, Ken Kamper of Hazelwood, Missouri, and James Denny at the Missouri Department of Natural Resources provided expert information about the construction of the Boone home in St. Charles County. Tom Isern aided with the bibliography.

At Iowa State University, Wayne Pedersen, Susan Congdon, and Mary Jane Thune provided their customary excellent service for interlibrary loan requests. Becky Jordan in Special Collections at Iowa State aided the location of the illustrations. My research assistants Stephanie Carpenter and Kirk Hutson kept the project moving when I had to give attention to other matters. I am thankful for their loyal and professional support.

I am also grateful for the aid of my wife, Mary Ellen Hurt, who read the manuscript and offered valuable advice for its improvement.

Last, this research was supported by a Richard S. Brownlee Award from the State Historical Society of Missouri in Columbia.

NATHAN BOONE AND THE AMERICAN FRONTIER

1

THE EARLY YEARS

NATHAN BOONE came into the world on March 2, 1781, the tenth child of Daniel and Rebecca Boone, at Boone's Station, halfway between Boonesborough and Lexington, Kentucky. This location one day would be the heart of the Bluegrass region, but in the late eighteenth century Boone's Station never became more than a cluster of log cabins for some fifteen to twenty families who had moved west to claim lands, raise their families, and live their lives free from the interferences of government and other institutions. This would not be the last stop for the Boones, who made moving a lifetime habit, but Daniel at the age of forty-six and Rebecca at the age of forty-two no doubt surprised themselves with the birth of yet another child after twenty years of marriage.[1]

From the beginning Nathan had a special relationship with his father, although Daniel was not at home for his birth. In November 1780, Virginia divided Kentucky into the three counties of Fayette, Jefferson, and Lincoln. By early spring, the people in Fayette County had elected Daniel as their representative to the Virginia legislature. Because the evidence is unclear and even contradictory, no one can be certain when he left to take his seat in the legislature, although he apparently had arrived in Richmond by April 1781. When Cornwallis's troops threatened to take the city, the legislature withdrew to Charlottesville, but a large mounted force under Sir Banastre Tarleton soon forced the legislators to flee. Boone, however, delayed too long, helping load the legislature's records onto a wagon.

When he left Charlottesville for Kentucky, British soldiers controlled the countryside and soon seized Boone and learned his identity. Tarleton held Boone for a brief time during which he reportedly was treated with "kindness and liberality," but the British either released Boone or he escaped, although he remained in British custody as late as June 17. By the end of August, however, Daniel had made his way home, anxious to see his wife and newly born child. Unknown to him, two of his daughters—Jemima, who had married Flanders Callaway, and Susannah, wife of William Hays—also had given birth during his absence. Rebecca and his daughters apparently had planned to play a trick on Boone when he arrived home, and almost immediately after he had entered the home presented him with three babies and asked him to pick his own child. Nathan later proudly recalled that his father "quickly recognized the right one." During the course of his childhood Nathan and Daniel formed a bond that would keep them together until his father's final stop on the Missouri frontier.[2]

But that came later. During the last two decades of the eighteenth century, Nathan Boone's world was crowded, noisy, and comfortably protective, but it was also a world of isolation, danger, and fear. At Boone's Station, Daniel had built a double-pen log house to shelter his five children who remained at home. Although Israel had reached his early twenties and would soon be ready to depart from home and while daughters Levina and Rebecca approached marriageable ages, sons Daniel Morgan, aged eleven, and eight-year-old Jesse Bryan would remain part of the household for several more years. At the same time, six other children of Rebecca's widowed uncle, James Bryan, also lived with the Boones and thought of them as grandparents. The Boone cabin was even more crowded with the addition of Will and Susy Hays who had several children and who lived with the Boones for a time during the early 1780s. Jemima and her husband, together with Daniel's brothers Samuel, Edward, and Jonathan and cousins in the Scholl family also lived at Boone's Station. All in all, approximately twenty people lived in the log house that had two rooms divided by a breezeway, or dogtrot. A loft above each room provided sleeping and storage space, while the women cooked outdoors.[3]

Despite the companionship and safety that family and friends could provide in an outpost on the frontier, Boone's Station enjoyed neither peace nor security. Although many of the Indian nations north of the Ohio River had ceded Kentucky and other lands south of the river to the British in the Treaty of Fort Stanwix in 1768, the Shawnees and Wyandots reserved the right to hunt south of the river, and trouble commonly occurred between Indians and whites, who each thought the other deserved to be killed on sight.

In 1781 violence and retribution defined Nathan Boone's world. At the time of his birth, his father already had experienced a host of confrontations with the Indians that taxed his skill at both diplomacy and war. Daniel had rescued Jemima who had been captured by the Indians in July 1776, he had saved Boonesborough from a surprise attack by a combined force of Indians and British soldiers in March 1777, and in February 1778 he had been captured by a band of Shawnees under Black Fish while he boiled water for salt at a place called the Blue Licks. On that occasion, the Shawnees took Boone north of the Ohio where they forced him to run the gauntlet before they adopted him into the tribe. At that time, Daniel had already lost his eldest son, James, who at the age of sixteen had been killed by the Indians on the family's move from North Carolina to Kentucky in October 1773.[4]

Although Nathan was too young to have remembered specific events, even as a baby he must have sensed the scurry of activity if not the apprehension around the Boone household during the spring and summer of 1782, as Indian attacks, spurred by the British in Detroit, increased in Kentucky. In May a Wyandot war party killed twenty-two men and a Captain Samuel Estill south of Boonesborough. In July Daniel pursued a band of Indians who had killed his friend Nathaniel Hart on the latter's farm near Boonesborough, but Boone's party could not catch them. By early August, a large force of Indians had crossed the Ohio River, and the frontier people in the Boonesborough area learned that "a very formidable army of English and Indians would come Quickly." Simon Girty, the white renegade and turncoat, served as one of the leaders of this war party. Before his raiders had crossed the Ohio, Girty urged them to make war unmercifully against the Kentuckians, saying: "Brothers the Long Knives have overrun your country and usurped your hunting grounds. They have destroyed the cane, trodden down the clover, killed the deer and the buffalo, the bear and the raccoon. The beaver has been chased from his dam and forced to leave the country." Girty, whose very name shot fear into the hearts of the frontier people because of his reputation for committing or permitting atrocities against both soldiers and civilians, dramatically told the Indians who gathered before him, "Were there a voice in the trees of the forest [it] would call on you to chase away these ruthless invaders who are laying it to waste."[5]

When Daniel, who served as a lieutenant colonel in the militia, learned that the Indians, led by British officers, had struck Bryan's Station to the northwest on the Elkhorn River, he helped lead a rescue party, recruited at Boone's Station, Boonesborough, Lexington, and Harrodsburg, to break the siege. By the time the rangers arrived the Indians had already departed because they could not take the blockhouse without artillery. Without waiting for reinforcements, Colonel John Todd, who commanded the rangers, led his men northeast in pursuit of the Indians who had at least a day's head start. Speed rather than caution governed his actions, and Boone became increasingly apprehensive by the time they reached the vicinity of the Lower Blue Licks. Boone knew Indian "sign," and he did not like what he saw. He suspected that the Indians were leading the Kentuckians into a trap. After the disaster that soon followed, Boone recalled that the Indians were "concealing their numbers by treading in each others tracks." He counted their campfires along the trail and estimated the war party to be at least five hundred men. Because such a large force made no apparent effort to conceal its retreat but instead littered the trail, Boone could see an ambush in the making. He knew that if the Shawnees had wanted to escape they could have already crossed the Ohio River. Instead, they left their campfires unconcealed, and they had not scattered in small groups. The situation called for the utmost caution, a characteristic alien to the Kentucky rangers.[6]

The rangers reached the Licking River on Monday morning, August 19, and Boone knew the place well. Hunters and settlers called it the Blue Licks. Here deer and other animals came to lick the salt from an outcropping of rock and mineral. Boone knew the land along the Licking as well as any man, and what he saw troubled him. On the north bank of the river, he observed several Indians walking about the fringes of wooded ravines that trailed down from higher ground. They smoked and acted unconcerned by the presence of the rangers. They were also beyond rifle range.[7]

Colonels Todd and Stephen Trigg, who commanded a contingent from Fayette County, quickly held a council and asked Boone, who had more experience with the Indians than any man among them, what they should do. Boone knew exactly what the Indians wanted. "Colonel," he responded, "they intend to fight us." They wanted, Boone said, "to seduce us into an ambush," and he warned Todd not to "run heedlessly into the trap so artfully set for us." With the Indian force larger than the rangers, who numbered approximately two hundred, Boone urged Todd and Trigg to break off contact, saying, "it is not prudent to pursue." Boone explained the reasons for his assessment, and he suggested crossing the Licking upstream and slipping behind the Indians from the rear. None of the officers at the council agreed.[8]

The Kentucky rangers, who already had a reputation for ardor as well as bad judgment and a lack of discipline, saw no need to wait. Major Hugh McGary, whose courage had been questioned at Bryan's Station, almost shouted at Boone, "By Godly what did we come here for?" Then, confronting Boone directly, he said: "I never saw any signs of cowardice about you before." With this challenge to his honor and courage, Boone lost his self-control and accepted McGary's dare to fight, saying "I can go as far as any man," and that no man before had called him a coward. McGary then spurred his horse into the water and called to his men "All who are not damned cowards follow me, and I'll soon show you the Indians." The Kentuckians, who were spoiling for a fight, rode their horses pell-mell into the river crossing; chaos rather than order prevailed. Boone joined his rangers saying, "Come on we are all slaughtered men."[9]

With the river forded the Kentuckians divided into three forces, with Trigg on the right, Todd in the center, and Boone on the left in command of the men from Boonesborough and Boone's Station. His son Israel crouched beside him as they moved toward the ridge, and nephews Thomas, Squire, and Samuel followed along with cousins Abraham, Joseph, and Peter Scholl. All "kept near to Boone," because, as one ranger said, they had "faith in him to get us out of trouble." The Kentuckians under Boone understood that trouble would soon be forthcoming and that it might be more than they could handle. They were right, and it came quickly and unmercifully.[10]

Most of the rangers under Boone dismounted, and they followed McGary up a pathway that led a half mile to the top of the hill that served as the lick. When McGary reached the crest with about two dozen rangers, the Kentuckians were met by a "terrific war whoop" which instantly spread to the surrounding wooded ravines on both sides of the summit. Suddenly a volley of rifle fire cut down McGary's men, who, one survivor reported, were "shot down like pigeons." Boone and his Kentuckians had not yet reached the crest, but they saw McGary's men going down. With the annihilation of McGary's rangers before his eyes, he later reflected that "It fell to my lot to bring on the attack." Boone then led the charge up the hill firing along with his men, pausing only to crouch and reload amid the dead men who had followed McGary up the hill and the rolling thunder of the combined rifle fire from both Indians and Kentuckians.[11]

As Boone led his men steadily up the hillside, he did not know that Trigg had been shot dead and Todd had been driven back from the center. Trigg's column had essentially ceased to exist and the rangers in the center had fallen back behind Boone's men. When McGary rode up to Boone and reported that "Todd and Trigg's line has given way, and the Indians are all around you," Boone looked down the hill and saw that the Indians had reached the river and were seizing the reins of their horses. During the constant firing, smoke from the black powder covered the hillside like a fog and muffled the screams of the attacking Indians and the groans of the wounded Kentuckians. The fighting quickly became hand-to-hand and from tree to rock to ravine as the Indians pushed the rangers back down the hill. In less than five minutes fifteen of the forty officers had been killed and more than forty of the Kentuckians lay dead, dying, or wounded. Some were able to flee when Boone gave the order to retreat, only to be met by the Indians who had reached the river behind them.[12]

The fighting along the riverbank became even more desperate as the Kentuckians tried to break through the line and swim across. Boone saw the chaos at the crossing and ordered his men to stay close together while he led them through the woods on their left to a better ford that he knew about. As his men ran through the trees toward the river and away from the fighting, he remained behind with his son Israel and several others to form a rear guard. When a riderless horse ran by, Boone grabbed the reins and pulled it up. He called to Israel, telling him to get on and ride out. But Israel shouted, "Father, I won't leave you." Boone turned away to look behind them only to hear the smack that a bullet makes when it hits flesh and bone. Behind him Israel lay "shivering" on the ground, shot near the heart. As he reached for the protection of his father, blood ran from Israel's mouth and his eyes glazed, and Boone knew that his son could not be saved. Holding him in his arms for the last time, Boone looked into his eyes, then rested him on the ground and fled into the woods and toward the river and the safety beyond.[13]

When Boone dove into the Licking about seventy-five yards downstream from the main ford, bodies were drifting by those of his men who had made it to the south bank and assembled to provide covering fire for the ones still struggling to make it to the river and through the water to the other side. Daniel's nephew Squire Boone lay crippled with a ball in the hip. Thomas, another nephew, had been killed, while six men remained missing and many others suffered a host of wounds from lead, knives, and tomahawks. When Boone crawled out of the water and up the south bank of the Licking, he saw his men not far away and rallied them around him. Knowing that the situation was hopeless and that to remain meant certain death, Boone ordered a retreat. They ran south with the other Kentuckians toward the safety of Boonesborough. The expedition to punish the Indians for crossing south of the Ohio and attacking white settlements had become a desperate and humiliating rout.[14]

Perhaps Nathan, at nearly eighteen months of age, sensed the apprehension of his mother when Boone rode with the expedition to the Blue Licks, and he may have noticed the grief of Rebecca when Daniel returned home and told her of Israel's death. Perhaps, too, he sensed the determination of his father when Daniel led a burial party from Boone's Station to the Blue Licks five days later. Nathan later recalled that his father told him that when the burial party approached the battle site on August 24, vultures circled above while others fed on the bodies, that had been scalped and mutilated. One man, who rode with Boone, reported that the smell of the dead was the "awfullest smell" he had ever known in his life. Although the identification of the dead proved difficult, if not impossible, because they had laid in the sun for so many days, Nathan believed that his father found Israel by identifying his clothing and buried him apart from the mass grave of the others. Boone later reported to the governor of Virginia that they had "Marchd to the Battle Ground again But found the Enemy were gone off So we proceeded to Bury the Dead—which were 43 found on the ground and Many more we Expect Lay about that we Did not See as we Could not tarry to Search very Close, being Both Hungary and weary and Some what Dubious that the Enemy might not be gone quite off."[15]

As the years passed Nathan heard his father blame himself time and again for the death of his son at the Blue Licks because he had lost his customary self-discipline and good judgment when McGary called him a coward. Instead of pressing his case for caution based on experience, he rashly joined the hotheads and rushed forward. But Boone's reasons for guilt may have been far greater than the sin of foolish leadership. Several days before the Kentuckians rode out, Israel had been sick in bed with a fever. When word arrived that a large Indian force had crossed the Ohio, the young Kentuckians at Boone's Station and Boonesborough hurried to sign up for the expeditionary force of rangers that would prevent their attack on the settlements. But Israel did not sign up and Boone was ashamed of his son and derided him for not joining the group. Delinda Boone Craig, Nathan's second child and eldest daughter, reported that Boone had said, "Israel, I did not hear your name when they were beating up for volunteers, and I had expected to have heard it among the first. I am sorry to think I have raised a timid son." Shamed by his father, Israel left his sickbed and enlisted. Nathan, however, later said that his father and mother tried to persuade him not to go. Whatever the case, Nathan observed thereafter that his father wept for Israel whenever he spoke of the Blue Licks.[16]

No one, of course, can say with certainty that the anxiety and grief that must have permeated the Boone home because of the Blue Licks campaign affected Nathan, who was little more than toddler. But the battle of the Blue Licks marked his early life with a culture of violence and a military tradition. At the same time his log home and family at Boone's Station gave him comfort and security. Although Nathan one day would leave his boyhood and Kentucky behind, both the military and family served as foundations for his life, and both demanded steadiness, reliability, and duty.

Nathan's family, like most on the frontier, made their living by raising a small patch of corn and tobacco and by keeping a few cattle and hogs to meet their subsistence needs. But Daniel disliked plowing and cultivating with a passion, and Rebecca had more than enough work raising their children. Consequently, they were indifferent farmers at best and poor ones at worst. Daniel much preferred to take his rifle and traps and disappear into the woods and to return weeks or months later with deer, beaver, and bear skins tied to his packhorses, all of which brought needed income into the Boone home. But the troubles with the Indians during the American Revolution and for more than a decade thereafter prevented him from making his long, cherished hunts. After the battle of the Blue Licks, however, the war essentially ended in Kentucky with the exception of periodic and isolated Indian raids, and Daniel, once again, got the urge to move on and try his fortunes elsewhere.[17]

Never a good businessman, Daniel had claimed thousands of acres with military land warrants issued by Virginia, and he obtained thousands of acres more by surveying tracts for speculators who paid him with lands. Daniel, however, never properly completed the paperwork or filed his claims, and he eventually lost all of his lands. By the autumn of 1782, he evidently had been pressured to leave his claim at Boone's Station because he did not have title to that land, and he had moved his family from that place to Marble Creek about five miles to the west, where he farmed. But his heart was not in it, and his farm was a rather sorry sight. Soon Boone had the urge to move again. In the fall of 1782, when his friend Simon Kenton invited him to settle at his newly founded village of Limestone, present-day Maysville, on the Ohio River about seventy miles to the north, Boone rode with his sons-in-law Will Hays and Flanders Callaway to investigate the possibilities.[18]

Boone liked what he saw. Although Limestone was no more than a few cabins huddled between the bank of the wide Ohio River and the steeply rising hills that marked the southern edge of the floodplain, the site had great possibilities for trade. Indeed, Limestone provided the best landing on the river for settlers bound for the Bluegrass country as well as a convenient place for those traveling downriver on flatboats to replenish their supplies. Boone fancied himself a tavern keeper and merchant who could make money from the river trade. When Daniel returned home and discussed the possibilities with Rebecca she agreed with his assessment of their financial situation and recognized the opportunity to improve their family life at

Limestone. Neither had been reluctant to move before, especially when the opportunity for a fresh start beckoned. So, in the spring of 1783, they loaded their belongings on packhorses, along with daughters Levina and Rebecca and sons Morgan, Jesse, and two-year-old Nathan, and followed the trace north to Limestone. At the age of forty-eight Daniel was excited about his chance to start a new life.[19]

In the course of their move, somewhere between the Blue Licks and Limestone, as they passed through an area of dense cane, several buffalo bolted from the thicket and ran across the trail, knocked over one of the packhorses, and caused the others to skitter and rear. The instant commotion gave everyone a fright until Daniel got the horses under control and looked about to make sure no other buffalo would stampede across the road. This excitement made an indelible imprint on Nathan's mind, and he recalled the event as his earliest memory.[20]

During the next six years, while the Boones lived in Limestone, the town never became more than a rough cluster of buildings with a few docks that made the loading and unloading of supplies from the flatbottomed "Kentucky boats" easier than when they tied up along the bank. Even so, Boone plunged into the task at hand with enthusiasm, building a "house of entertainment," a tavern. With help from his sons Jesse and Morgan, Boone dismantled an old flatboat in the custom of the frontier and used it and other lumber to build the tavern, which also served as the Boone home. He also acquired a warehouse along the river to store the goods offered and taken in trade.[21]

Soon Boone proclaimed that Limestone had become a "grate Landing place." Indeed, most settlers, traders, and long hunters would have agreed with a woman from Pennsylvania, who called the landing the "Best on the River." But she also considered Limestone itself "very Indifferent." Yet, in this small, ramshackle frontier community Nathan Boone passed into boyhood, forming his first memories of home, with his mother running the tavern kitchen with the help of several slaves who also looked after him. Periodically, Daniel purchased another slave to help Rebecca with her work while the slaves' children played with Nathan. Early in his life, then, Nathan learned that slavery was an accepted relationship between whites and blacks.[22]

While Nathan learned about the relationship of whites and blacks in a slave society, the frontier as a western rather than southern experience shaped his early years. Life around the Boone home was fast paced with traders and hunters unloading packs of deerskins and furs for trade with his father. On one occasion, Daniel sold 1,790 deer and 729 bear skins that he had taken in trade. Although Boone had little money, the frontier economy operated efficiently and profitably based on trade in kind—barter—based on cash prices. Long hunters and nearby farmers brought skins, furs, ginseng root, corn whiskey, smoked hams and bacon, and pickled pork to Boone's warehouse or store. Many immigrants, who left the river at Limestone or who merely stopped on their way downstream, also bought or traded for needed items such as cornmeal, salt pork, skillets, and blankets as well as other housewares, dry goods, and staple food supplies. Powder, lead, and skinning knives always proved popular items for exchange. Boone stored the hides, furs, ginseng, and country produce in his warehouse and sent periodic orders by post to merchant suppliers in Pittsburgh, Philadelphia, and Louisville. Boone also bought horses, which he kept with those he raised on his lush pastures in the Bluegrass. Periodically he would send a herd over the mountains to an eastern market.[23]

During all of the trading activities and the coming and going of the men who took a meal and stayed the night at the Boone tavern, Nathan watched and listened as hunters talked about the trails in the backcountry, running traplines, and judging horseflesh, while farmers visited with Daniel about land surveys, the prices and prospects for the corn crop, and the value of their slaughtered hogs in trade. By the time he reached eight years of age, Nathan's world was one of boots and saddles, the sight of freshly skinned and drying hides, the smell of sweat, callused hands and sun- and wind-burned faces, the aroma of whiskey, and women baking bread, washing clothes, and roasting venison, pork, and beef.

Although the Peace of Paris in 1783 brought a formal end to the War for Independence, the Indians in the Old Northwest refused to accept defeat on a piece of paper when they had not been beaten on the battlefield. They adamantly contended that the lands north of the Ohio River belonged to them, and, with British encouragement, they lashed out at the settlers who crossed the river onto their lands. More than a few of the twelve thousand settlers who landed at Limestone between 1786 and 1788 used Boone's tavern and warehouse to provision their settlements across the Ohio and the landing as their last port of embarkation.[24]

With increasing frequency after the American Revolution, the Shawnees and Wyandots crossed the Ohio River to strike settlements in Kentucky, and the militia retaliated in kind north of the river. Between 1783 and 1787, Indians killed an estimated three hundred settlers and stole some twenty thousand horses along the Ohio. At Limestone, Indian raids were constantly on the minds of the inhabitants, and Boone, as the commander of the local militia, had the responsibility for defense of the settlement. Opposition in Limestone forced him to "desist," however, when he tried to prevent further animosity between Indians and whites by ordering the return of horses to the Shawnees that had been stolen by a renegade group of Kentuckians who had crossed the river for a raid. Kentuckians wanted retribution, not fairness, when they dealt with the Indians, and Boone disappointed them when he advocated evenhandedness. Still, they always sought Boone's advice and help when they feared an Indian attack.[25]

When Daniel talked to Rebecca about the Indian raids, especially the killings and rumored threats of a major war, Nathan sensed the fear in the adult world. He watched and heard his father and mother talk about a raid in force against the Shawnees that the Kentuckians planned for late September 1786. And, before Daniel led a company of eight hundred men across the river into the Ohio country on the night of the 29th, he probably gave Nathan a hug and admonishment to be good while he was gone before he disappeared among the assortment of men and horses at the assembly point.[26]

About two weeks later when Daniel returned, Nathan was fascinated and more than a little frightened by the prisoners, mostly women and children, that the Kentuckians brought with them. He no doubt listened intently as Daniel told his mother about sacking the Shawnee villages long the Miami River valley far to the north and the murder of Chief Moluntha by McGary to avenge their defeat at the Blue Licks. Nathan also stayed close to his father, who had the responsibility of providing food for the Indian captives from his tavern and warehouse, and he likely watched as Daniel distributed the provisions during the next ten months while the Indian prisoners were held at Limestone.[27]

Because Boone had the most experience in dealing with Indians and because he served as the commander of the local militia, he had the responsibility of arranging the exchange of Indian prisoners for white captives held by the Shawnees north of the Ohio River. Neither the Indians nor the Kentuckians made substantive efforts to trade captives during the autumn and early winter of 1786, but in February of the next year Nathan watched as his father made preparations to send a French Canadian trader and his Shawnee wife across the Ohio to spread the word among the Shawnee villages that the Kentuckians wanted to exchange prisoners. On March 4, 1787, Shawnee Chief Noamohouoh reciprocated by leading a small party, including three captive white children as a sign of goodwill, across the river to Limestone.[28]

Six-year-old Nathan saw the white children who were now dressed like Shawnees, who spoke their language and seemed to be neither Indian nor white. He also probably heard his father talk to the militia in Limestone and with his mother about the terms for exchange that Noamohouoh brought from Captain Johnny, a young war chief, who spoke for many Shawnees. Because Daniel provided a room for Noamohouoh at the Boone tavern, Nathan saw the discussions for the exchange and the friendly manner in which his father dealt with the Shawnee chief. When Colonel Robert Patterson, who commanded the Kentucky militia in that area, refused to exchange Nohelema, whom they considered a queen among the Shawnees and an invaluable captive, for three children, Nathan surely saw his father angrily rant about his lack of authority while everyone expected him to do his duty by facilitating the prisoner exchange. In the end, Nathan also learned that persistence brought rewards. In late March, Daniel gained authority to send Nohelema home with Noamohouoh, and in April the reciprocal nature of Indian relations brought a Shawnee by the name of Captain Wolf to the Boone tavern with nine more captives to exchange for Indian prisoners under Boone's care.[29]

On August 20, Captain Johnny, along with Blacksnake, Captain Wolf, and several other Shawnee leaders, appeared across the river from Limestone with a large number of white captives and offered to exchange them for Shawnee prisoners held by the Kentuckians and to make peace. Nathan watched as his seventeen-year-old brother Morgan crossed the river by boat with two Indian captives as a sign of goodwill and with instructions from his father. Then Daniel, along with several officers and a contingent of militia, crossed over and made arrangements with Captain Johnny for a major prisoner exchange.[30]

When the white men, women, and children began ferrying across the Ohio to Limestone, Nathan likely watched as they landed and were swept up in tearful and joyful reunions with their families. Perhaps too he saw that some of the captives who had been among the Shawnees for a long time did not enthusiastically return to white society and that several children cried for their Indian parents who had adopted them. One seven-year-old girl, however, arrived without anyone to greet or claim her. She had been a captive only a few months, and she had not yet been acculturated into Shawnee society. Her name was Chloe Flinn, and Daniel took her home where Rebecca gave her clean clothes and cared for her. Late in her life she remembered that she had been playing on an Indian's bearskin rug with other children when a friendly man stretched out his arm and called for her to climb up behind his saddle and "he would take her home." During the next few months while Daniel searched for her parents along the Kentucky side of the river, Nathan played with her and no doubt asked her about her experiences among the Indians. He had never had a sister about his same age, but his experience with the commotion of the extended Boone family prevented any feelings of imposition by her presence. From Chloe, Nathan perhaps sensed that the whites could move between two cultural worlds and that differences could be understood. When Daniel found her relatives, Nathan was sad to see her go.[31]

Before the prisoner exchange ended, however, Daniel invited the Shawnees to cross the river for a feast with roasted beef and whiskey, and they accepted. The celebration converged on the south bank of the Ohio near the Boone tavern, with Shawnees and whites mingling about all to the marvel of Nathan. When night fell Nathan probably ran about the crowd both excited and a little frightened as Shawnee men danced around a large campfire, as one observer noted, "hideously painted in their grandest style for war" while an Indian beat a rhythm with a stick on a pair of old saddle bags. As the evening wore on, Nathan also surely observed that whiskey changed the behavior of Indians and whites, and if he did not see it, he no doubt heard his father tell his mother about preventing trouble by a drunken Kentuckian who threatened to reclaim a horse that he recognized among the Shawnee mounts even if he had to kill and scalp every Shawnee at the celebration. And, Nathan learned that his father and Simon Kenton had seen the "trouble brewing" and defused the situation by purchasing the horse for a keg of whiskey. Although he did not yet understand the term, Nathan began to learn by observing his father that diplomacy could prevent problems from getting worse and even solve them, but it required calm, clear, controlled thinking in times of crisis.[32]

The peace that followed the prisoner exchange was neither secure nor long lasting. Many of the Shawnee villages had refused to sign the treaty at Limestone and continued to press their attacks against white settlers both north and south of the Ohio River. The Kentuckians retaliated in kind, and talk of ambushes, scalpings, retribution, and a new Indian war permeated the conversation at the Boone tavern and home. Nathan, however, saw that despite the fear of Indian attack his father considered himself a friend of many Shawnees, and he perhaps learned that good and evil were not necessarily absolutes and that both characteristics could be found among Indians and whites. And, at the age of seven, Nathan saw that Blue Jacket, one of the most feared and admired war chiefs among the Shawnees, could be held in respect and that friendship could transcend cultural animosities.

Blue Jacket, known to his people as Weyapiersenwah, had participated in the Battle of Point Pleasant under Cornstalk on October 10, 1774. A decade later Blue Jacket ranked second only to Cornstalk as a Shawnee war chief. After the prisoner exchange at Limestone in 1787, Morgan went hunting with Blue Jacket, crossing to the north bank of the Ohio River on several occasions, and Daniel and Blue Jacket became acquaintances. Although Blue Jacket pledged to spare Limestone from any attack and the further capture of its settlers, he did not see anything wrong with stealing horses from the settlers in the vicinity of the village.[33]

In the spring of 1788, Blue Jacket led the Shawnee raiding party that attacked Strode's Station and stole eight or ten horses. Before the Shawnees could reach the Ohio, however, their pursuers caught up with them north of the Licking River. Although the Shawnee scattered and escaped, Blue Jacket was ridden down and beaten.

Blue Jacket, however, saved his own life by calling out "Boone! Boone!" Rather than kill him on the spot, the Kentuckians took Blue Jacket to Limestone to see whether Daniel knew anything about the man. When they arrived Daniel was no doubt embarrassed to see his son's hunting companion hauled before him for stealing horses. Nathan perhaps watched as his father locked Blue Jacket in a cabin, with his hands tied "hog tight." Then, the entourage returned to the Boone tavern for food and drink, during which time the Kentuckians recounted the Shawnee attack on the station, their pursuit of the raiders, and the capture of Blue Jacket. As the evening wore on they became drunk and fell asleep. When they awoke in the morning, Daniel excitedly reported with great concern that Blue Jacket had escaped. "A knife happened to be sticking in the logs near him," Boone reported, and Blue Jacket worked around until he got it, cut the rope with which he was bound, and "cleared out" just about daybreak.[34]

The Kentuckians were surprised that Boone had been so careless, and they quickly pursued Blue Jacket. Nathan no doubt watched and listened as angry men rushed and shouted about as they saddled their horses and rode out of Limestone in search of the Shawnee war chief. But, other than finding his leggings in the woods, they could not locate his trail and Blue Jacket made a safe crossing of the Ohio and returned to his village several days later. Perhaps Nathan also heard his father confide to his mother about what really happened; if so, Nathan never reported what his father said about the escape and his role in it. But Nathan could not help but see that the matters of right and wrong often depended on perspective and that respect, friendship, and loyalty were principles of consequence for both whites and Indians.[35]

Nathan also learned something of the wider world beyond Limestone at this time. In 1787, Daniel had been elected to the state assembly by the settlers in Bourbon County. Soon after the prisoner exchange he took Rebecca and Nathan via keelboat upriver to Redstone on the Monongahela and then by road to Richmond where he sat in the assembly from October to early January. In Richmond Nathan went about town with his mother a bit awed by the hustle and bustle of a capital city with the legislature in session and where wagons driven by slaves and white farmers brought great loads of brown, sweet-smelling tobacco to the warehouses for sale and where a host of merchants plied their trade. Whether Rebecca enrolled Nathan in a school remains uncertain, and he never mentioned any education at this time. If he did not attend school in Richmond during the autumn and early winter of 1787, he probably passed his days leisurely exploring the streets near their lodging with neighboring children.[36]

After the Boones returned to Limestone early in 1788, Daniel took a keelboat with fifteen tons of ginseng root, known as "sang" on the frontier, up the Ohio past Pittsburgh and into the Monongahela, reaching Redstone, Nathan remembered, in "cherry time." Then Boone, along with his sons Morgan, Jesse, and Nathan, and Rebecca loaded the root into wagons and hauled it on the road that led to Hagerstown, Maryland, where he sold it. Wild ginseng grew in the woods, free for the taking; physicians and apothecaries bought it to make medicine, and ginseng could be exported to China where it was used as an aphrodisiac. The frontier people commonly dug it to make a little money.[37]

Although Nathan had been too small to help considerably, he walked the deck of the keelboat and tried his hand at hefting the polls and pulling the oars. When the boat began to take on water after a log drifting in the strong Ohio current smacked the side and loosened the boards, he too got a fright as his father and brothers steered it to the bank, bailed water, and made repairs. When the ginseng sold for less than half the amount Daniel had anticipated, because it had been damaged by the water, Nathan perhaps began to understand that earning a living on the frontier was fraught with uncertainty and that money made family life more comfortable, while the lack of it caused privation.[38]

Although disappointed with their lack of success selling ginseng, Daniel and Rebecca decided to make the best of their trip by returning to the Boone homestead in Exeter, Pennsylvania. One resident remembered the arrival of the famous frontiersman, saying, "He and his wife came from Kentucky by horseback, and their little son rode behind his father the whole journey." A ride of several hundred miles over reasonably good roads was of no consequence to Boone, but for seven-year-old Nathan the trip from Hagerstown, perched behind the saddle with his hands on his father's waist, seemed a long and tiring adventure. But when the Boones arrived in Exeter, they rented a house for several months, and Nathan enjoyed playing in the yard and about the town with distant cousins and neighboring children. When they asked where he came from, Nathan no doubt told them a bit about Limestone, the Indians, their adventures on the Ohio, his trip to Richmond, and most of all, his father.[39]

The Boones stayed in Exeter visiting family and old friends until the late summer of 1788 when they returned to Limestone. Later a woman who met the Boones in Exeter recalled that Rebecca was "very pleasant and sociable, and spoke very freely of their affairs." She remembered Daniel as "stern looking, very taciturn and gloomy." Nathan may have noticed his father's unhappy demeanor, but the comfort of his family life seemed unchanged. If anything, it got better for Nathan. In the fall his father took him along with Morgan and Jesse into the woods to dig ginseng to ship upriver to an eastern market. For the first time, Nathan helped make camp and tend the fire, and he lay on the ground under a blanket that kept him warm against the cold night air. He heard the call of the owl and saw the stars splashed against the sky, and he began to learn how men lived in the open and around camp as they hobbled their horses, made coffee from water taken from a nearby stream, collected wood, and tended a meal roasting over the fire or sputtering in a skillet. In doing so, Nathan also started to understand, as his father had long ago, that the wilderness need not be feared, that men could make their way in it far removed from the comforts of home, and that they could feel at peace in it. From this time until the end of his life, the emptiness and solitude of the frontier would meet an emotional need in Nathan that was both learned and inherent, and it would beckon him as much as it did his father.[40]

The lure of the wilderness that Nathan was just beginning to sense and understand now pulled strongly within his father. By late 1788, Daniel's real estate speculations had proved a failure although the frontier people held him in great respect for his military and diplomatic leadership. Moreover, his efforts at trading horses and selling ginseng never provided the profits that he sought. Still, Daniel achieved modest success as a tavern keeper, merchant, and shipper and by so doing provided adequate food and clothing for his family. Even so, Limestone had lost its appeal, and in 1789 he sold his merchandise at the store and moved his family back up the Ohio to its junction with the Kanawha River, which ran down from

Virginia's western mountains, where the village of Point Pleasant hugged a piece of land that protruded into the Ohio as it swept by from the north.[41]

Boone located a cabin on Crooked Creek not far from Point Pleasant for his family, which still included Morgan and Jesse. The rich lands along the Kanawha and the Ohio beckoned settlers and the tree-lined hills and silent but ever-moving waters created a beauty unmatched on the frontier. One traveler observed that "Point Pleasant is a most beautiful place and very rich land." Although the Point, as it was known, had only "very few inhabitants" and "indifferent buildings" when the Boones arrived in the spring of 1789, it already had become a regular stop for settlers moving downriver in Kentucky boats. With three sons and a wife to support, Daniel soon acquired a building and began anew as a frontier trader and shipper.[42]

Boone's reputation attracted considerable attention and business, and Nathan had free run of the store, where hunters and trappers brought their deer, beaver, and bear skins for trade. Venison hung from the rafters while bear bacon dripped grease onto the floor. When the hides and pelts piled high and crowded the store, Nathan helped his father and brothers separate them into small stacks and tie them with ropes for Morgan and Jesse to take upriver by keelboat to Pittsburgh. In the summer of 1792 Nathan helped his father and brothers pack deer skins and bear skins along with an assortment of fox and otter pelts and two barrels of ginseng for sale to Matthew Vanlear, a merchant with whom they frequently traded at Hagerstown, via the Ohio and Monongahela Rivers and an overland road.[43]

Nathan watched his father quickly become immersed in the daily life of Point Pleasant not only as a merchant but also as a surveyor who earned a modest income by working for settlers along both sides of the Ohio and up the Kanawha. Daniel also became acquainted with the "principal people" of the area. In October 1789, at the first meeting of the county court for Kanawha County, Boone was elected lieutenant colonel of the militia, the third ranking officer in the county. Nathan no doubt listened and watched as his father planned the defense of Point Pleasant which, until the Battle of Fallen Timbers in 1794, remained vulnerable to Shawnee raiding parties that crossed the Ohio River to strike the isolated settlements to the south. He surely listened with alarm when his father told about the killing and scalping of Rachel, the daughter of his old friend John Vanbibber, and the capture of his son Joseph by a raiding party of Shawnees. At that same time the Shawnees captured Vanbibber's sister near the Point and killed her husband and children. More than a little apprehension was felt in the Boone home when Morgan reported that he and Tice Vanbibber had several narrow escapes from the Indians who chased them while they were hunting. Nathan also experienced both fear and excitement when his father told him about holding a canoe ready after hearing a rifle shot and seeing Morgan running through the woods toward him.[44]

In 1791, Daniel's reputation as a leader once again gained him election to the Virginia assembly. As a representative of Kanawha County this was Boone's third election to the assembly, and it would be the second time that he took Rebecca and Nathan to Richmond while the legislature sat in session from October through December. On this trip Richmond made an indelible impression on ten-year-old Nathan. He probably not only heard his father discuss the pending separation of Kentucky from Virginia and the desire of the settlers in that region to be admitted as a sovereign state, but he also remembered warm and intimate family time with father and mother close and attentive. On one occasion Nathan recalled going into the assembly and telling the sergeant at arms that he had an important message for his father. When Daniel hurried out of the chambers, worried about the possibilities of an urgent request from his son, Nathan greeted him by asking if he could have some spending money while he walked about the town. On another day, he went on a picnic along the James River with his father and mother. Nathan fondly remembered that his father bought oysters and his mother roasted them over a campfire. When the sun began to set the autumn chill gave Nathan the shivers, and Daniel beckoned him to sit close, and he put his arms around him. For Daniel, hardship in the wilderness had been a way of life, but now as he held his son in his lap and as they watched the flames, they talked of what they had done and what they would do. Their closeness and comfort overpowered all thoughts of cold and past privation.[45]

When the Boone family returned home over the Midland Trail, which linked the Kanawha and Shenandoah Valleys, they visited with Henry Miller, a boyhood friend of Daniel's. During their stay, Daniel observed that the horns on one of Miller's bulls would make a fine powderhorn. In an affectionate gesture to his old friend, Miller killed the bull and gave Daniel one of the horns. As they sat about the log house, Boone engraved the horn with his name and the year, fitted both ends with a plug, attached a lanyard, and gave it to Nathan as a souvenir for their trip. Nathan cherished the gift for years and carried the powderhorn until he lost it in Missouri, while making a run for his life from a party of hostile Indians who had just taken his furs.[46]

As a militia colonel and merchant at Point Pleasant, Daniel amply provided for his family. By 1792, Boone reported taxable property of two horses, one slave, and five hundred acres of land. With sufficient capital at hand and with Jesse married and Morgan frequently gone hunting or searching for speculative opportunities in lands, Daniel and Rebecca apparently committed themselves to the education of Nathan, then aged eleven, by sending him to a Baptist school in Kentucky. Nathan lived with his sisters Jemima Callaway and Susannah Hays, both of whom lived on farms a few miles from Boone's Station. The school was located between the Callaways and the Hays, who lived about two miles apart, all in all a short daily walk to and from the classes of the Reverend John Price. Nathan returned home two years later, accompanied by Morgan and three of his brother's friends who had been visiting in Kentucky. Thereafter, Nathan never attended school of any kind. At the age of thirteen, though, Daniel now began to take him into the woods to hunt, and father and youngest son soon became inseparable.[47]

As Daniel Boone increasingly picked up his rifle to escape the irritations of the merchant business and the river trade at Point Pleasant, he realized that he missed this part of his earlier life more than he had imagined, and he began to long for the solitude of the woods and a home far removed from the commotion of life in a frontier town. The more he thought and talked about it to Rebecca, the more he was convinced that they should give up the store at the Point and move back into the woods. As a result, sometime during 1793, Daniel moved his family about sixty miles up the Kanawha where they occupied a log house at the mouth of Campbell's Creek. It is to this location and home that Nathan returned at the age of thirteen after his schooling in Kentucky.[48]

Daniel and Nathan spent most of the autumn of 1794 hunting deer and bear and checking their traplines along the Kanawha River valley and its tributaries. Now his father taught him how to set a trapline for beaver, skin the carcasses, and stretch the pelts over a frame made from grapevine. They ate beaver tail and venison roasted over an open fire, and they even dared to cross the Ohio River near Point Pleasant to hunt deer. Although many white settlers had already settled in Ohio, the Shawnees angrily claimed that land as their own, and they made trespassing a life-threatening mistake whenever they caught whites north of the river. So Daniel and Nathan moved quietly and carefully through the woods, and Daniel shot a few deer for their hides to sell back at the Point. During this and other hunts, Nathan had the responsibility of tending the camp. On one frosty morning with leaves falling, however, when Daniel was away from camp scouting in the woods, he heard a rifle shot from the vicinity of the camp. Boone ran back to the site thankful to find not that a Shawnee raiding party had killed or captured Nathan but that the boy had shot a buck that had wandered near the camp. Nathan fondly remembered his first deer and that his father was both surprised and proud of his son.[49]

After Nathan had killed his deer, he hunted regularly with his father as an equal. Before they returned home from Nathan's first trip across the Ohio, however, Nathan learned about the dangers of hunting in the woods that the Indians claimed as their own. Daniel discovered that a party of Indians had located their camp, and they quickly loaded the canoe with their bear and deer skins, venison, and supplies and drifted into the current of the Ohio River under the cover of a dense fog. Daniel told Nathan to lie down in the canoe and cover himself with their blankets while he guided it from the stern, quietly dipping the paddle in the water until they were out of danger. This experience gave Nathan considerable fear, and he urged his mother and father to move back to the relative safety of the Bluegrass, later recalling that he had become accustomed to the "quietness and safety of the interior" while attending school in that region.[50]

Daniel did not oppose Nathan's urging to move back to Kentucky. He had never been one to remain anyplace for long, and Morgan offered him a tract of wooded land on the Brushy Fork of Hinkston Creek about a dozen miles from the Blue Licks along the Maysville

Road in present-day Nicholas County. The lure of his four daughters and their children, who lived in the Brushy Creek vicinity, also proved a compelling attraction for Daniel and Rebecca. Sometime during the spring or summer of 1795, Nathan and his parents loaded their possessions on a Kentucky boat and floated down the Kanawha and into the Ohio for their trip back to Limestone. There, they piled their belongings into a wagon and made their way south to Brushy Creek where they settled on a tract of unimproved land, located about six miles east of Millersburg. Daniel and Nathan quickly went about the task of building a log house and clearing and plowing several acres of bottomland to have both shelter against the coming winter and a late corn crop in the fall. For the next two years, Nathan and Daniel planted corn in the spring and hunted deer and bear along the Big Sandy during the autumn. In the fall of 1796, Nathan, Daniel, Jesse, and Flanders Callaway killed a total of 156 bears. They sold the skins for two dollars a piece, and they smoked the meat and rendered the fat into oil for sale in the spring.[51]

Daniel and Nathan, however, were usually disappointed on their hunts. By the mid-1790s, the Bluegrass region had been sufficiently settled so that most of the game had either been killed or driven away. When they sat about their campfire during the autumn evenings Daniel would reflect to Nathan that when he had been captured by the Shawnees in 1778 "you would not have walked out in any direction for more than a mile without shooting a buck or a bear. There were then thousands of Buffaloes in the hills in Kentucky; the land looked as if it never would become poor; and to hunt in those days was a pleasure indeed." But now the buffalo were gone and only a few deer browsed in the forest glens, and Nathan, Rebecca, and Daniel lived a hardscrabble life eking out a living from the land rather than from the bounty of the hunt. Civilization had caught up with the Boone family, and it changed their way of life.[52]

At the age of seventeen Nathan decided that hunting in central Kentucky offered no future, and sometime during the spring or summer of 1798 he left Brushy Creek with cousin Jonathan Bryan to clear unimproved land, which his father owned about a half mile above the mouth of the Little Sandy, near present-day Huntington, West Virginia, on the Ohio River. This tract, however, proved too heavily timbered and Nathan decided to raise their first crop on land that they could clear easier about ten miles back up the Ohio where they had found rich bottomlands covered only with small trees and a light undergrowth of grape vines. After clearing eight acres with more work than they first thought would be necessary, they planted and raised a "fair crop." Nathan also trapped beaver along Blaine's Creek and hunted buffalo in the area, and he spent time clearing the land for a cabin and a few acres of cropland on the Little Sandy, all the while urging his parents to join him. The bottomland was black and rich, only a few settlers had drifted into the area, and the deer were plentiful in the nearby woods. The Little Sandy would provide a fresh start for his father and mother. They could make a go of it there, he no doubt told them. Brushy Creek offered nothing that could not be left behind, and they would still be close enough to his sisters and their children for the grandparents to see them occasionally. The time was right for another move. All they had to do was pack up and come.[53]

Daniel liked what Nathan told him, and the offer of a new start with his son on the Little Sandy was just what he needed. With the settlements pressing Boone and his favored way of earning a living turned unproductive, he fell into debt and began to lose the lands that he had acquired for surveying during the past few years for nonpayment of taxes. Faced with public humiliation and the frustration of being unable to provide a living for his family in the manner that he knew best, Boone and Rebecca joined Nathan on the Little Sandy sometime during October or November of 1798, just a few weeks before the Mason County sheriff arrived at Brushy Creek to arrest Daniel for nonpayment of an obligation for which he had been sued in court.[54]

Perhaps Daniel and Rebecca now realized that their lives had changed in a dramatic but subtle way. Instead of providing a home for their youngest child, they now had begun to look to him for their care. The strong bonds between father and son, forged in the cabins and towns where they had lived, and in the woods where they had hunted and shared a blanket, campfire, and meal, had become unbreakable. The new beginning that Nathan offered proved reason enough to follow him, but the attachment between father and son was overwhelming. Where Nathan would go Daniel would now go also, and where the father went the son would follow.

Nathan and his mother and father, however, did not stay at their farm on the Little Sandy for long. By the spring of 1799 they were on the move again, but this time their relocation involved more than a relatively short resettlement in Virginia or Kentucky. Instead, they cast their eyes on the distant Spanish-held Missouri. Both Nathan and Daniel had known about the potential of the rich lands in Missouri for some time. Two years earlier, in 1797, Morgan had scouted the Missouri country and located a broad floodplain with rich, black soil along Femme Osage Creek, which emptied into the Missouri River in the St. Charles District. Missouri was far removed from Kentucky and western Virginia, which Daniel now considered too crowded to tolerate, and the Femme Osage country, located approximately forty miles west of St. Louis and twenty miles southwest of present-day St. Charles, was only a little more isolated during the late eighteenth century than it is today.[55]

Morgan, Nathan, and Daniel knew that the Spanish were offering large land grants without property taxes for Americans who would settle in the Missouri country to help block British expansion south from Canada. Before Morgan returned to the Little Sandy to report what he had found, he visited Lieutenant Governor Zenon Trudeau and asked about the compensation Spain would provide if his father led a party of settlers to Missouri and whether they would be required to profess the Catholic religion. The governor, who knew about Daniel's success in opening Kentucky for settlement, assured Morgan that Spain would provide liberal land grants for Boone and those who came with him. So far as religious requirements were concerned, the frontier was a big place where regulations were difficult to enforce and where individual freedom was a way of life. In other words, if the Boones were not Catholics, they should not worry about it.[56]

After his meeting with Morgan, Lieutenant Governor Trudeau wrote to Daniel and urged him to come to Missouri with as many families as possible. He promised Daniel a thousand arpents of land (about 850 acres), even though Spanish law limited individual grants to eight hundred arpents. For each family that accompanied him, Spain would grant between four hundred and six hundred arpents. Morgan then left four slaves to build a cabin at his site along the Femme Osage and returned to the Little Sandy, possibly carrying Governor Trudeau's letter, and he arrived sometime during the autumn of 1798.[57]

Both Daniel and Nathan listened with excitement to Morgan's account of the Missouri country and his grant along the Femme

Osage. There, Morgan reported, deer abounded and beaver, otter, and mink waited to be trapped. Missouri looked like the Kentucky country when Daniel first crossed the mountains thirty years ago. Governor Trudeau's letter beckoned with opportunity for a fresh start in a new country. For Daniel, Missouri offered the chance to return to the life that he loved best. Nathan could come too, they would build a house, plant a patch of corn for meal and hominy, and hunt and trap together in a new land. Creditors could be left behind, and they would not need to worry about crowding from other settlers. Missouri was a big country and far away. It would take time before many settlers crossed the Mississippi, and the Femme Osage was far removed from the river traffic, anyway. The Missouri frontier offered freedom where they could do as they pleased.

They talked. Morgan told his story again and again. They read Trudeau's letter again and again. The more they talked and thought about Missouri the more Daniel became "disheartened" with Kentucky where the people had "got too proud." As he told one acquaintance, he was "unwilling to live among men who were shacked in habits," and he only wanted "to hunt for beavers in some unfrequented corner of the woods." Missouri was such a place with few people and considerable forest and streams. Daniel was convinced that they should go. What did Nathan think? Should they do it? They would have more land in Missouri than they could ever acquire along the Little Sandy or in Kentucky, and the title would be guaranteed. Thus, they would not have the problems that came with poorly surveyed lands and conflicting, overlapping ("shingled") claims that plagued their holdings in Kentucky. If he and Rebecca moved with Morgan, would Nathan come?[58]

Nathan and Daniel no doubt talked it through during the warm autumn days as they harvested their corn crop and hunted deer in the nearby woods with the leaves turning brilliant reds and yellows. They discussed it as they sat by the fire when the winter wind swept down the Ohio and chilled the land. By spring they had agreed: They would pull up stakes and move to Missouri. Once they had made their decision, Nathan and Daniel worked quickly to prepare for their move, choosing which household items, supplies, and tools to take. About a half mile from their cabin, they cut down a giant poplar and sawed off both ends and trimmed the branches. The trunk measured a good fifty feet with a five-foot diameter, and they went about crafting it into a dugout or pirogue with adz, ax, and fire. Although the wood proved soft and workable, the size of the trunk kept them at their work until September. Then the loading began.[59]

An abundance of activity kept the riverbank by Nathan's cabin noisy and in a nearly constant state of commotion as they loaded the canoe. Squire Boone, a younger brother of Daniel, had decided to go along in another pirogue with several of his sons; this added to the hubbub. Additionally, friends of Daniel, Nathan, and Morgan also planned to migrate with the Boones, thereby adding several more pirogues to the flotilla. When they embarked in the middle of September, Nathan and Morgan guided their pirogue laden with packs and gear while their mother sat in the middle to help balance the canoe. Daniel struck overland with a hired man and several slaves, driving a herd of cattle, horses, and hogs along a trail that bordered the Ohio River.[60]

The Ohio River took Nathan and the Boone entourage north before making a sharp bend and a long meander past present-day Portsmouth and on toward Limestone and Cincinnati. There, it dropped sharply south past Louisville in a twisting course toward a junction with the Mississippi south of present-day Cape Girardeau. Nathan did not make it that far, however. As the noisy flotilla drifted with the river and as he and Morgan led the assembly guiding their pirogue with rudder and paddle, he began to have serious misgivings about whether he had made the right decision. It was not that he did not want to move to Missouri with his father and mother, but rather that he was, in a sense, going alone. Not long after he built his cabin at the mouth of the Little Sandy in Kentucky, he had met Olive Vanbibber, who lived about twenty miles up the Ohio River and who, by all accounts, was a beautiful woman.[61]

Nathan was taken by Olive's good looks and pleasant personality, and she was attracted to him. She was born on the banks of the Greenbriar River in Kentucky on January 13, 1783, to Peter and Mary Vanbibber. Her family moved to Point Pleasant when she was two, and after the death of her father on October 10, 1796, Olive and her mother moved to the north bank of the Ohio River above the mouth of the Little Sandy. Now at the age of sixteen, she caught Nathan's attention, and he soon became infatuated with her and then in love. They saw each other as often as time and distance permitted, and she was more than a little disappointed when he told her about his impending move to Missouri, and Nathan was himself morose. He told her that he was glad that he knew her and that he would miss her. She, too, was fond of him and wished him well. Would he write? He would. He told her to take care of herself. She would try.[62]

As the current swept the Boone party south and west, Nathan thought of Olive and their conversations during the months that he had known her, and his longing became too great to bear. When they docked at Limestone, Nathan was glum. There, the excitement of their move intensified because Daniel's daughters Susannah and Jemima, and their families including seventeen grandchildren, joined the group. The assemblage now became even more hectic, with children crying, the packing and repacking of needed items, and melancholy goodbyes to three Boone children who chose to remain behind—Jesse, Levina, and Rebecca. The farewell would be the last time that Daniel and Rebecca would see these children. Neither would return to Kentucky. When the pirogues finally drifted out of sight, they were gone forever.[63]

But not Nathan. When his father met the flotilla at Limestone with the livestock, they talked. He told him that he wanted to go back and marry Olive and bring her to Missouri. Would she marry him and come, Daniel asked? Nathan did not know. If she would not do either, what would Nathan do? Would he stay or follow? Nathan was unsure. They sat and talked, but there was not much to say. He told his mother how he felt. She was not surprised. Most of her other children had already married. It seemed a natural state of affairs for young people on the frontier. But Nathan was her youngest, and she could not help but feel a twinge of sadness. Both Daniel and Rebecca told him to do what he thought best, but Nathan remembered that his father "grieved" because "he had nothing to give him and [his] wife with which to commence the world."[64]

Nathan perhaps said and surely thought that he did not care about a present and that he just needed to see Olive and that he would come as soon as he could. Then, while Daniel got the herd on the trail again and as Morgan organized the pirogues for their journey downriver toward Missouri, Nathan bought a marriage license in hope that Olive would agree. He started back by horse on the seventy-five-mile journey. When he reached her cabin door, Olive was no doubt surprised and happy to see him. She also knew what his presence meant. Would she marry him and follow his family to Missouri? She would. Now? Well, as quickly as possible. On September 26, 1799, a week after Nathan returned from Limestone, they married. Five days later on October 1, Nathan and Olive saddled up and tied their packs on several horses and headed west. Sleeping under the stars the newlyweds snuggled under their blankets before their campfire as the autumn nights turned chill. They ate deer that Nathan shot and the parched corn that Olive prepared from the food pack. After riding through Lexington and crossing the Ohio at Louisville then angling northwest to Vincennes, they held up at least a week while a lame horse got over its soreness. Then, Nathan and Olive followed the trail west across Illinois toward the Mississippi River where, in late October, they crossed to St. Louis.[65]

Many years later, when Olive was an old woman and entitled to reflect on the past with fondness and nostalgia, she did neither. As a product of the frontier, Olive had a toughness and pragmatism that made life in the West not only possible but matter-of-fact. She recalled her experience moving from a cabin on the Ohio River to Missouri with Nathan saying: "On the first of October, without any company but my husband, I started out to Missouri." When they reached the Mississippi, she remembered: "My husband rowed and I steered and held the horses by the bridle. It was rather a perilous trip for so young a couple. I was just sixteen, my husband eighteen."[66]

Born and raised on the frontier, Nathan and Olive moved west with it. They would know no other life but that of the frontier for as long as they lived.

2

MISSOURI

NATHAN AND OLIVE did not linger in St. Louis when they crossed the Mississippi River in late October of 1799, although the relative bustle of the town that served as the Spanish seat of government and formative center for the fur trade made them think about a layover for a rest before they completed the last leg of their journey. Instead, they struck overland for St. Charles, which they reached by crossing the Missouri River in a skiff with Nathan rowing and Olive once again holding the bridle reins of the swimming horses. Here, the French-speaking inhabitants gave them the sense of passing into another country, but the presence of several dozen slaves and a village population of only a few hundred reminded them of the frontier country from which they came. Indeed, with the exception of St. Charles, the Missouri frontier seemed little different from Kentucky. It was a rough and uncultured land with a lack of sophistication or pretention. One French traveler who passed through St. Charles about this time wrote, "The ordinary occupations are hunting and trading with Indians, and it would be difficult to find a collection of individuals more ignorant, stupid, ugly and miserable." Still, St. Charles was thirty years old when Nathan and Olive passed through, and it had become a well-known site for hunters and trappers to sell their skins, buy supplies, and drink whiskey. Certainly St. Charles had rough social edges, but no more so than other frontier towns that had been involved with the fur trade in Kentucky. It did not shock Nathan and Olive, who apparently did not consider it out of the ordinary and who made no comment about the single street, several dozen log houses on each side with gardens, bakehouses, and barns out behind. Nor did the men who wore leather leggings and the women who dressed with deerskin aprons and moccasins strike them as peculiar. Still, the houses of the French must have looked odd compared to the American frontier houses the Boones were used to seeing; the French set their logs perpendicular rather than horizontal and used thatched roofs rather than split wooden shingles.[1]

Perhaps the roughness of society in St. Charles had no apparent effect on Nathan and Olive because they were in a hurry to pass through the town. With their destination near, they were anxious to reach the Femme Osage River. From St. Charles, they followed the Missouri River southwest about twenty-five miles to where Morgan's home occupied a bluff a mile back from the north bank of the Missouri. There, his slaves had built a double-log house and cleared and planted about fifteen acres for the Boone family. That winter, the Boones lived on cornmeal and the deer and turkeys that Nathan, Morgan, and Daniel killed.[2]

During their first few weeks in Missouri, Daniel and the unmarried men in the Boone party claimed lands, as provided by their concessions from the Spanish lieutenant governor, near the mouth of the Femme Osage, an area that soon became known as Bachelor Bottom and that now has been largely reclaimed by the Missouri River. Nathan, however, did not locate and survey any lands because he had not reached St. Louis with his father's group, and only those present, that is, those whose names could be placed on an enumerated list, received a concession from the Spanish government. Soon thereafter, on January 20, 1800, however, Nathan secured 800 arpents, or about 680 acres, on the north bank of the Femme Osage, about four miles upriver from Morgan's place. He acquired this tract by trading a horse, saddle, and bridle, with an estimated value of $120, to Robert Hall, who had received it as his land concession from Lieutenant Governor Zenon Trudeau dated January 26, 1798, for immigrating with Daniel. Nathan moved onto this land soon after Hall left the area sometime before October 1, 1800, because he harvested the corn crop that year. In the agreement Hall reserved the right to return within twelve months to reclaim this land by paying for any improvements that Nathan had made plus his initial investment. If he did not return within the allotted time Nathan had full title to the land and could "hold it for Ever." Nathan did not worry about Hall's return because people routinely came and went on the frontier. Nathan also claimed 420 arpents along Loutre Creek in St. Charles County. Although the circumstances of this acquisition are unclear, this concession from Lieutenant Governor Charles Dehault Delassus was dated December 10, 1799. Nathan had it surveyed on February 4, 1804, and he received a certificate of survey on March 25, 1805. A Board of Land Commissioners, which Congress established on March 2, 1805, to sort out Spanish land titles after the Louisiana Purchase, however, rejected Nathan's claims. Although the board granted Nathan's concession of 800 arpents on February 13, 1806, it rescinded its ruling on December 1, 1809, when Frederick Bates held for the board that the "claim ought not be confirmed to Robert Hall, or his legal representatives." The Board of Land Commissioners also ruled on July 31, 1810, that Nathan's claim of 420 arpents should not be confirmed, probably because he had not lived on this land and cultivated it as required by previous Spanish law.[3]

While Nathan waited for confirmation or rejection of his land claims he quickly began the task of building a log cabin and clearing about eight acres of timber for cropland along the Femme Osage. He intended the cabin to be temporary until he could erect a substantial log house like Morgan's, but the results of his efforts were more tenuous than he had planned. Rather than take time to lay a plank floor, Nathan set the corner logs on stones on a level piece of earth, and the shingles that he split with mallet and froe were not sufficiently lapped to shed water. As a result, when it rained the water dripped down onto the floor and turned it to mud. On one occasion, when he was away from home, the rain made a small pond inside the cabin. Olive then took matters into her own hands and with a young slave woman laid down poles from saplings and a bed of elm bark to cover the mud floor and keep their feet dry, a considerable achievement for a pregnant teenager on the frontier. When summer came in 1800, Nathan erected a substantial log house, and they moved out of the cabin. Not long thereafter, Daniel built Nathan a workshop where Nathan could repair his traps and guns as well as those of his neighbors. In time, he disposed of his tools and Olive used the shop for her loom, adding a fireplace which she also built with the aid of her slave woman. They cut the logs for the chimney with a saw and laid the stones for the hearth. Where Nathan sometimes made do at home, Olive often followed and put things right.[4]

In February of 1800, when the days began to warm and the maple sap started to flow, Daniel and Rebecca joined Nathan and Olive, and they tapped maple trees and boiled the sap down to sugar. Nathan and Daniel enjoyed this time together in the chill air of late winter. Father and son also explored the area and hunted up the Femme Osage River valley. They had land of their own, comfortable houses, and game in the woods. The Missouri frontier was everything that they had hoped it would be, and spring soon brought planting time. Once the corn crop was in the ground, Nathan took ax in hand and went about clearing more land and making minor repairs on the log house. Olive worked in the garden and endured the discomforts of pregnancy. Nathan went into the woods regularly to shoot a deer or turkey for the table, but the ax work and his hunts to provide food merely passed the time until winter returned and he could go into the woods with traps and rifle in the manner of his father for an extended or "long" hunt.[5]

When the autumn came in 1800, Nathan followed the example of his father and, along with Isaac Vanbibber, hunted south of the Missouri along Bourbeuse Creek; he did not return home until January. On this trip, Nathan did not take his traps because he wanted to replenish the meat supply for his family. It was a good hunt, and he and Isaac hauled a considerable weight of venison and turkeys, along with the meat and skins of eight or ten bear, on their packhorses. When spring came Nathan plowed a few acres and planted corn but, like his father, his heart was in the woods, not in the fields. During the late summer and early fall of 1801, he hunted again along the Bourbeuse with Morgan. They shot deer for the skins, which brought forty cents per pound in St. Louis. With each skin averaging about two and a half pounds with the hair scraped off, they made a "pretty fair hunt." Nathan preferred this way of making money best of all. Like his father he was proving himself to be an indifferent farmer and a good hunter. He could make his way in the woods, track and hit what he aimed at, and he could support his family by doing it. The land returned only a pittance and required a lifetime of toil, but the woods provided bounty with meat, skins, and furs; although a long winter hunt often brought hardship and privation, it gave Nathan Boone the life that he understood and loved. Scion of his father, the fruit proved true.[6]

During the late fall of 1801, Nathan and Morgan also made a distant hunt. Each took a pack of traps and trailed two horses. They crossed the Missouri and headed for the Niangua River 150 miles to the southwest. There, they found the beaver plentiful and set their traplines, working both sides of the river until January, by which time they had packed a hundred pelts and a number of deerskins. Although they had gone deep into Osage country, they did not see any Indians. When spring came, Nathan hurriedly planted his corn and returned to the Niangua with William Lamme to take more beaver, which they sold to two hatters from Lexington, Kentucky, who arrived in St. Charles or St. Louis later that spring to buy furs.[7]

Nathan's trapping and hunting expeditions now became more frequent and his farming activity fell by the wayside. In mid-September 1802, Nathan and William Lamme once again headed deep into Missouri. They crossed the Missouri River and hunted the Pomme de Terre River valley about forty miles west of the Niangua, but they did not linger. Nathan wanted to make the major part of their hunt along the Grand River to the north of the Missouri. There, they ran their traplines until early spring, caching the skins as they worked along the river. By late March when they packed up to return to the Femme Osage, they had taken some nine hundred beaver, but they had lost about one hundred pelts to Indians who had discovered one of their caches. Compared to Kentucky, where a catch of two hundred beaver would have been considered a good winter, trapping on the Missouri frontier exceeded his greatest expectations. Neither Nathan nor Lamme saw any Indians during the course of this long hunt, and they returned home about April 1. Nathan then repacked the beaver pelts and took them to Lexington, Kentucky, where he sold them for two dollars each. With approximately eight hundred dollars in his pocket, far more than he ever expected to earn in any year by farming, Nathan committed himself to earning a living by roaming the backcountry with a rifle rather than by taking a plow in hand.[8]

In September 1803, Nathan was back on the Niangua with William Lamme, James and John Callaway, and another man. They hunted deer and set their traplines with some success, but a party of Indians discovered them and stole four of their horses one night. Although they had lost their packhorses, Nathan decided that they should continue their hunt, and they headed west until they reached the Kansas River. They camped on the southeast side of the Kansas at the mouth of the Wakarusa River. Although they had a "good hunt," the Indians in the area kept watch on them and stole a "considerable" number of their furs before Boone's party returned home, but they did not have any direct encounters with them.[9]

Nathan and Matthias Vanbibber returned to the Kansas River in the fall of 1804, trapping along the Grand River on their way. Before they reached the Kansas, Nathan and Matthias had taken fifty-six beaver and twenty-two otters, and they ran their traplines without discovery. Early one morning, however, a party of twenty-two Osages "hellowed" their camp. Nathan and Matthias were about a hundred yards away and came quickly and with apprehension. They had good cause to be alarmed. Not only was this their first direct contact with the Osages who made the Missouri country their home, but this tribe had become increasingly resentful of white intruders on their lands, and Nathan and Matthias clearly were outnumbered. Without ceremony the Osages asked them about their catch, and Nathan told them that it had been fair and pointed to the fur packs. Nathan suspected that their chances of keeping the furs were slim, but he tried to talk his way out of a bad and potentially dangerous situation by using the diplomatic skills that he had learned from his father. Nathan told the Osages that he and Matthias worked for the Chouteau brothers out of St. Louis and that the marks on the traps and the furs identified them as the property of the Chouteau's fur trading company. The Osages knew the Chouteaus, for they had traded their furs to them for some time, and although they had no desire to steal from a dependable trading partner, the Osages suspected that Nathan told less than the truth. Without much contemplation, they collected the furs and strapped the packs over one of Nathan's horses, and grabbed the reins of the other two horses. Before they departed, however, the leader of the group told Nathan and Matthias that they had better "clear out" of this country because another party knew about their presence and was looking for them. The next time, they might not be so lucky as to lose only their horses and furs. With that chiding, the Osages galloped off.[10]

Not long after the Osages departed and while Nathan and Matthias were trying to decide what to do next, the other party of Indians appeared at a distance and called to them. Nathan and Matthias did not return their greeting but instead ran for the woods along the riverbank where they hid. Although this second group of Indians called to them several times, they soon departed because they could not find anything worth stealing from the camp. After some time, Nathan and Matthias decided that they could safely come out of hiding, and they moved their camp about ten miles up the Grand River. The next morning Nathan shot a deer, but the shot attracted four Indians, two on horseback and the others on foot, who surrounded and threatened them with their guns. The Indians professed to be Sacs and demanded something to eat at Nathan's camp. By the time that they had roasted and eaten some of Boone's venison, the Indians had determined that Nathan and Matthias did not have anything of value worth taking except their rifles, which they tried to wrestle from them. Nathan and Matthias were able to maintain possession of their weapons, and the Indians gave up after a brief struggle.

Although unable to take the rifles from Nathan and Matthias and apparently not wanting to shoot them, the Indians had ordered Boone and Vanbibber to leave the camp with them. The Indians wanted the two men to walk in front but they refused to do so, suspecting that they would be shot in the back. As they walked alongside their captors, Nathan and Matthias talked in low voices about their possibilities. Nathan believed that if they were taken far, the Indians probably would try to kill them during the night when their guard was down. And, they agreed, at the first sign of trouble they would each shoot one Indian and attack the other two with their knives.

Nathan and Matthias walked side by side for some distance all the while watching the movements of the Indians. Soon, they came to an open prairie where two more Indians joined them. Now, however, their plan for self-defense could not be executed because the odds had turned against them. Uncertain about what they should do next, both agreed to wait and see, especially because the Indians now began speaking Osage. If they were not Sacs, Nathan and Matthias believed they still might be able to talk their way out of their predicament by convincing the Indians that they were merely trappers working out of St. Louis for the Chouteaus and not freelance trappers who were taking Osage furs and intruding on their lands.

After a brief discussion between the Indians, one of them walked up to Nathan and struck him in the face with the ramrod from his rifle. Boone reeled backward and both he and Matthias cocked their rifles and held them ready to fire. Although his face throbbed with pain, Nathan had learned from his father that there was a time to run and a time to fight and sometimes it was best to do neither. This last alternative often required the most self-discipline and courage. Both Nathan and Matthias as well as the Osages decided to wait and see what would happen next. The Indians, who stood only a few feet from Nathan and Matthias, clearly understood that if they pressed their intimidation any further two of them would surely die. With the odds not as favorable as they would like, the Osages ordered Nathan and Matthias to "go," but Nathan returned the order by commanding them to depart first.

No one moved, and nervous eyes glanced about. Finally the Osage leader told Nathan that his men would depart if he gave them some powder, lead, and flints. Nathan agreed, provided the Osages laid down their rifles and came up one at a time to receive their portion. After the six Osages had been handed their gifts, they moved off with two watching and walking backwards until their party disappeared from sight toward the north in the undulation of the prairie. Once the Osages were gone, Nathan and Matthias struck off at a hard run in the opposite direction, and they continued their flight until after dark. That night Boone and Matthias slept in a rock cave, but they did not build a fire and they had nothing to eat. Although both had ample powder, they only had five bullets between them. Moreover, their heavy blanket coats had been taken by the second party of Osages. In the chill night air of late November, each spent a cold and sleepless night. In the morning, Nathan shot a turkey, which provided two meals at the expense of one of their priceless bullets. Although the roasting meat and a small campfire brightened their spirits, snow began to fall and deepen their misery.

They traveled south at a hard pace through bitter cold for the next two days. When they struck the Missouri, they crossed over the ice and headed downriver. Snow followed them. After several days it was knee-deep. The extreme cold affected their gun barrels and sights, so their rifles would not shoot true. They trembled from hunger whenever they took aim, and they wasted their last four bullets shooting at a buffalo and a deer. Then they cut up their ramrods, but the short pieces made poor bullets and they could not kill game with them. As a result, they traveled seventeen days without eating meat, and they survived only by eating the grapes and "haws" that they found in the thickets.

During this frozen trek, the knifelike wind and cold became a greater enemy than the Osages, and both Nathan and Matthias knew that the weather would kill them as surely and as unmercifully as any Osage war party. As they fled eastward, they kept asking themselves one question: Will we make it? As they hurried through the crusted snow, time also became their enemy as they trembled from the cold and weakened from the lack of food. The Femme Osage seemed a thousand miles away. Only speed would save them.

One day, amidst the snow and cold, they discovered a tree that someone, probably Indians, had used for target practice and they dug out the smashed bullets, built a fire, and heated the lead enough to reshape four balls. Then, they continued east for three or four miles, where they discovered several Indian "cabins" along the river about a half mile below present-day Rocheport. Nathan and Matthias decided to build a fire in one of the houses and rest until morning. Upon entering a house, however, Nathan discovered a large cougar, which he shot without hesitation. While the cougar roasted on a spit Nathan and Matthias cut its skin into two pieces and fashioned vests with the fur turned inside to give them some warmth against the cold. Then they ate the meat, which Nathan remembered tasted "sweet and cattish."

The next morning, after they had traveled three or four miles, they discovered the track of a man in the snow, and Nathan and Matthias followed it, not knowing whether it had been left by an Osage or white trapper. A mile and a half later they entered the camp of a half dozen white hunters who were weather-bound. All of the hunters were friends of Nathan and Matthias, and one of them, James Callaway, was Boone's nephew. By this time, their legs were nearly bare because they had cut off their deerskin leggings to patch their moccasins, which had worn out quickly on the frozen ground and snow. Their friends hurried to give them new moccasins, pants, and blankets as well as ammunition, and they rested a week around the campfire eating buffalo and deer meat.

The discovery of James Callaway's camp saved Nathan's and Matthias's lives, but they still had a hundred miles of hard travel through more cold and snow before they reached home on the Femme Osage. Now, however, the weather moderated, and they had adequate powder, lead, and clothing. As they followed the Missouri River eastward, they shot deer and turkeys when they needed meat, and they kept reasonably warm in their new clothes. When Nathan's hand touched the door of his home and he entered, much to the delight and relief of Olive, it was Christmas Eve. Years later, Olive remembered the moment with her customary wit and propensity for understatement by saying: "It was the first Christmas he had spent at home since our marriage. I had to thank the Indians for that."

Nathan lingered the remainder of the winter recovering from his prolonged exposure to the harsh winter weather during his flight home from the Grand River area. Later in life he attributed his rheumatism and a host of aches and pains to that experience. Indeed, it marked his body and constitution for all time. It did not, however, weaken his spirit or desire to range far along and beyond the frontier in pursuit of both beaver and Indians. In contrast, Matthias Vanbibber never recovered from the ordeal. His health failed, and he remained bedridden for most of the next two or three years before he died. Nathan, however, regained his health, and plotted the recovery of his horses, traps, and furs from the Osages.

Little more than a year later, on December 13, 1805, Nathan sent a petition to William Clark, commander of the territorial militia, requesting $168 for the beaver and otter pelts and traps that the Osages and Kansas took from him on December 3, 1804, "by force of arms" as well as $90 in compensation for the loss of five horses and several "steal" traps under similar circumstances to a "party of Kansas and Kaw Indians" on November 1, 1805. The federal government did not pay this claim for more than twenty years, but if nothing more it indicated to Clark that Boone was a man who knew well the Missouri frontier and who might be of service in the future.[11]

The Osages, who called themselves the Children of the Middle Waters and the Little Ones, controlled the lands, mostly in Missouri, between the vast forests to the east and the sprawling plains to the west. Essentially the Osages occupied the Ozark Plateau and the prairie fringe between the Missouri and Arkansas Rivers during the last half of the eighteenth century. Prior to white settlement east of the Mississippi River, the Osages lived in the lower Ohio River valley, but stronger tribes pushed these Dhegian-Siouxian-speaking people west during the seventeenth century. Once they had left their enemies behind, these Siouxian people divided into five groups— Osage, Kansa, Omaha, Ponca, and Quapaw. The Osages, like their relatives in the other tribal groups, were a horticultural and hunting people who lived in villages, which they relocated whenever the nearby wood supply or their garden plots for corn, beans, and squash became depleted. During the spring and autumn they migrated to the central Great Plains between the Smoky Hill and Arkansas Rivers to hunt buffalo. In the meantime, they lived in long houses with wooden frames made from saplings, which they covered with grass mats and, by the nineteenth century, buffalo hides. These houses often measured forty feet or more in length with widths and heights of about twenty feet, much in the building tradition of the cultural groups that lived in the East. These long houses usually provided shelter for about a dozen family members, including kin.[12]

The Osage men shaved their heads except for a strip called a scalp lock in the middle, while unmarried women braided their hair. Both men and women tattooed their bodies, the latter to signify honors won by their husbands during war or the hunt. Osage men and women also painted their bodies for both ostentation and ceremonies and both wore jewelry in the form of silver rings, strings of beads, and pieces of bone stuck through their ears. One observer reported that: "Their ears, slit by knives, grow to be enormous, and they hang low under the weight of their ornaments with which they are laden." Osage men and women also wore necklaces, arm bands, and silver bracelets and "a profusion of rings on the fingers." The Osage taste for body ornaments, especially silver rings, indicated their contacts with Spanish traders to the south as well as their dependence on those relations to maintain a preferred lifestyle.[13]

The Osages organized socially into the earth and sky clans, the first of which symbolized war and the second, peace. They further subdivided their clans into divisions, each of which having specific ceremonial or military functions. The Osages also maintained a patrilineal heritage for the determination of clan membership, although upon marriage the couple lived with the wife's family. Regardless of their membership in the various subclans, the Osages worshipped an all-powerful and all-prevailing spirit that was everywhere—Wah' Kon-Tah—the Mystery Force. This great spirit had created the Osages and all things in the universe, and the Osages were deeply devoted to Wah' Kon-Tah, rising before dawn each day to learn his will through a prayerful reverence.[14]

The Osage also organized politically according to a class of leaders and commoners, both of which were determined by inheritance, wealth, and tradition, although bravery in war enabled individuals to gain status and power that would not have been possible otherwise. Two chiefs, one each from the earth and sky clans, wielded political power based on heredity, and they came from elite kinship groups while a few lineages controlled the tribal council. The chiefs kept order, were in charge of healing the sick, and directed the buffalo hunts. The tribal council also dealt with village matters and diplomacy and war.[15]

By the mid-eighteenth century, the French had discovered the Osages, who traded them beaver pelts for guns, powder, and lead, which made their hunting easier and their chances of success more certain. The French also used their contacts with the Osages to help discourage British expansion from the north and east. After Spain gained control of French territory west of the Mississippi River with the Peace of Paris in 1763, which ended the French and Indian War, Spanish traders made contact with the Osages and began to exchange horses, mules, and other items for furs. The Spanish, however, tried to control the Osages by restricting the weapons trade that opened the door of economic opportunity for British traders from Canada. The Spanish attempted to block contact between the Osages and these traders and to prevent British influence on the tribe by encouraging the Sacs to attack them and keep the Osages and the British apart. In 1795, Lieutenant Governor Zenon Trudeau wrote: "The Sacs, who are very numerous, hunting on the Missouri killed ten or twelve Osages after having shaken hands with them and promised peace. I believe that it is very important that these two nations are continually in discord in order to stop the communications of the Osages [with the British] upon the upper Missouri."[16]

The Osages quickly became dependent on the fur trade to provide them with both essentials and luxuries, such as knives, metal cooking equipment, blankets, needles, thread, beads, and fishhooks. While the Osages periodically fought to ensure control of their traditional hunting lands, they also soon became reliant on fur traders working out of St. Louis for essential goods. The fur trade became so important to both the Spanish and the Osages that Governor Baron de Carondelet granted a monopoly to trade with the Osages to Pierre and Auguste Chouteau in May 1794. By August of the next year, the Chouteaus, who had considerable experience dealing with the Indians in Spanish territory, had built a trading post on Halley's Bluff near the Osage River in present-day Vernon County. Called Fort Carondelet, the facility was at best a rendezvous for the trappers and traders who worked for the Chouteaus as well as a source of supply for the Osages. Soon, thousands of beaver pelts and otter and bear skins passed from Osage hands to the Chouteaus at Fort Carondelet. Thus, while the Osages controlled travel and trade along the Missouri, Arkansas, and Red Rivers during the eighteenth century, they no longer lived a life free from European constraints. Indeed, the Osage economy and social and political systems would necessarily change to accommodate the effects of European intrusion on their lands. Yet even though Osage dependency on European suppliers increased, the tribe remained a formidable force that Lieutenant Governor Trudeau estimated could field a war force of 1,250 men. Spain's decision to authorize the establishment of Fort Carondelet and award the Chouteau family a monopoly of the lucrative Osage trade indicated the failure of its efforts to control this powerful tribe. Now, Spain would rely on unrestricted trade rather than economic or military coercion to influence the Osages.[17]

By 1800, however, white American trappers, such as Nathan Boone, and other Indian people were beginning to encroach on Osage lands. The Sac and their relatives the Fox (Mesquaki), pressured by westward-moving settlers, began to establish villages on the northern edge of Osage territory and to hunt south of the Missouri. The land between the Des Moines River and the Grand and Chariton Rivers now became a neutral ground that separated the Osages to the south and the Sacs and Foxes to the north, with each group driving the other away if they ventured too far south or ranged too far north.

On the western and southwestern fringe of Missouri, the Delawares and the Shawnees, who had been encouraged to move west by the federal government, established new villages and claimed lands that restricted the traditional range of the Osages. To the south, the Cherokees, Choctaws, and Chickasaws also began to hunt at will in the Ouachita Mountains and Ozark Plateau, further violating Osage territory.[18]

The aggressive Sacs exchanged their furs for essentials, particularly rifles, powder, and lead, with Canadian traders at Prairie du Chien, while the Osages conducted a similar business with Auguste and Pierre Chouteau. Both the Osages and the Sacs were well supplied by their benefactors by the end of the eighteenth century, but they were relatively equal in strength and, despite periodic raids against each other, they held their respective territories in a stalemate of mutual power. At the same time, Kickapoo and Potawatomi raiding parties crossed the Mississippi River and struck Osage hunting camps in northeastern Missouri for the purpose of stealing horses and furs and taking prisoners. In the spring of 1799, Kickapoo raiders attacked an Osage camp while most of the men were away bear hunting; when the Kickapoo departed, forty-five Osages, mostly women and children, lay dead. Six years later, during the early winter, a band of Potawatomis killed thirty-four women and children and took sixty prisoners at another Osage hunting camp.[19]

The Osages struck back hard and with a ferocity that made their enemies pause and ask the Spanish for protection. During the autumn of 1792, the Osages attacked intruders from the Delaware, Shawnee, Potawatomi, Miami, and Peoria nations with such vengeance that these people collectively complained to Lieutenant Governor Zenon Trudeau in St. Louis that "We were attacked on every side by the Osages who killed us and stole our horses. . . . We appeal to you, my father, to . . . keep them and prevent them from killing us and stealing our horses." This plea had little effect on the Osages who continued to strike their enemies at will long after the Missouri country became a territorial possession of the United States with the Louisiana Purchase in 1803. While the Osages engaged in defensive maneuvers to protect their lands to the north and east, they continued their traditional practice of raiding along the Red River valley and striking the Wichitas and stealing their horses. The

Osages also competed violently and successfully with the Pawnees to control the buffalo country south of the Smoky Hill River in present-day east-central Kansas.[20]

When Boone moved to Missouri and began to venture into the Ozark Plateau in search of deer and beaver skins, the Osages were not only the largest tribe in this region, with about 6,300 people, but they were also the most powerful tribe, with approximately 1,500 fighting men. They had established a strong trading relationship with the Chouteaus, and they were intent on keeping competitors, either whites or Indians, from encroaching on their lands to take the furs they considered their own. In 1804, Thomas Jefferson knew that the Osages were the most powerful people in the prairie-plains transition area west of the Mississippi River when he wrote: "The truth is they are the great nation South of the Missouri, their possession extending from thence to the Red River."[21]

Despite this sprawling territory, the Osages lacked the unity necessary to make a strong stand against those who ventured onto their lands and hunting grounds. By the late eighteenth century five bands lived in three general areas. The Big Osage resided near the mouth of the river that bore their name in central Missouri, while the Little Osage camped along the Missouri River more than a hundred miles to the west. The others lived along the Arkansas River to the south. The Osages in Missouri spoke for the tribe, and they had the closest contacts with the Chouteaus for trade and with the Spanish government via various officials in St. Louis. By the beginning of the nineteenth century, however, the southern Osages essentially led independent economic and political lives from their relatives in Missouri, in part because the Chouteaus had attempted to dictate tribal leadership by recognizing Pawhuska, also known as White Hair, as the sole leader and spokesman for the tribe. Instead of creating political unity for the Osages and logistical harmony for their fur trading business, the Chouteaus merely further divided the tribal groups and created ill will among them. In April 1800, White Hair reported that the Arkansas band had "withdrawn from his authority." Although Lieutenant Governor Charles Dehault Delassus both threatened and bribed them to recognize White Hair as the single leader of the Osages, the Arkansas band ignored him.[22]

The Spanish also attempted to force the Arkansas Osages to join the Missouri bands to simplify the logistics of the fur trade. Soon thereafter, the Americans also failed to achieve tribal consolidation. This failure, however, was due more to intertribal rivalries than opposition to Jefferson's plan to make room west of the Mississippi for the eastern tribes. At this time, traders operating out of New Orleans also attempted, with some success, to lure the Arkansas bands into their range of influence and away from the Missouri villages and St. Louis. Thus, while the Osages confronted white encroachment on their lands, their lack of unity prevented a solid military front at a time when they had the greatest need for cooperation.[23]

By the early nineteenth century, the Osages were also weakened by an economy that extracted a heavy price from their lands and increasingly became dominated by American political power. They had become so reliant on American trade goods that they began to range farther into the southwest to hunt and steal horses. They also killed beaver, otter, bear, and deer in Missouri by the thousands. In 1806, the northern Osage sent forty-three thousand dollars' worth of furs through St. Louis to eastern markets at a time when traders paid only forty cents per pound for deer skins and not more than two dollars for bear hides while other small animal pelts brought only twenty-five cents each.

While the Osages depleted their hunting grounds in Missouri and beyond, immigrant Indians also attempted to gain access to the lucrative fur trade, and they increasingly crossed onto Osage lands. The federal government, however, insisted that the Osages remain at peace with their ever increasing neighbors if they wanted to maintain trade relations. Because the Osages desired to continue their trade with the Americans more than they wanted to strike their enemies, they obeyed federal instructions to such an extent that by 1805, Zebulon Pike contended that they had become a "nation of Quakers, as it respects the nations to the north and east of them."[24]

It was to the Osages, then, that Nathan Boone rode in the spring of 1805 in search of the furs, horses, and traps that had been taken from him during the previous winter. He left his home on the Femme Osage when the weather warmed, and he traveled alone, stopping first at the Big Osage town on Pomme de Terre Creek about six miles from the Osage River. When Nathan rode into their village past the long houses, where the women, with tattoos and red paint daubed along the part of their hair to symbolize the path of the sun, watched with suspicion and caution as they went about their household tasks. The men, many of whom had elaborately decorated their bodies with yellow, green, and white paint, also watched as he made his way to the center of the village. There, White Hair met him. Boone nodded and White Hair offered a noncommittal greeting. White Hair asked Boone, what did he want? Nathan replied that he had come for the horses, furs, and traps that the Osages had stolen from him. White Hair did not know anything about Boone's loss, but he asked if Nathan knew who took his possessions. Boone looked about those gathered but he could not recognize anyone as he later recalled "owing to their various painted countenances and changes of rude dress." Still, he persisted. The thieves had been Osages, he said. They spoke Osage, and they dressed like Osages.[25]

White Hair could see no reason to pursue the matter. After all, Boone had been on Osage land, trapping beaver that belonged to his people. The frontier was dangerous as everyone knew. The Sacs often raided and hunted south of the Grand and other tribes often encroached on Osage lands. Anyone could have made the theft. No, Boone said, the men were Osage. If they were not here, he would look elsewhere. Although the Osages occupied several villages, he would go to them all until he regained his rightful property. Although Nathan did not have much hope of recovering his traps and furs, the horses could not be hidden as easily and with a turn of luck, he might get them back. White Hair told Nathan that he was free to try.[26]

At that point, when both Nathan and White Hair remained stubborn in their positions, a trader in the surrounding crowd spoke up and told them that he had heard that a party of Little Osages, who lived in another village about a half dozen miles away, had robbed him. White Hair agreed that a party of Little Osages might be responsible and as a sign of goodwill he sent several men to seize Boone's horses at their village. If Nathan's horses had been there by the time the recovery party arrived, his presence and purpose had become known and the horses were gone. Boone, however, would not accept failure, and he remained among the Osages for seventeen days, traveling among their villages, asking questions, and looking for his horses among the pony herds. But, with the exception of recognizing two of his traps, he found nothing, and he returned home disappointed. He had, however, learned that firmness brought results among the Osages and that courage earned their respect.[27]

Although Nathan preferred the solitude of the wilderness to domestic life, he was not always knee-deep in cold water setting beaver traps, skinning deer, or dealing with Indians. When he was not on horseback heading for the Niangua, Osage, or Grand River country, children, home, and family life occupied much of his time. In late May of 1800 Nathan and Olive traveled with his parents and assorted friends and relatives to St. Charles, where Brother L. Lusson, Priest of the Recolet of St. Charles, married Morgan Boone and Sara Griffin Lewis, the fourteen-year-old daughter of John Lewis and Elizabeth Harve, who lived at the Post of St. Andrews, otherwise known as the Bon Homme settlement on the south side of the Missouri. Nathan and Olive signed the witness list and returned home to the Femme Osage. Little more than a month later, on July 3, 1800, Olive gave birth to the first of their fourteen children. They named him James in honor of Nathan's brother who had been killed by Indians during his parents' trek from North Carolina to the Kentucky frontier. Daniel and Rebecca were both happy and grateful, although their remembrance of the past tempered their spirits. Nathan was glad that he could honor his parents by naming his first son for a brother that he had never known but who had meant so much to his parents.[28]

While tending to the business of family and building a house, Nathan also began a new venture far to the west. During his flight from the Osages during the winter of 1804, he and Matthias Van-bibber had passed a salt spring along a creek that drained into the Missouri River about 150 miles from the Femme Osage. Salt was an essential mineral, being used in considerable quantities by the frontier people to preserve their pork, which along with venison served as a dietary staple. Nathan had heard his father talk about boiling water for salt to supply the Boonesborough community in Kentucky, and he had seen others make salt prior to his move to Missouri. With a little ingenuity and work, Nathan thought, he could make money at the salt springs and help provide for his family during the summer months when he gave up the hunt and trapline because beaver and deerskins were not in their prime.[29]

Nathan needed considerable help to boil the water and ship the salt down the Missouri to markets in St. Charles and St. Louis, and he asked Morgan to lend a hand. Morgan agreed, and sometime during the spring or early summer of 1805, they headed west with a half dozen men and packhorses laden with heavy kettles. When they reached the springs or lick, they built a fireplace or furnace from nearby rock. It extended thirty feet with a width of about five feet. The walls rose four feet and the top remained open in order to hold their forty kettles over the flames. Once the furnace had been completed, they cut and stacked wood, dipped water from the fast-flowing spring, filled the kettles, and started the fire.[30]

Soon they were producing between twenty-five to thirty bushels of salt and burning nearly a cord of wood per day. By frontier standards a bushel of salt weighed fifty pounds, and it brought as much as two and a half dollars. Nathan figured he could earn more than sixty dollars per day based on a production of twenty-five bushels per day. Given this rate of return Nathan and Morgan could easily pay their workers fifteen dollars per month and still pocket considerable profits. Even so, boiling water for salt was hot, tiring work. With approximately three hundred gallons of brine required to manufacture a bushel of salt, the men were constantly at work carrying water, cutting wood, and scraping the "bittern" pans that collected the salt at the bottom of the kettles. Then they had to pack it and, at first, send it down the Missouri in pirogues that they crafted by hollowing sycamore trunks. Later, keelboats carried their salt to the settlements along the river and St. Louis.[31]

Their work went well and the location became known as Boone's Lick. Before long Nathan and Morgan had enlarged their furnace and built a new one that gave them the ability to boil sixty kettles, employ as many as twenty men, and produce a hundred bushels of salt daily. By 1808, however, Nathan spent less and less time at the lick because of his obligations as a government surveyor and army guide as well as his preference to hunt and trap whenever possible. Consequently on August 15, he made a three-year agreement with a John Zumwalt and a man by the name of Murdough to work the furnace for him. Boone provided forty kettles, two carts, four oxen, three axes, and a flatboat, and Zumwalt and Murdough agreed to send him fifty bushels of salt per month with delivery at Gardner's Landing on the Femme Osage.[32]

Although it is not clear how well this lease arrangement worked out, trouble with the Indians apparently endangered the operation of the saltworks from the beginning. In December 1805, Territorial Governor James Wilkinson wrote to Secretary of War Henry Dearborn: "I am info[rmed] that the salt works of a son of old Dan Boone, about one hundred and fifty miles up the Missouri have been broken up." The Indians he reported had "killed or carried away the cattle and destroyed the salt works." Although Nathan's losses may not have been as great as the governor assumed, the Indians caused him more trouble than he wanted. And during the summer of 1808, Nathan had to agree not to hold either Zumwalt or Murdough responsible for "accidents" caused by the "savages" that might keep his salt making business out of production. During the months that followed, the Indians made the operation increasingly dangerous and ultimately unprofitable. In order to provide the workers with a consistent supply of fresh meat, for example, Nathan periodically contracted with drovers to deliver a herd of cattle to Boone's Lick. The Indians, probably Osages or Sacs, who hunted the area, considered the cattle to be theirs for the taking. They killed the cattle that wandered too far from the camp's grazing area, and they stole others, including the oxen that the men used to draw loads of wood to the furnace stack. Although Nathan and Morgan could temporarily provide their workers with deer, replacing lost oxen proved serious and expensive. First, they had to send word back to the settlements in the St. Charles vicinity that they wanted to buy trained oxen and then those had to be driven to Boone's Lick—all of which cost a considerable amount of time and money. Consequently, after four years of enduring the frequent losses of their beef cattle and oxen, Nathan and Morgan decided their salt business did not provide sufficient returns and, in 1811, they sold their operation to a James Morrison.[33]

During the few years that Nathan and Morgan operated the furnaces, they followed a route that eventually wore down to a trail, called a trace, that linked Boone's Lick in present-day Howard County to the St. Charles and Femme Osage communities. In time, it became known as the Boone's Lick Road and bore heavy traffic when settlers began moving into central Missouri following the War of 1812, with settlers passing through Warrenton, Jonesburg, and Danville then skirting about eight miles north of Fulton and Columbia before reaching the Boone's Lick country.[34]

Despite the relative success of the salt business, Nathan made more money as a surveyor after the United States acquired the Louisiana Territory in 1803. This opportunity came after Congress created the Territory of Louisiana, essentially present-day Missouri, on March 3, 1805, based on the Northwest Ordinance of 1787. With a territorial government in place, the surveying of the public domain could begin, although the land office in St. Louis did not offer public lands for sale in Missouri until 1818. Perhaps as early as the fall of 1806, when Silas Bent arrived in St. Louis as principal deputy surveyor, Boone contracted through the territorial government to help survey the newly acquired lands in present-day St. Charles, Lincoln, Warren, and Montgomery Counties. He also conducted extensive survey work that subdivided the two common fields that belonged to St. Charles and that became known as "Boone's Survey."[35]

Nathan worked under the Land Law of 1800, also known as Harrison's Frontier Land Act, which required federal lands (public domain) to be surveyed and divided into 640-acre sections. The government would then sell these in 320-acre blocks at two dollars per acre. Nathan had learned the skill and art of surveying from his father in Kentucky and Virginia, and to conduct the work as accurately as possible, he hired ax men to clear the line of sight for his circumferentor, a special compass with sight vanes mounted on a tripod, and to mark the "bearing trees" that would help show the corners of his surveys. He also hired chain men to hold the poles and call off the distances measured while he sighted and drew up the plat maps and recorded the physical features of the area. But Nathan took more care than his father, partly because of federal requirements that surveyors make allowances for magnetic variation and to run correction lines to accommodate the convergence of meridians and thereby more accurately locate the corners of sections and quarter sections, techniques that his father had not practiced but that resulted in the most accurate surveys possible at that time. For this work the General Land Office paid surveyors such as Boone at the rate of three dollars per mile, but he had to pay the chain and ax men as well as cover all of his expenses. With thrift, however, a surveyor could make money, and the work provided a steady and reliable income. Nathan liked surveying. He enjoyed the sense of accomplishment, and he relished his time in the woods and open country, even if he was not hunting or trapping, provided, of course, that the Osages and the other nearby tribes remained at peace. By the summer of 1805, however, peace at home and abroad became increasingly uncertain.[36]

3

THE OSAGE EXPEDITION

B Y THE AUTUMN of 1805, the Osages, Sacs, and Ioways were causing considerable trouble for the traders and settlers who ventured into central and western Missouri. In all likelihood, hunting parties from one of these tribes were the ones who stole and killed Nathan's cattle at Boone's Lick. By the early nineteenth century, the Osages especially had gained a mean reputation among the white settlers in Missouri. Osage warriors stole horses, killed cattle, plundered homes, and threatened lives. The chiefs could not control their young men, who believed only force, not accommodation, would protect their lands from white encroachment. In early December, Governor James Wilkinson decided to send an officer to the Osage villages to warn them to keep the peace. Otherwise, the governor feared their raids would lead to a general war "at no great distance of time."[1]

Indeed, the danger of an Indian war increased with each passing year as the western tribes attempted to halt the migrating frontier people, and the British, operating out of Canada, encouraged them to resist white settlement and to protect their lands and the British fur trade. In early March 1808, Frederick Bates, recently the acting territorial governor and now territorial secretary to Meriwether Lewis, who had just arrived in St. Louis to assume the duties of governor, reported that "the Osage Indians have, and are now committing depredations." Although they had not killed anyone, Bates informed Lewis that they stole the horses and destroyed property of the frontier people whenever possible. On one occasion: "Furniture was split to pieces with their Tomahawks; feather beds ript open and destroyed, and everything which could not be carried away rendered useless to the owners."[2]

Because the "wicked young men" of the Osages and Sacs had a propensity to commit "bad deeds" and because the frontier people, such as Nathan Boone, were becoming increasingly fearful for the safety of their families, the Territory of Louisiana organized a militia in 1804 to provide for local defense. Two years later, James Wilkinson, who served as territorial governor, appointed Nathan to the rank of ensign in the Sixth Company of the militia in the District of St. Charles. As an ensign Nathan ranked third in command of his company behind his father, who received the appointment of captain, and Joshua Dodson, who became the lieutenant. Nathan's commission indicates the reputation that his family had for helping settle the frontier and the recognition of his own experience in the backcountry as a trapper and hunter. By 1806, no one knew the western forests and river valleys of Missouri better than Nathan Boone.[3]

Territorial legislation creating the militia required all male inhabitants in the district between the ages of sixteen and sixty to serve. Each man had to provide his own weapon and to attend six musters annually. As an ensign Nathan had the responsibility of helping organize the required four musters for the company, and he participated in the battalion muster held each April and the regimental muster each October. On muster days Nathan also had the responsibility to get the militiamen onto the drill grounds by eleven o'clock to be ready for the roll call a half hour later. He then had to report the names of the missing so that the adjutant general of the district could levy a fine.[4]

The militia were not required to drill on muster day, but just prove that they could show up when called. Given the independent nature of militia that were organized across the frontier, the chore of assembly often proved difficult enough. Still, this practice was important because the law provided that the militia could be called into service by the governor or the commander of any district to thwart an invasion or Indian trouble. Failure to obey a call to arms or to disobey the command of an officer, such as Nathan, meant court-martial for cowardice and desertion. In 1807, a revised militia law authorized the governor to call the militia into service for no more than sixty days and reduced the maximum age limit to forty-five. It also required three hours of drill on muster days and ordered the officers to wear the uniform of commissioned officers in the U.S. infantry. In addition, the act raised the company musters to seven and set the company strength at a range of thirty-eight to seventy men. Nathan's Sixth Company then became part of a battalion composed of two to four companies, while four to eight companies could be organized into a regiment. With so many small companies, battalions, and regiments, Nathan served as one of many officers in the militia. Yet his family name and his considerable experience as a long hunter and trapper gained him immediate recognition as a leader and an officer who stood out among many. At the age of twenty-five, then, Ensign Nathan Boone in the militia of the Territory of Louisiana, began what became a long military career distinguished by his recognition of duty, acceptance of responsibility, and knowledge of the frontier.[5]

In 1808, Nathan's experience on the far western frontier of Missouri and as an ensign in the militia brought him to the attention of William Clark, who only two years before had returned from his expedition to the Pacific Northwest with Meriwether Lewis. Clark now served as U.S. Indian agent and brigadier general of the militia of the Louisiana Territory, and Lewis held the post of territorial governor. At this time the federal government was attempting to keep the western tribes loyal or at least neutral to the United States as its relationship with Great Britain deteriorated; Britain had been impressing American seamen into its Royal Navy and seizing American goods as contraband that could aid France in its continuing war with its perennial enemy. In 1808, then, to lure the tribes on the upper Missouri from British influence, the War Department planned to establish good relations with them through trade. In order to do so, the department began establishing trading houses, called factories, where an agent or factor would conduct the fair exchange of merchandise with the Indians for furs, skins, and other goods.[6]

On May 17, Superintendent of Indian Trade John Mason sent a letter to George C. Sibley, newly appointed Indian factor for the Osage, in which he explained the purpose of this policy. Mason wrote: "The principal object of the Government in these establishments being to secure the Friendship of the Indians in our country in a way most beneficial to them and the most effectual & economical to the United States." Mason instructed Sibley to "be conciliatory in all your intercourse with the Indians & so demean yourself toward them generally and toward their chiefs in particular, as to obtain and preserve their Friendship & to secure their attachment to the United States." By so doing, the federal government would not only establish a presence among the western tribes, but also gain their friendship and goodwill, which would smooth the way for additional land cessions from the Indians.[7]

On the Missouri frontier the federal government needed a fort to serve as a trading location to gain influence over the increasingly hostile Osage, Sac, Ioway, and Kansa people. Pressed by the rapid encroachment of white settlers on their lands and lured by British traders from the North West Company operating out of Canada, these western tribes posed a dangerous threat to government plans for the peaceful acquisition of their lands and their removal to more isolated and confined locations. At first, Clark and Lewis thought a post for trade and defense could be established near the Indian villages on the Osage River, but the water flow did not permit navigation during most of the year. Consequently, they decided to build a fort on the Missouri. Clark and Lewis believed that a fort on the river would provide a central and easily accessible trading location for the Indian people who lived in the prairie-plains transition area. It would enable the federal government to exert its influence over them, lure them away from Canadian traders, and tie the tribes to the federal government in time of peace. A military bastion at this location would also enable the army to strike deep into Indian country in time of war.[8]

By June 1808, the Missouri frontier had become so dangerous for white traders, hunters, and settlers that Governor Lewis announced that no licenses to trade with the Osage and other tribes would be issued until permanent forts could be built. A month later he notified Secretary of War Henry Dearborn that White Hair, the principal chief of the Osages, could not "govern" his people, and that federal authorities "must therefore take such measures with rispect to them as we deem most proper." Lewis then decided that White Hair should "withdraw the well disposed part of his band . . . retire to Fire Prarie, [an open area along the Missouri River near present-day Sibley] and leave the malecontents to their fate." At the same time, he told the Shawnees, Delawares, and Kickapoos in the St. Louis vicinity not to attack the Osages who withdrew from the hostile bands. Lewis also told those tribes, as well as the Ioways and Sacs, that the hostile Osages were "no longer under the protection of the government of the U'States, and that they were at liberty to wage war against them if they thought proper, under this restriction only, that they should attack in a body sufficiently large to cut them off completely and drive them from their country."[9]

Lewis would have peace in the Missouri country by separating the Osages into two groups—those who wanted peace and those who wanted war. He would provide for the protection of the former and ensure the destruction or removal of the latter. Quickly Lewis sent runners to the various Indian nations to explain his policy of both peace and war, and he was pleased to learn that the Shawnees planned to assemble a war party of twelve hundred men a few miles above the mouth of the Gasconade on the Missouri River for the purpose of attacking the Osages. Lewis believed the attack would be successful because only about seven hundred hostile Osages would remain in their villages after White Hair withdrew those who wanted peace. The *Missouri Gazette* predicted a "warm and important campaign."[10]

While Lewis planned for an Indian war against the Osages, William Clark knew just the site needed for such a fort where the peaceful Osages could gather, live, and trade, which would enable both persuasion and control. He had passed it on June 23, 1804, on his expedition up the river. About thirty miles east of present-day Kansas City, near the town of Sibley, Clark observed a portion of the south bank that rose seventy feet above the river. Here the river narrowed and the current made a relatively big and quiet eddy that his boats had used to make the poling of the expedition's keelboats easier. Clark recognized the importance of the site for future use and wrote in his diary, "This will be a good site for a fort and trading house with the Indians." Here the guns of a fort could command the river and all traffic would depend on American permission. Only those traders who held licenses issued by the federal government would have access to the fur trade beyond, and any hostile force, native or foreign, that descended the river to strike the settlements in Missouri would meet a formidable foe. At this location, the federal government could build a fort that would be the most western point of defense for white settlements in Missouri.[11]

On July 1, 1808, Governor Lewis recommended Clark's site to Secretary of War Dearborn. Lewis reported that the fort could be located on the southern bank of the Missouri at a place known as Fire Prairie, located about three hundred miles upriver from the mouth of the Missouri and approximately fifty or sixty miles from the Osage villages. Here, the Osage trade could be well established and supplies could easily reach the fort. Lewis wrote, "from this place we can ascend or decend at pleasure, while on the Osage river difficulties of the navigation are such (that even admitting the Indians were friendly) as would always embarras the trade considerably." Lewis also noted that Fire Prairie was "convenient to the Kanzes as well as to the principal hunting grounds of the Ioways and Saucs." He believed that by "compelling several nations to trade at the same establishment they will find it absolutely necessary to live in peace with each other." Ultimately Lewis believed that a fort located at Fire Prairie "would in the course of a few years be very instrumental in bringing about a permanent peace between the nations on the lower part of the Missouri." Accordingly, he ordered the Osages under White Hair to assemble at Fire Prairie for the purpose of making a treaty.[12]

Fire Prairie became the logical location, because the federal government wanted to sign a land cession as well as a peace treaty with the Osages and to consolidate that tribe near a fort and trading house on the Missouri. In order to establish the post Clark planned to send a company up the Missouri on keelboats laden with twenty thousand dollars' worth of trade goods while he led another party across land to the site. Accordingly, on August 7, 1808, Captain Eli Clemson left Fort Belle Fontaine with eighty-one soldiers and several civilians, including the government factor George C. Sibley. Although only twenty-six years of age, Sibley had served two years as the assistant factor at Fort Belle Fontaine near St. Louis, and he had earned a reputation for hard work and attention to detail. Still, his preference for wearing cutaway coats and silk vests no doubt caused Captain Clemson and his regulars to view him with a jaundiced eye. Although Clark had great confidence that Clemson could locate the site for a new fort, he was less sure about his own plans for an overland route and skeptical that Clemson's men alone could

In 1807, William Clark became brigadier general of the militia for the Louisiana Territory and principal Indian agent headquartered in St. Louis. Clark learned of Nathan's reputation for hunting and trapping in the backcountry of Missouri and, in 1808, he asked Boone to guide an expedition to Fire Prairie to treat with the Osages. *State Historical Society of Missouri, Columbia.*

handle trouble if it came from a large attack by the Indians. Lewis eased Clark's fears by ordering twenty cavalry and sixty mounted riflemen from the militia to accompany him. Although this force would provide some comfort, Clark also recognized that he needed someone who knew the far reaches of the Missouri frontier to lead his force to the rendezvous with Clemson.[13]

Clark did not inquire long about who he should ask to lead his expedition. Everyone in the St. Louis and St. Charles areas knew that Nathan Boone had hunted, trapped, and explored the western country from the Grand River on the north to the Marais des Cygnes on the south and to the Smoky Hill in the west. If anyone knew the lay of the land, the creeks and streams, the fords, the woods, the game trails, and the Indian camps, it was Nathan Boone. Clark sent word to Boone requesting a meeting, probably at Fort Belle Fontaine. When Nathan arrived, Clark explained the purpose of the mission and their need to contact the Osages and bring them into his camp to sign a treaty and consolidate the tribe under federal watch and influence. Did Boone know the site on the Missouri where he wanted to build a fort? Yes, he had seen it before on his hunts. Could he lead a force there as quickly and as directly as possible in order to arrive about the same time that Clemson reached the site? Nathan no doubt responded that the route was direct and not difficult, but an overland trip across some 250 miles of unmarked terrain would take time. Could Nathan, Clark probably also asked, find the Osage villages and bring their inhabitants in to talk and sign a treaty? Yes, he likely said, he knew where to look for the Osages who would be to the south along the Marais des Cygnes. Whether they would come in was another matter. Did Clark have an interpreter? Yes, the half-breed Paul Loise. Did Boone know him? Yes. What Clark wanted, he said, was for Nathan to lead him and his company of rangers, that is, mounted riflemen, to the site of the new fort and bring in the Osages.[14]

Boone accepted Clark's offer although he may not have had a choice. Although much of Nathan's military service between his appointment as an ensign in the territorial militia and his service as a captain of volunteers during the War of 1812 is, at present, impossible to trace, Nathan now served as a captain of the St. Charles rangers. In 1804, the first militia act for the Territory of Louisiana authorized the governor for the District of Louisiana to raise volunteer, mounted, and uniformed troops for special services. Three years later, the law was amended so that volunteer rangers were relieved from militia duties, and they were authorized to receive arms and other military equipment from the federal government for as long as they served. These rangers were also required to be prepared to mobilize quickly.[15]

As an officer of the St. Charles rangers, then, Nathan may have been ordered, rather than asked, by Clark to guide the expedition to the Missouri and the Osages. In late July, however, the *Missouri Gazette* reported: "It is with heart felt pleasure we announce the patriotism displayed by the St. Charles troop of horse, a few days ago; they offered their services to accompany Gen. Clark up the Missouri, in order to protect and assist in the building of the intended Fort." No matter. This was the life that Nathan loved best—ranging far out on the frontier away from civilization. As a settler and militia man, he was also keenly interested in keeping the peace with the Osages and other tribes to ensure the safety of his own family as well as for the settlers who were beginning to move farther west, beyond the St. Charles District.[16]

Clark ordered the rangers, to assemble in St. Charles on August 25, 1808, where, according to the law, they mustered at eleven o'clock. With this departure date, Clark planned to arrive at Fire Prairie at the same time that Clemson's keelboats reached the fort site. A half hour later they rode out with Nathan in the lead, followed by Clark, then Captain Mackey Wherry and Lieutenant James Callaway, and with the rangers behind riding two abreast. They rode through rolling country with occasional meadows of high grass, and they crossed several branches of Dardenne Creek as they made their way west at a fast pace through present-day Warren County. By evening they had traveled twenty-one miles, far better than the eighteen miles that the U.S. Cavalry would later average on the Great Plains, while trained cavalry riding over good roads could be expected only to cover twenty to twenty-five miles per day. After making camp near a pond and settlement, probably about seven miles south of present-day Wentzville, many of the nearby residents, some of whom had family members in this troop of rangers, visited the camp.[17]

Nathan had hoped for an early start the next day, but a heavy fog prevented the men from locating several horses that had wandered from the herd during the night. By seven o'clock, however, they were ready and "marched" northwest through timbered land interspersed with grassy plain until they crossed the Peruque. Boone knew the land well, and he led the rangers roughly along the divide that separated the streams that flowed north into the Mississippi and south into the Missouri. Nathan took the soldiers west, crossing Indian Camp Creek and the Eagle and May Forks of Big Creek. Late in the afternoon, after covering twenty-two miles, they stopped at Cuivre Creek for the night. Clark noted in his diary that this wooded area was "good Second rate land."[18]

The next day, Boone led the men out of camp at 6:30 A.M. Boone took Clark and the rangers essentially along present-day Interstate 70, near Wright City, Jonesburg, High Hill, and Danville, crossing Charette and Bear Creeks and passing over a trail that led north to an Ioway village. Nathan took them to a campsite near a salt lick on the east bank of the Loutre River. Although not as productive for making salt as his springs to the west, he claimed this site, known as Loutre Lick, as his own. After three days, Nathan had led them at a consistent pace, and the rangers covered another twenty-one miles. During the day, Clark sent out a hunting party, which brought back several deer and two turkeys that the men divided and roasted over their fires.[19]

At seven o'clock in the morning of Sunday, August 28, Nathan showed the rangers a ford that he used to cross the Loutre River. Then, they passed through a plain near present-day Williamsburg. They saw elk grazing several times during the day, but Clark's hunters could not get close enough for a shot. They camped on the nearly dry headwaters of the Auxvasse after traveling twenty-five miles. The next morning they crossed into present-day Boone County, named after his father, and forded Cedar Creek. By now, however, Boone's pace over uncharted country without trails began to take its toll. By noon on August 29, Clark noted in his diary that several of the horses were "much gaded," but that the country was "handsom." By the time Nathan led the rangers to a campsite on the east bank of Roche Creek, they had traveled another twenty-three miles since morning, and one horse had died.[20]

When Nathan moved alone, running his trapline or hunting deer for their skins, he traveled at this pace, and neither Clark nor the rangers were beginners when it came to experiencing the hardships of the frontier. If anyone complained about the rate that Boone set, Clark did not report it. Even so, both men and horses began to tire. By August 30, several men were sick, but Nathan did not slow the pace, leading them across Roche Creek, a branch of the Moniteau River, and over a large Indian trail, through woods of oak, hickory, and walnut that Clark reported were "tolerably thick," sixteen miles in all, before they stopped and "nooned it." Here, Nathan told Clark that the lands to the south were "salt bitter," while the country that rolled away to the north was "fine." They traveled another nine miles and camped near Salt Creek, 132 miles out of St. Charles.[21]

Despite the two sick men, who gripped their reins and endured what must have felt like a forced march at best, Nathan led the rangers across Bonne Femme Creek in present-day Howard County. Two miles west of New Franklin, Clark's hunters killed a buffalo, a bear, and three deer. About three o'clock, they dropped down into the floodplain of the Missouri River and followed it through "delightfull lands" and "glades" until they reached the "Cart Road" that Nathan's men had used to transport salt from his lick about two miles to the north. Clark sent two of his soldiers to the lick, who reported that men were at work boiling the brine from the springs. Then, they proceeded a short distance and camped on the east bank of the Missouri opposite present-day Arrow Rock. Clark noted in his diary that the river was two hundred yards wide. Darkness had now descended, and the river was dangerous even during daylight. Nathan would lead them across in the morning.[22]

In the late summer heat of 1808, the Missouri ran wide and shallow. Nathan went first, sitting loose in the saddle as his horse entered the lazy current and headed for a "fine" rocky landing below a hill that rose about ninety feet above the west bank. The others followed. Although the crossing went with little difficulty, it took time. Clark recorded that they "Commenced Crossing early," but the last ranger of the eighty-man force did not reach the west bank of the Missouri until 11:30 A.M.—all in all, a major achievement. Now they were six days and 155 miles out of St. Charles. They had ridden hard behind Nathan, and Clark knew that his men needed a rest. After ordering them to fire off their guns, to celebrate their feat as well as to identify any weapons that had damp powder, the rangers cleaned and reloaded their rifles. Then, they camped and made breakfast at the top of the hill near where the village of Arrow Rock now stands.

Here, the black, fertile land of the floodplain and the gently rolling hills that lifted away from the valley would draw a host of settlers not long after the expedition passed. By 1810, seventy-five families lived in the vicinity of Boone's Lick and Arrow Rock. One traveler who made his way upriver in 1811 reported that the settlers in this area came down to the bank to watch his keelboat pass upriver. "They are," he wrote, "generally persons in good circumstances, most of them have slaves." One settler, Braxton Cooper, reported that the upland beyond the river was the "most beautiful ever beheld." Nathan had crossed this country many times, and he no doubt appreciated its beauty, but he did not linger to enjoy it now. At 1:00 P.M. the expedition moved west through thick undergrowth and scattered timber and into open grassland for a thirteen-mile ride before they camped for the night near the Salt Branch of the Lamine River, west of present-day Marshall.

September 2 dawned warm and cloudless, and Nathan had the men saddled and headed across country at 7:00 A.M. They entered rolling prairie and rode past an abandoned Osage village. Elk and deer browsed on the tall grasses, and they saw signs that buffalo had grazed and bedded there. Clark, who could never spell correctly or consistently even in the same sentence, called the area "Rich & Butifull," but he, too, had tired after they traveled "late" into the evening, headed for a campsite Boone knew along the Lamine River. Darkness had nearly fallen when they reached the bend on the river where Nathan wanted to stop. Although they had traveled for fifteen hours and made camp about ten o'clock, Nathan was apprehensive about the possible presence of an Osage or other Indian hunting or war party in the area. The rangers picketed their horses and posted guards to watch through the night. Despite this precaution Nathan thought the force might have been spotted by now. Clark agreed and sent a rear guard back along the trail. Although the guard traveled back nearly to the place of their noon rest stop, they did not discover anyone watching their trail or any campfires lighting the September darkness. With the exception of the rear guard, the rangers had followed Nathan for twenty-five miles that day, and sleep on the ground under their blankets came quickly.

The next morning Boone struck out early, heading "nearly West," passing through prairie and across Tabo Creek. Clark observed that Boone had led them into country that was "thinly timbered tho' sufficient for Settlements and verry rich." This was part of the country that Clark intended to purchase from the Osages. Like Boone, Clark knew full well that the land, timber, and navigable streams, along with the commercial value of the salt springs in this area of Missouri, would soon lure a host of settlers and support a large population. However, Boone must have also known that their expedition to the Missouri to treat with the Osages would soon end the way of life that he loved best, because once Osage lands came into the possession of the federal government, it would not be long before farmers turned under the prairie grasses and cattle drank where he once set his beaver traps. Boone also knew that the westering settlers could not be stopped—whether for good or ill, he could not say, since he was part of that great movement. Certainly, his life was about to change, and he knew it and accepted his fate. The only thing that could be done was to do his duty.

On Sunday morning, September 4, Nathan could see Fire Prairie, a rolling brushy plain, in the distance. Fire Prairie Creek, which drains into the Missouri about six miles below present-day Sibley, had more mud than water at the ford that Nathan wanted to cross, so the rangers cut brush to make a bridge to keep their horses from sinking in the muck. Then, as Clark wrote, "we crossed with ease." Nathan then led the expedition toward the Missouri, about three miles away. There they discovered a man by the name of Pursley, whom Captain Clemson had sent to meet Clark's expedition. Pursley told Nathan and Clark that Clemson had gone about three miles upriver to the bluff where Clark wanted to build the fort. Pursley also told them that the Osages had discovered Clemson's flotilla and that a dozen of them had waited with him for Clark's arrival; as time had passed, however, they "got scared and ran home." Now that the Osages were aware of their arrival and their intent to build a fort and trading post, Nathan and Clark knew that word would quickly spread among the Osages, who would soon want a meeting. But all of that would come a little later; Nathan's men still had to complete the last leg of their journey. Before they rode the final few miles, a hard driving rain soaked the rangers, but their chilled spirits soon warmed when they entered Clemson's camp, where Nathan and Clark found everything in "good order." By Clark's calculation, they had ridden 247 miles from St. Charles; to celebrate their arrival and, perhaps, their endurance of Nathan's hard pace, Clark ordered a feast, with every man getting two days' rations of pork, flour, and whiskey.

While the rations of salt pork roasted over open campfires and while bread fried in pans and the men sipped their whiskey and relaxed, Nathan and Clark talked about the next day and the treaty negotiations with the Osages. Since the Osages had not met them as he hoped they would, Clark likely said, the only thing to be done was to bring them in. He asked, Where would they be? Would they be heading north from their camps to meet them at this site? Should they wait a few days? No, Nathan thought not. If the Osages were not here yet, they were not coming. Since the government was compelling them to meet and sign a treaty, they would delay as long as possible, and they would not come willingly because they knew that they would be required to make a considerable cession of their lands. They would only lose in any treaty meeting that had been forced on them. He would be surprised if they had left their villages located on the Marais des Cygnes River.

Nathan did not tell Clark anything that he did not already know. They no doubt had talked about the problem around the campfires on their ride out to the fort site. Clark was impatient. Lewis had given him a mission, and he intended to do what his friend and superior had asked. He wanted to do it quickly and efficiently. So only one thing could be done. Go get the Osages, Clark told Nathan. Find them and bring them in. Leave tomorrow morning. Knowing how hard Boone traveled, Clark calculated that Boone would take about three days to reach the Osage villages. Tell White Hair, Clark said, that "if they wished to take protection under this fort to come." Boone was to remind them that if they failed to do so, they would be an enemy of the United States and that they could not expect friendship and leniency in any future meeting. Or, as George Sibley remembered the conversation, "Recommending them very Strongly to do So, and avoid the fatal consequences of Refusing."[23]

Clark did not need to tell Nathan to leave early and to return as soon as possible. By the time the early morning sun began to warm Fire Prairie on Monday, September 5, Nathan and Loise had ridden far to the south of the campsite on the Missouri River. Boone angled slightly southwest. Nathan knew the land well, and he also understood that the Osages would be waiting. Moreover, from his experiences in dealing with them, he realized that the young men would be obstinate and probably in a foul mood with little desire to be accommodating. While Nathan rode south, he thought about what he would do when he reached the Osage villages.

While Clark waited for Nathan's return he supervised the construction of the post. His layout included blockhouses at the corners for defense, three measuring eighteen and one twenty-four feet square. Beyond the fort, but still protected by eleven-foot high palisades, he planned a house and store for the factor. The officers' quarters and barracks would utilize one side of the palisades for their outside walls. A fifth blockhouse, located north of the factor's store and overlooking the river, provided advance warning in case of attack.[24]

Clark's plan provided for the essentials of security and trade but the rangers worked reluctantly at best. With nearly half of them

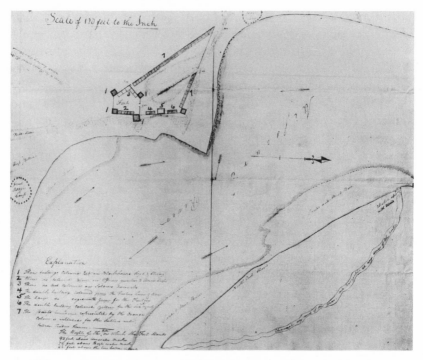

In 1808, when Nathan Boone accompanied William Clark and a contingent of militia and soldiers to Fire Prairie along the Missouri River, the men began building a post, which soon became known as Fort Osage. Clark made this sketch of the fort while he waited for Boone to arrive with the Osages for a treaty council. *State Historical Society of Missouri, Columbia.*

members of the militia, rather than belonging to the regular army, they balked because they had volunteered for escort duty not carpentry, and they went about their work lethargically and not without questioning the orders of their officers. On Wednesday, September 7, Clark noted in his diary that the "Militia works reluctantly and much difficulty to get them to do anything." By Friday, however, morale had improved and Clark noted: "The men turned out to day with more Cheerfullness than usial and earlier."[25]

While the men worked they saw no signs of Indians, but Clark and Clemson expected the Osages to arrive soon, and they pressed the construction in order to have adequate protection for their men, who would soon be outnumbered. Sibley, however, saw no need for

THE OSAGE EXPEDITION   67

apprehension. On September 12, the day Boone arrived with the Osages, he wrote: "How cheerful and pleasing a sight it is to see 200 men cutting a village out of an almost impenetrable forest."[26]

About September 8, Nathan reached the junction of the Marais des Cygnes, Little Osage, and Marmaton Rivers, known to the Osages as the "Place-of-the-Many-Swans," where they made their villages, and he located the Osage town of White Hair. By the time Boone and Loise rode into the first village, the runners had already spread the word of his arrival to the other villages along the valley. White Hair and the other leaders asked their visitors, Why had they come? Boone replied and Loise translated that the Osages had promised to meet Clark on the Missouri. Why had they not gone to meet him? They had changed their minds, the Osage leaders responded, and they had no intention of sitting in a treaty meeting where they would lose their land. Boone should go. Nathan, however, told the chiefs that Clark had given him orders to bring the Osages to the Missouri. He could do nothing else; his duty required him to take the Osages back with him. No, the Osage leaders replied; they had no intention of going to the Missouri, but they would take Boone's request before the tribal council.[27]

The discussion in the tribal council did not go well for Nathan. The more the Osages talked about going to meet Clark on the Missouri the more angry they became. The Osage leaders ordered him out of the council, saying that they had not sent for him; as Boone later recalled, they treated him "rudely." When Loise translated the council's order for them to get out, Nathan responded with a sharp, stern voice. No, he said, they would not leave until the council told him whether the Osages would go to Fire Prairie to meet with Clark.[28]

The council debated the move once again. White Hair reminded the members that he had told Clark as early as 1805 that a few of the young braves had killed some of the "frontier people" and that he could not control them. Moreover, he reminded the council that Clark had urged the "peaceable portion" of the tribe to join him on the Missouri River, where he would build a fort for their protection. Clark would also build a trading house to supply them with blankets, knives, clothing, powder, flints, and lead. White Hair, who was the principal chief, commanded respect, and the council listened to him, but they did not all agree. The best solution that White Hair could gain was the reluctant assent of the council to let those who wanted to go with him leave the Osage camps for Fire Prairie.[29]

Boone was satisfied with the answer of the council. The next morning White Hair and Walk-in-Rain, another chief, led several hundred Osages north toward the Missouri, with Nathan showing the way. Although many Osages remained behind, Boone knew that Clark would let White Hair and Walk-in-Rain speak for the entire tribe, and the treaty sought by the federal government and Governor Lewis could now be achieved. Still, the Osages could change their minds and return at any moment to the Marais des Cygnes, so he hurried them along the trail. Most of the Osage women, children, and old people could not keep up with Boone's accustomed pace, but he continued ahead with White Hair and Walk-in-Rain and several lesser chiefs and warriors, while the others followed their path.[30]

Boone and his advance party of fifty-five Osages reached Fire Prairie and Clark's campsite during the evening of September 12. White Hair and Walk-in-Rain then informed Clark that all of the Osages would soon arrive to live near the fort as they had promised. The chiefs also told Clark that the Osages lived in poverty because whites, Choctaws, Cherokees, and Chickasaws intruded on their land and killed their deer and trapped their beaver, and they asked Clark for protection. Clark reported that the chiefs informed him that "they had collected all of the horses which they could find of those, their bad men had taken from the white people." Clark received the Osages in a "friendly manner," listened, and promised them that he would speak to them in the morning and showed them a nearby campsite. While Nathan made his report to Clark about the mood of the Osages regarding the treaty, the Indians, in Clark's words, "appeared anxious" to make a treaty, and they "Sung and Danced the greater part of the Night."[31]

At nine o'clock the next morning, White Hair and Walk-in-Rain, together with a delegation of other Osage leaders, walked down from their campsite to Clark's quarters, where the men were at work erecting blockhouses. Amidst the chopping sounds of ax and adze, Clark, with Boone looking on, "informed them what was about to be done by the government." The Osage delegation was not being invited to negotiate a treaty that involved the cession of lands and a promise to keep the peace. Rather, Boone had led them to the fort, where Clark would dictate the terms of agreement. Not all of the Osage leaders liked what Clark told them, nor were they pleased with the tone of his voice. But they listened because they had no choice. Clark, however, thought that the meeting went well and reported to Secretary of War Dearborn that the Osages "declared their emplicit Confidence in me and their perfect Satisfaction and approbation to every article and would at any time Sign those articles."[32]

Clark first reminded the Osage that they had been in "frequent habits" of committing murder, robbery, and theft on the frontier people who were citizens of the United States in the Louisiana Territory. Before he left in three days, Clark told the Osages, they had to agree to stop "all such like acts in [the] future." Clark also informed their leaders that he would help them prevent the misconduct of their people by running a line between the lands of the United States and the Osages beginning at the fort and extending south to the Arkansas River. All lands east of that line would belong to the United States. This land cession would help the federal government pay for the losses of property by its citizens at the hands of the Osages, who could not afford to pay for what their "bad men" had stolen. The federal government would consider this exchange fair, provided, Clark said, that the Osage "would conduct themselves properly in [the] future." For this land cession, they would be protected by the soldiers at the fort, and they could easily trade with the government factor. In addition, the federal government would provide the Osages with a blacksmith, mill, and plows. The government would also pay the claims against the Osages for the stolen horses and property that had not been returned. Clark told them to consider his proposal and to "consult among themselves" and return the next day, at which time he would have a treaty prepared for them to sign. If, however, they were displeased with the offer, he told them to speak out and "if any thing Dwelt on their minds to speak it & not be bashfull."[33]

With that invitation to speak their minds, the chiefs held a quick discussion and told Clark that they "assented" to his proposal and that he was doing them a "great" service. They would be ready to sign the treaty tomorrow. With this pleasant sign of success, Clark began work on the treaty, but before he had it "framed," he conferred with the chiefs several times during the evening. At one of those discussions, White Hair told him that the Spanish had contacted the Pawnees and the Kansas and that Basil Vasseur, a trapper and fur trader who operated out of St. Louis, had convinced the Arkansas River band that "all which had been told by the White Hair and [Governor] Lewis were lies."[34]

Nathan did not worry about the Arkansas Osages, although he had not communicated with them. He believed the Missouri villages would sign a treaty primarily because they had little choice. To remain outside of the protection of the United States meant an escalation of the violence that would lead to open war at a time when the Osages were divided over tribal leadership. The Arkansas band could afford to be obstinate because they lived farther away and, for the time being, distance kept them beyond the encroachment of the frontier people on their lands, the reach of the army, and the diplomatic skills of its government ministers. Clark hoped that Boone was correct in his assessment of the Osages' necessity to sign a treaty, because he wanted to bring the negotiations to a conclusion and to return to St. Louis as quickly as possible. "I am verry unwell," he wrote, "with Desentary, which I have had for Some time and now [has] become very Serios." Clark and Boone slept little that night. Clark worried about his health and made numerous trips to the latrine, while Nathan rested as best he could while the Osages "danced hollered and Sung the great part of the Night."[35]

When the Osage leaders arrived at the fort on the morning of September 14, Clark attempted to impress them by having the officers and rangers parade on the level ground that extended back from the fort. Then he read the terms of the treaty to them. In the words of Clark, the treaty required the Osages to "ceed, Convey & Relinquish all the land east of a line South drawn from where we then Treated to the R[iver] Arkansas & amounting to Thirty Milion of acres of excellent country, including the settlements below the Missouri." The Osage leaders, however, balked when they learned that the treaty would require them to give up their hunting lands above the Grand River. Clark, however, had prepared for this possibility with a contingent plan in Article 10 that would prohibit whites from hunting west of a line that ran from Arrow Rock to the Arkansas without the permission of the president. Perhaps in deference to Boone, this provision would prevent any "misunderstanding" in the future between whites and the Osages and end the "great disturbance & complaints" that white hunters made after they had been "robbed, plundered & Sent naked in cold weather without any means of procuring food." Clark then told the Osages, however, that even though these lands would now belong to the United States, they could hunt on them safely and that all traders had to operate out of the fort at Fire Prairie. They could no longer travel to the Osage villages. This provision would enable greater governmental control of the Indian trade and help prevent disagreements, unfair practices, and British intervention. They would no longer need to fear the tribes who had contested ownership and hunted on those same lands in the past. The Osages would now be the favored people of the United States in this area, and they would no longer live in "continual dread of all the eastern Tribes whom they knew wished to destroy them & possess their Country."[36]

White Hair, who had always been accommodating to the demands of the federal government, as well as Walk-in-Rain and the other "principal men," found considerable merit in what Clark told them. Now, they requested that Clark "not let a whole nation suffer for the bad Conduct of a Fiew who were then willing to reform." They were now ready to come under the protection of the United States. Then, with the provision that allowed them to hunt unhindered on much of their ceded lands and, after the treaty had been read and interpreted twice, they signed "with great apparent pleasure." All of these negotiations and explanations had taken the "greater part of the day" by the time the last chief had signed, with Boone and the officers witnessing the ceremony. Then Clark ordered the firing of the fort's four cannon and a copy of the treaty given to each chief, and the celebration began to honor the negotiations. Clark gave a rifle to each principal chief and to the Big and Little Osages one hundred pounds of powder, two hundred pounds of lead, and fourteen carottes of tobacco along with knives, blankets, and paint to divide among themselves. Clark also told the Osages that if they obeyed the treaty provisions, he would ask the government to distribute twelve hundred dollars in goods among them next year at the fort, with five hundred dollars in merchandise to the Little and Great Osages and one hundred dollars in goods to each of the two "Great Chiefs." The Osages could not resist this generous act. Clark wrote that: "This unexpected present pleased those people gratly, they paintd danced and Sung all Night." Clark was delighted with the treaty negotiations, especially because the meeting hardly involved give and take wrangling. Clark had gotten the treaty that he wanted. Perhaps the ease by which he achieved it surprised even him, because he considered the Great Osages a "vicious and obscene" people, while the Little Osages were "friendly and well disposed."[37]

The next day, Thursday, September 15, Chiefs White Hair and Walk-in-Rain left the post with half of their people on a return journey to the Marais des Cygnes, where they would collect the remainder of their villagers in order to bring them back so that they could live "under the protection of the Fort." One blockhouse was finished, except for the upper floor and daubing between the logs; four other blockhouses were well under construction; two houses for the factor's goods were nearly finished, along with a blacksmith's shop, a workshop, and a sutler's storehouse; the barracks were begun; and two thousand feet of lumber were sawed. With this progress underway and the Osage treaty successfully completed, Clark prepared to leave the fort under the command of Captain Clemson. Reuben Lewis, the subagent, would also remain and oversee Osage affairs. Clark told Nathan and the rangers to prepare to leave the fort at ten o'clock on Friday, September 16.[38]

At sunrise the next day, Nathan waited on his horse while Clark had the orders for the troops read aloud. By the time the horses had been collected and the troops organized, the sun had reached its zenith. Then Nathan led sixty men eastward under the command of Captain Mackey Wherry. Clark, "being too unwell to ride," would descend the river to St. Louis by boat, along with several other sick rangers and soldiers and a guard of twenty men. For Nathan and his men the ride back to St. Charles proved uneventful. Although the rangers had not known precisely where Boone was leading them on the way out to Fire Prairie, the trail left by their eighty horses now marked the way back. Still, the journey was not easy and Nathan and his men traveled as fast back as they had come, with the incentive now to return home as quickly as possible. They reached Arrow Rock at ten o'clock on Monday after traveling about sixty-five miles as the crow flies in two days. Clark was waiting there with his two boats. The river had fallen since their trip out, and by early afternoon Clark reported "all crossd well [and] drew their provisions of pork & six rations of whiskey and set out."[39]

Clark reached St. Charles on Thursday, September 22, although it is not clear when Nathan led the rangers into the town, where they disbanded and headed for home. By the time he arrived at the Femme Osage the weather had turned cold with a strong north wind, and the treaty had already begun to crack.[40]

Clark believed that the treaty that he had negotiated with the Osages provided for the needs of the United States and the tribe. He reported that the Osages "expressed much anxiety to become more closely under the protection of the United States than they had been." Clark, however, had failed to understand that White Hair and Walk-in-Rain, though respected chiefs, did not speak for all Osages. An Osage delegation soon arrived in St. Louis to return, as the treaty required, a herd of horses that they had stolen, but they became argumentative upon learning the precise terms of the agreement. These Osages protested the terms of the treaty and complained that Clark's interpreter had misled White Hair. They also told Governor Lewis as well as Clark that White Hair did not have the authority to make a land cession treaty that gave away, as Clark put it, "50,000 Squar Miles of excellent country," without consulting the tribal council. Clark "felt a little surprised" to learn that some Osages objected to the treaty, but they were well justified because their political decisions had to be based on consensus. Moreover, the Osages were divided over White Hair's claim of leadership, and some questioned his authority to represent them in negotiations. Many Osages also preferred a post located closer to their villages on the Osage River rather than far to the northwest on the Missouri. Others who had been at Fire Prairie also contended that they had only agreed to let whites hunt on their land—they had not ceded it.[41]

Clark insisted that the Osage leaders understood the terms of the treaty because his interpreters had carefully explained the provisions to them. In a letter to Secretary of War Dearborn, dated September 23, 1808, Clark reported that "no unfair means had been taken on my part to induce the Osage to seed to the United States such an extencive Country for what is conceived here to be so small a Compensation, when in reality their Compensation when taken into proper view is fully adequate." He also contended that the Osage had "chearfully approved the land cession and that every individual of the Little Osage nation, and a great majority of the Great Osage were perfectly contented and favorable to the Treaty." Lewis did not doubt the ability or integrity of his old friend, but he knew the treaty would be worth nothing if all Osages did not accept it.[42]

In the end, Clark helped resolve the crisis by telling Lewis that although he thought the terms of his treaty had been fairly negotiated and freely accepted, "those articles of the treaty entered into with the Great and Little Osages were conditional, and well calculated as a preparatory step to a more favorable one." As a result, Lewis agreed to rewrite and renegotiate the treaty to reconcile Osage objections and ensure harmony among the tribe as well as to achieve the desired land cession. Lewis, in consultation with Pierre Chouteau, wrote the new treaty, which he thought was "more consistent with the wishes of the Government," perhaps because it provided for the cession of Osage lands located north of the Missouri River, which Clark's treaty had not included. Upon completion, Lewis planned to send Chouteau back to the fort at Fire Prairie to explain the terms and to use that "extensive influence" that he had "long possessed over those nations" to gain Osage approval.[43]

On October 3, 1808, Lewis sent a copy of the treaty to Chouteau along with a letter. In it, he told Chouteau

> This draft of a Treaty, you will observe, contemplates something more than the restoration of peace: It gives to the great and little Osage, the most efficient security, in our power to bestow: It assures to them, for their exclusive use, the lands west of the boundary line: It separates those who sanction it, from the vicious and the profligate, whom no treaties can bind, whom no menaces can intimidate, and by whose ungovernable conduct, the peace of both nations is perpetually endangered. It enables us also, to reduce to submission, without bloodshed, those who persevere in hostility, by withholding from them the merchandize necessary for their support.

Lewis was confident that the treaty revisions would accommodate the needs of both white settlers and hunters and the Osages. "By these arrangements," he told Chouteau, "we shall also obtain a tract of country *west* of our present settlements, and *East* of the hunting boundary of the Osage, sufficient for the purposes of our white Hunters, and for such Indian Nations, as have long been on terms of intimate friendship with us. Thus, will our Frontier be strengthened and secured, with the least possible expence to the government."[44]

The new treaty reaffirmed the pledge of the federal government to protect the Osages, establish a permanent trading post at Fire Prairie, and provide the tribe with a blacksmith and mill. Lewis also made adjustments regarding hunting grounds, the surrender and punishment of Indians and whites who broke the laws of either nation, and the return of stolen property. In addition, the treaty provided that the Osages would neither sell land to private citizens of the United States or to any foreign power without the approval of the federal government, nor provide arms to any tribe at war with the United States. The federal government would pay a maximum of five thousand dollars in claims against the Osages for the theft of horses and other property. Upon signing the treaty the Osages would receive goods valued at twelve hundred dollars and an annuity in merchandize of fifteen hundred dollars.[45]

Lewis bluntly insisted that the Osages sign the treaty to remain friends and allies with the United States. Lewis told Chouteau,

> Those of the great and little Osage who refuse to sanction this Treaty can have no future hopes, that their pretensions to those lands now claimed by them, will ever be respected by the United States: For, it is our unalterable determination, that if they are to be considered our friends and allies, they must *sign* that instrument, *conform* to its *stipulations,* and establish their permanent villages, near the Fort erected a little above the Fire Prairie.

If they refused to sign the treaty, Lewis authorized Chouteau to stop all trade with the Osages and to notify him by special messenger so that he could "place the frontier in the best state of defence and make the necessary preparations for an expedition against them." Moreover those Osages who did not sign would not be permitted to trade with government agents at Fire Prairie or with private traders.[46]

The Osages had little ability to argue. They were hostages to American trade, and they could not withstand a war levied by the combined tribal force that Lewis had prepared to send against them. If they rejected the revised treaty, they would not be able to easily replace American with British traders operating out of Canada or Spanish traders who entered the southwest via Mexico, and they would lose much of their land in a war. The result would be a significant reduction in their standard of living. The Osages recognized that they had no choice but to exchange land for protection and trade. If they did not do so they would lose to both white settlers and other Indian nations. Consequently, on November 10, 1808, the "chiefs and warriors" of the Big and Little Osage "touched the feather," making a cross with a quill pen, and thereby approved the treaty modifications. Fort Osage was also now formally christened with ceremonial cannon fire.[47]

On August 31, 1809, the Arkansas band of the Osages approved the treaty in St. Louis, but the U.S. Senate did not ratify it until April 28, 1810, primarily because President James Madison did not submit it to that chamber until January 16, 1810. Then, the Senate delayed action until it was certain that Chouteau had the authority to negotiate a treaty with the Osages. George Sibley, who observed the negotiations at Fort Osage, reported that Chouteau's threat to cut off trade "awed" the Osages and caused them to sign the treaty. But he noted that while "a very unusual number of them touched the pen; many of whom knew no more the purpose of the act than if they had been a hundred miles off; and I here assert it to be a fact . . . the treaty is not fairly understood by a single Osage." Even so, the Osages made their camp near the fort during the winter of 1808–1809, but in the spring many returned to their old villages along the Osage River. Although the Little Osages who remained at the post planted a corn crop, Captain Clemson wrote by that time "it was visible in their every movement, that they began to grow tired of their new residence, a great number of them returned to their old towns, the fall & winter of 1809–10."[48]

The Osages had good reason to violate the treaty and move away from the fort; its small garrison could not protect them from attacks by the Sacs, Foxes, and Ioways. At the same time, the trading post lured those northern tribes into the area. As a result, most of the Osages soon drifted away from the fort and the Missouri River, but they continued to trade their furs and skins at the post. Consequently, government officials and settlers alike worried about the loyalty of the Osages if war came with Great Britain.[49]

Despite lingering fears about Osage loyalty, with the signing of the revised treaty, the Osages came into the American camp, and, thereafter, they remained friends of the United States. Their loyalty and friendship proved essential not only for the protection of white settlers on the Missouri frontier but also because American relations with Great Britain had begun to deteriorate rapidly due to their altercations at sea. Even more important to the settlers in Missouri, British agents operating from Canada attempted to lure the western tribes away from American influence with the intent of using those nations against the United States in time of war. Nathan Boone would soon be thankful that he had played a major role in the winning of Osage friendship for the United States and with it a lasting peace between both nations.

On June 16, 1809, Nathan received $46.50 for guiding Clark and the St. Charles rangers to Fire Prairie. He welcomed the money, although the payment had been delayed by bureaucratic paperwork, and he felt satisfied that he had performed his duty honorably and well. Most important he had played an important role in bringing the Osages and Clark together to make a treaty—a treaty that ceded to the United States the lands that make up nearly the entire state of Missouri. With his aid, the federal government effectively used its power to gain Indian lands through the cession treaty process. By so doing, Boone helped the federal government provide lands for western settlement as well as security for a portion of the frontier. Still, this would not be the last time that he served as an agent of the federal government to keep the peace on the frontier. The Osage expedition had given him considerable experience in dealing with the Indians in an official capacity, as well as working with army regulars and militia. The diplomatic skills that he learned at Fort Osage would serve him well the remainder of his life; however, as the United States drifted closer to war with Great Britain, Nathan's next service on the Missouri frontier would require fighting, not negotiating.[50]

4
WAR

THE OSAGE TREATY calmed but did not quiet the winds of an Indian War that swept across the American frontier in 1808. In Missouri, the frontier remained a middle ground where Indian and white cultures clashed as tribes competed for the same hunting grounds, confronted settlers, and swayed with British influence. Although claimed by both, the frontier was controlled by neither Indians nor whites. To make matters worse, in late November 1808, Missourians heard that France had declared war against the United States, a rumor that caused "considerable apprehension." Although this alarm quickly proved false, the Indian menace did not go away. As a result, Governor Meriwether Lewis announced a general order issued by Secretary of War Henry Dearborn on November 28, 1808, which authorized the enlistment of 377 men for the militia in the Territory of Louisiana. These Missourians, out of a general call for 100,000 men, would help defend the frontier against hostile Indians. Lewis ordered the District of St. Charles to enroll 41 riflemen, while the District of St. Louis would provide 77 infantry and 21 riflemen, the District of Ste. Genevieve 77 infantry and 19 riflemen, the District of Cape Girardeau 77 riflemen, the District of New Madrid 57 infantry, and the District of Arkansas 21 infantry. Lewis ordered those designated as riflemen from the St. Charles, St. Louis, and Ste. Genevieve districts to form one company and the riflemen from Cape Girardeau a second, both of which would constitute a battalion under a Major Cook of the

Ste. Genevieve district. The infantry from St. Louis would also constitute a company while their counterparts from the District of Ste. Genevieve would organize another and the Districts of New Madrid and Arkansas a third, all under the command of Colonel Auguste Chouteau of St. Louis.[1]

To ensure readiness, Lewis ordered the riflemen from the Districts of St. Charles, St. Louis, and Ste. Genevieve to muster in squads under company officers in their respective districts once each month. Because of the sparse and scattered population in the New Madrid and Arkansas districts, the infantry would muster every three months. Lewis informed the militia that they would "perform any duty, which may be, by him deemed necessary for the defense or protection of the frontiers of Louisiana and the adjacent frontier of Indiana." Lewis wanted the volunteer companies to "hold themselves in readiness to march at a moment's warning" of an Indian attack. The governor also ordered the inhabitants of the St. Charles district to erect as many stockades and blockhouses as Colonel Timothy Kibby and Majors Daniel Morgan Boone and James Morrison, the field officers of the militia, deemed necessary to provide adequate defense against an "invasion of the savages."[2]

Nathan was not subject to this enrollment or expected or pressured to enlist because Lewis exempted him and all the rangers who had participated in the Osage expedition during the autumn. However, Nathan was concerned about the increasing hostile Indian activity in the St. Charles district. In late March 1809, isolated attacks on the frontier people became increasingly common, and the settlers often retaliated against friendly Indians. By early April, Nathan and his fellow Missourians had learned that Tenskwatawa, brother of Tecumseh and known as the Prophet, was "stirring up the savages against the United States" and that British agents were encouraging the Indians to do "bloody work" among the frontier settlements. The Winnebagos, who lived along the Illinois River just east of the Mississippi, reportedly were distributing wampum belts among the Indian villages to enlist support for a general Indian war. The Sacs also contributed to the fears of the settlers because they became increasingly brazen as horse thieves. In order to prevent mutual attacks and help keep the peace, Governor Lewis ordered whites to stop settling on Indian lands, but they did not listen or heed.[3]

Although the frontier people continued to settle where they pleased, the governor's call for the mobilization of the militia created a flurry of activity. In early April, Lewis sent 140 riflemen north to strengthen the garrison at Fort Madison, which had not yet been completed at a site about twenty miles above the mouth of the Des Moines River in present-day Iowa. On April 21, Lewis ordered a general rendezvous for the militia companies on May 4, and he reminded the men that "the Commander in Chief fondly hopes that every exertion will be made by those volunteer companies to equip themselves with good horses, arms, etc. such of the dragoons as have no Swords and Pistols, will arm themselves as *Mounted Riflemen*."[4]

By early June, however, reports from Fort Madison indicated that the Sacs and Foxes had backed away from war because the militia units had frightened them. This report proved little more than wishful thinking. The Sacs and Foxes had temporarily buried the tomahawk because the British and the Prophet counseled patience. The time had not yet come for a major strike by the western tribes. Missourians were also pleased to learn in mid-August that the Shawnees and Delawares living in the Cape Girardeau area had given up liquor and had committed themselves to learning agriculture in order to live in the tradition of small-scale white farmers. These tribes reportedly had established a court to try criminals, and they had executed three men with a tomahawk and burned their bodies on a stack of wood before some one hundred onlookers. Violence permeated the Missouri frontier for both Indians and whites.[5]

Although construction of a new post that would be called Fort Belle Fontaine, located about twelve miles northwest of St. Louis, began in April, it did not give nearby settlers much sense of security, and the conflict between white and Indian cultures continued unabated into 1810. In July a band of Potawatomis, allegedly under the influence of the Prophet, stole horses on Loutre Island and killed four men who pursued them. Other killings in the area kept the frontier people fearful of a general Indian attack through the late summer. When Benjamin Howard arrived in St. Louis to assume his post as territorial governor on September 17, following Meriwether Lewis's apparent suicide, he could do little to ease the fears of the residents and the frontier people beyond the city.[6]

While the tribes to the north and east continued to menace the frontier, and while Missourians mobilized for defense, the Osages grew restive because the federal government did not protect them as it had promised in the treaty. On February 21, 1811, George C. Sibley, the Indian factor and agent at Fort Osage, notified William Clark that the Osages "complain" that they had suffered from unprovoked attacks by the Ioways, Otos, Sioux, and Potawatomis who "Robbed them of their horses, and murdered their People . . . and have nearly, if not quite, compelled them (the Osages) to the last Resort, the Tomahawk and Scalping Knife." Clearly, the Osages approached desperation, and Sibley told Clark that if the federal government would not redress its wrongs, they wanted a free hand to defend themselves and retaliate.[7]

Sibley's letter helped, because by early March the soldiers at Fort Osage were aiding the tribe against the Ioways by ferrying war parties across the Missouri for their raids to the north. When the Osages returned they brought back Ioway scalps to show their success. On May 5, 1811, Sibley also reported to Clark that when the Osages caught an Ioway spy within three hundred yards of the fort he was "instantly cut into at least 50 pieces." Sibley also noted that a group of noisy and excited Osages stormed into his bedroom to show him the severed head of the Ioway spy.[8]

While the Osages fought their Indian enemies on the western frontier, other tribesmen continued to attack the settlers near Boone's home in the St. Charles District, all of which indicated that they had taken the tomahawk in hand and gone to war. In late June 1811, with the killing of whites "within the sound of the drum of Bellfontaine," the editor of the *Louisiana Gazette* in St. Louis reported that the settlers along the Missouri and Mississippi Rivers had been thrown into "consternation," and he expected to hear of "prompt measures being immediately taken . . . to repell any further attack." Governor Howard planned just that action, and on July 10 traveled to St. Charles on a visit to the settlements along the Missouri River north and west of St. Louis for the purpose of selecting sites for blockhouses and other fortifications. On September 12, Howard also reappointed William Clark as brigadier general of the territorial militia, and both men worked closely to organize the militia and supervise the construction of blockhouses, which one contemporary called "simply strong log houses, with a projecting upper story, and with loopholes for musketry."[9]

Despite the mobilization of the militia and the building of fortifications for the protection of both settlers and soldiers, the Indians remained unimpressed and committed to driving the white settlers from the frontier. By late August, Missouri farmers were afraid to venture far from their cabins and their cornfields often went uncultivated. As war parties threatened, Lieutenant Colonel Daniel Bissell at Fort Belle Fontaine wrote that the "white frontier has been much alarmed." William Henry Harrison's defeat of the Shawnees at Tippecanoe in Indiana on November 6, 1811, did not end the Prophet's influence among the tribes that now hunted and raided along the Missouri River, but by himself Boone could do little more than aid his brother Morgan in the construction of nearby blockhouses. Neither Nathan nor anyone else knew the extent of the Indian alliance that seemed to be organizing against them, but they kept abreast of the latest news of the Prophet's attempt to form an Indian confederacy that would regain tribal lands and return his people to traditional ways of living independent of white civilization.[10]

On November 21, 1811, when Frederick Bates informed the militia that the "present crisis certainly does require our utmost vigilance," Boone could not help but agree. Although not part of the militia on active duty, and with the frontier now too dangerous for trapping, he probably ranged to the west and north, scouting for sign of impending Indian trouble. If he was not part of the group of spies that Governor Benjamin Howard "ordered upon the most exposed part of the frontier to prevent surprise should the Prophet's party pursue their hostilities further," Nathan was at least sought out for his opinions on Indian movements and frontier defense. Those seeking his advice included militia officers, such as his brother Morgan, and perhaps government officials, such as William Clark, as well as Governor Howard and Secretary Bates. Given Boone's knowledge of the frontier and the Indians who now roamed across it in war parties, he could not long remain out of formal service. When spring came, and with it renewed Indian attacks, Nathan was ready for military duty.[11]

In early January 1812, Governor Howard received a letter from Prairie du Chien in present-day Wisconsin informing him that the Indians had taken up the tomahawk and that runners from Tecumseh were uniting the tribes in the Illinois country. Howard knew that Winnebago and unidentified war parties had been plundering and killing settlers along the Mississippi, and on January 13, he notified Secretary of War William Eustis that "our difficulties with the Indians are not at an end, and my own opinion is that so soon as the winter is over we have much danger to apprehend from them." Howard did not believe that the army and militia should wait for the Indians to attack first. Rather, he favored a preemptive strike in the spring against the hostile Indians camped along the Illinois River. He believed that "untill some of those tribes are punished we shall not have a durable peace with them." Governor Howard also told Secretary Eustis that while he kept a "considerable portion" of militia ready to strike, he wanted authorization to use a detachment of regulars stationed at Fort Belle Fontaine to help prevent a surprise attack on the Missouri frontier. Secretary Eustis, however, apparently did not respond to that request.[12]

By mid-February, Governor Howard had learned that "formidable combinations of the savages" would soon attack the Missouri frontier, and he feared the worst. On February 13, William Clark wrote to the secretary of war that the mail from the east had not been delivered for nearly two months and that the Indian attacks continued to worsen. Clark reported that: "The Winnebagos are Determined for War," and that they had asked the Sacs and Foxes to join them in attacks on Fort Madison, Chicago, and the upper settlements of the frontier. Although the Sacs and Foxes had refused that request for the moment, the threat from the Winnebagos could not be ignored. Governor Howard urged the frontier people to remain cautious and "secure themselves in Blockhouses," and he asked the War Department to launch a major campaign against the "marauding savages" and their British allies. By the early spring of 1812, then, the majority of both Indians and whites favored the use of violence to force the other side to accept their wishes and will.[13]

With little help coming from the War Department, William Clark urged Howard to raise two special companies called rangers at federal expense to patrol both sides of the Mississippi River. These rangers would be kept in "continuel motion" with spies sent out to warn of any danger to their flanks and rear. Each company would be strong enough to "cut off" war parties of the usual size. If a large war party threatened to attack the settlements, the rangers could provide ample warning to the militia for mobilization against an Indian army. Clark also informed the secretary of war that he intended to draw a line on the map beyond which the friendly tribes should not pass, "without Certain signals which will be known to the rangers" as well as written permits from their agent. This line would run from Fort Osage to the Des Moines River, far west of the current Indian boundary line that extended north from the mouth of the Gasconade on the Missouri to the headwaters of the Jeffreon. The white settlers, however, were not the only frontier people in danger. Earlier, a friendly group of Sacs asked Clark for protection from the hostile tribes, but he denied any responsibility for their safety. Instead, he told them that the settlers were "much enraged on the frontier against all Indians" and that if the whites came across the Indians they would "perhaps kill" them.[14]

On the same day that Clark wrote to Secretary of War Eustis, Governor Howard learned that nine members of a family by the name of O'Neal had been killed by a Kickapoo and Potawatomi war party about eighty miles above Fort Belle Fontaine on the Salt River. In response the governor asked Lieutenant Colonel Daniel Bissell, commandant at the fort, to build a blockhouse for the protection of both soldiers and settlers. Howard did not ask for a permanent deployment of an entire company of regulars; rather, he requested their temporary presence until he could raise a company of rangers, who, along with a small contingent of regulars, could safeguard that area of the frontier. Bissell complied with Governor Howard's request and sent two officers and thirty men well equipped with ammunition, provisions, and tools to the site of the O'Neal family killings to build a blockhouse and to "give every Protection to the Distrest Settlers, in their power."[15]

On March 17, Governor Howard received good news from Secretary of War Eustis who authorized him to raise a company of rangers. Two days later, he informed the secretary that the Indian hostilities were the worst on the frontier since 1794 in the Northwest Territory. "I think nothing can prevent a strong combination among the Indians against us now," he wrote, "but a succession of quick campaigns, against those that are avowedly hostile, or display of efficient, defensive measures—The latter I think would have a tendency to deter those, that are decidedly inimical to us, from attempting further mischief, and would determine those who are wavering to remain neutral." In addition, Howard recommended the swift pursuit of all war parties by mounted rangers. To expedite this plan of defense, since he feared a major Indian campaign in the spring, Governor Howard informed the secretary of war that he had already authorized the formation of a company of mounted riflemen, rangers, to be commanded by Captain Nathan Boone.[16]

Governor Howard had planned to send the rangers under Boone to patrol the frontier in the early spring, but news of Indian attacks during the winter necessitated quick action. Accordingly, on February 6, Howard authorized him to raise a company for three months' service and to take the field as soon as the last man had signed his name. Before Boone had organized his company, however, Howard received authorization from the War Department to raise a company of rangers for service in the U.S. Army. The terms of federal service were to be for a year. Howard realized that if he acted on this order and raised another company it might take three months and that the best men had already enlisted to ride with Boone. Consequently, the governor altered the terms of service to meet expediency. He authorized three months of federal service for the men, during which time they would be equipped and paid by the army, while the officers would serve for one year.

On March 3, Nathan, along with First Lieutenant William T. Lamme and Ensign David Barton, mustered forty-one men at St. Charles. Two days later Boone and the rangers rode toward the Mississippi River, which they were to reconnoiter until further ordered. Sixteen days later the remainder of his newly enlisted company mustered at St. Charles and followed Second Lieutenant David McNair the next day to meet Boone at Buffalo, a blockhouse that his men had erected for the protection of local settlers, possibly with the aid of Lieutenant Colonel Bissell's regulars, about two miles south of present-day Louisiana, in Pike County close to the Mississippi River.

Governor Howard intended for Boone's rangers to build another blockhouse at the mouth of the Jeffreon River and for the army to garrison it with regulars. This fort would serve as a place of deposit for provisions and command passage on the Mississippi. Here, the regulars would secure the boats necessary to transport the rangers back and forth across the Mississippi River as they made their four-day patrol from the Missouri opposite the mouth of the Gasconade River to about forty-five miles above the mouth of the Illinois. This section of the frontier was the most exposed to hostile Indians, and Howard hoped that with the establishment of a "respectable garrison" at Peoria, the Indians could be kept under control. He also hoped that Boone's rangers would receive their pay in "good time."

Boone's Indian and military skills were now put to the test in an area of the frontier where friends and enemies could not be easily determined. Some of the Winnebagos and Kickapoos professed friendship, but other tribal members wantonly attacked and killed whites in the Illinois River country. Moreover, the Indians east of the Mississippi in the area where the rangers would be patrolling had divided into many bands, each with a chief who pretended from "vanity or design" that he spoke for the entire nation. Boone would have difficulty separating friend and foe, and he had only experience to guide him. West of the Mississippi the frontier people were "alarmed in the extreme." There, his rangers would help them build blockhouses for protection in time of Indian attack.

While Boone and the rangers began their patrols and blockhouse construction, Governor Howard prepared to give them as much military support as possible. By mid-March, he had three companies of cavalry and two companies of mounted riflemen well equipped and ready to march when ordered, and he had a "considerable portion" of militia requisitioned as infantry, organized and ready to muster at a moment's notice. Howard also urged the secretary of war to send four hundred muskets for distribution among the settlers on the Missouri frontier. He did not believe, however, peace with the Indians could be secured until the army provided a permanent garrison at Prairie du Chien and held the British traders in check. Howard also asked the War Department to require all American traders to conduct their business with the Indians only at designated places where their actions could be policed.

By the time the War Department authorized the commission of Nathan Boone as captain of a ranger company on March 28, Boone and his rangers had been patrolling the frontier for more than three weeks. But, while notification proved late, it made his work legal because the legislation authorized the War Department to raise six companies of rangers for the protection of the frontier, and President Madison designated one company for the Territory of Louisiana. With Boone's commission came orders for him to enlist four sergeants, four corporals, and sixty privates, all to serve for twelve months unless discharged sooner. The rangers were to equip themselves with good rifles or muskets and side arms as well as with clothing, horses, and provisions. In return for military service under the umbrella of the U.S. Army, they would be paid seventy cents per day if on foot and one dollar per day if mounted. The officers would receive the same pay and subsistence per day as the officers of the line. If Boone accepted the commission, the secretary of war told Governor Howard, he was to complete the necessary paperwork—the muster and payrolls.[17]

As the days of winter bled into the early spring, the threat of an Indian war kept the frontier people fearful, watchful, and close to home and Boone's rangers on the move. On March 21, the *Louisiana Gazette* reported that the Kickapoos and Winnebagos had killed settlers to the north and that Potawatomi war chief Main Poc would soon lead a Potawatomi war party against the Osages while striking the whites along the way. Governor Howard and the frontier people heard other reports that the hostile Indians were distributing black wampum belts, symbolizing war, at the council fires from the Sioux to the north to the head of the Wabash. The editor of the *Gazette* contended that "as long as there is a British subject suffered to trade within the lines of our territories" the Indians could not be trusted to keep the peace. The only sign of encouragement that all would be well came from the Missouri rangers. The editor reported that: "The new company of rangers now doing duty in the district of St. Charles are, perhaps, as fine a body of hardy woodsmen as ever took the field." Boone and his rangers knew that their "constant and rapid movements" would keep them from returning home for a long time.[18]

Boone's rangers, who began patrolling the Missouri frontier between Loutre Island and the Illinois River country, were a group of fifty-three hard men, including the officers, who knew how to sit a horse for hours over rough terrain, and who often had more familiarity with their rifles than with their families. They were also a tough-handed lot, with callouses testifying to their practical knowledge of the workings of an ax and saw. During the fifteen months that Boone led the rangers across the frontier they would have cause to use all their skills.

After Boone's rangers built what became known as Buffalo Fort, they quickly went about the business of erecting other blockhouses along their route in Missouri. They built Fort Howard about seventeen miles north of St. Charles on the east bank near the mouth of the Cuivre River, approximately two miles south of present-day Winfield in Lincoln County. This post was one of the largest fortifications constructed by the rangers and nearby settlers. The rangers cut, sawed, and raised the logs and set the pickets during the three weeks required to complete it. Covering one and a half acres, the oblong fort ran north and south with blockhouses on all of the angles except the southeast corner. When completed Fort Howard could provide safety for thirty families. Nathan may also have helped Morgan build Boone's Fort, the largest and strongest blockhouse in the area, on Page Bottom of the Femme Osage. Twice between 1812 and the end of the war, Nathan's wife, Olive, fled to that shelter during the dead of night when neighbors warned of an Indian attack.[19]

Boone's rangers also built Stout's Fort about one mile south of present-day Auburn in Lincoln County as well as Fort Pond near Wentzville in St. Charles County. Nathan's men may have ranged as far west as the Boonslick country and helped construct Cooper's Fort. This fortification, located across the Missouri River from Arrow Rock, about two miles from his salt-making operation and near the ford he had led Clark and the rangers across in 1808, consisted of several log houses and a large stockade that could protect twenty families. Boone's men, together with the regulars and other ranger companies, built additional forts during the War of 1812, which formally began with the declaration by Congress on June 18.[20]

Few of the forts constructed by the rangers proved more than a blockhouse with rifle ports that served as temporary safety for local settlers in time of Indian attack. In some cases, such as Buffalo Fort, settlers burned and abandoned the structures when they learned that the army could not provide a permanent garrison. Other forts fell into decay or were dismantled by settlers when the rangers and regulars no longer needed those sites for their patrols after the Indian danger passed. During the war, however, these blockhouses met a military need and gave some peace of mind to nearby settlers. John Gibson, who served under Boone, reflected that "we went into Building forts in Different places over the country to keep the Indians from murdering our helpless women and children. . . . we finished all those garrisons in the year 1812 and had our women and children out of danger of the wild Savages."[21]

Boone's rangers gave the frontier people a badly needed sense of security, and the settlers praised his men for building fortifications to protect them; they also valued the patrols. In early May 1812, Boone's rangers discovered a band of Indians about ten miles from Fort Mason and gave chase, but they lost them when night fell and a heavy rain obscured the trail. Joseph Charless, editor of the *Louisiana Gazette,* commended Boone and his men for this vigilance, saying, "Captain Boone has given a good account so far of those who have visited our frontier, and no doubt will continue to do so." Another Missourian described Boone as a "remarkable woodsman who could climb like a bear and swim like a duck." Boone and his rangers, then, were tough men with the skills necessary to live under harsh conditions far removed from the comforts of the settlements, and they had reputations for hitting their targets. For many, the rangers were "gallant and hardy," especially after time dulled memories; for others, however, the rangers were ruffians who took what they wanted and did as they pleased while treating civilians with considerable contempt and disrespect.[22]

On June 7, 1812, before much of the work building blockhouses could be completed or the patrolling became routine, however, the term of service expired for Boone's rangers. To ensure no lapse in the defense of the frontier settlements, Governor Howard sent another ranger company, commanded by Captain James Callaway, Nathan's nephew, to cover his patrol for fifteen days. Callaway's rangers rode out of St. Charles at 6:00 A.M. on June 4, headed for Fort Mason. By that time, the governor had already recruited thirty men from the St. Charles District for another ranger company to serve under Nathan. Boone did not return to St. Charles to help. Instead, the governor told him: "I shall take upon myself the trouble of recruiting the men as the moment is too critical to draw you from your command, to be employ'd in recruiting." Between June 18 and July 1, seventy-one men enlisted in the new ranger company. William T. Lamme and David McNair remained as his first and second lieutenants respectively. All recruits enlisted for twelve months, their duty extending from June 7, 1812, to July 15, 1813. Governor Howard recommended to the secretary of war that the officers be paid the same wage as their equals in the cavalry, which would exceed that received by the infantry. Boone's new company promised to be the most efficient in the service of the United States because of his leadership and the company's composition of "young, a-live, enterprising men." One observer noted that: "It is astonishing with what promptness the company was raised, equipt, and marched." Many of the rangers joined again, "although they had returned only a few days from an arduous service of three months." In June 1812, Morgan Boone and Daniel Musick also organized and commanded ranger companies to give Nathan's men some help patrolling the frontier.[23]

Before Nathan's new ranger company mustered at St. Charles and took the field, however, his first company escorted Governor Howard and a detachment of about twenty regulars from Fort Belle Fontaine to an area some 120 miles north of St. Louis. There, the governor scouted for a site to erect a fort that would be on the boundary line between the Sacs and Foxes and "us." Boone did not believe that the country provided a suitable location for a strong fortification, and Governor Howard moved his contingent south and began the construction of Fort Mason at a site that Nathan believed well suited for defense. The governor believed that Fort Mason would serve the rangers well, because the Indians were "collecting at different points to be ready in the event of war." While the construction of Fort Mason continued about nine miles south of Hannibal, Boone and Governor Howard hurried back to St. Charles for the muster of the new company of rangers on June 18.[24]

When Nathan's second ranger company mustered, it rode to Fort Mason and relieved the other men under his command. At Fort Mason Boone took a new oath of office administered by Lieutenant John Campbell and immediately ordered his command out on patrol, after explaining his operating procedure of sending spies thirty miles ahead of a column while others ranged three hundred yards in front and along the flanks. Boone's second ranger company also went about the task of building blockhouses during the summer of 1812, and they prepared for a major Indian attack. Nathan had learned from the command in St. Louis that the Winnebagos, Kickapoos, Potawatomis, Shawnees, and Miamis had declared war on the United States. He also knew that seventy hostile Winnebagos, Ioways, and Otos were terrorizing isolated settlements between Boonslick and Fort Osage, while more than a hundred Sacs had camped above the Salt River. If a combined or coordinated attack came from the Indians, Boone's rangers would be the first line of defense, and the odds were not with them. Fortunately for the frontier people in Missouri, the Osages remained loyal.[25]

Still, Boone's rangers had deception on their side, and they used it to their advantage. By the early summer of 1812, the rapid movements of the rangers led the Sacs and Foxes, who posed the greatest danger to this part of the frontier, to believe this force was far larger than in reality. In June Lieutenant Campbell reported that two Sac and Fox chiefs informed him that they thought several companies of rangers had been stationed at Fort Mason. Campbell, in turn, reported that "the Indians on the Mississippi say that the soldiers about this post are as thick as the trees in the woods." Campbell believed that the rangers' seemingly superior numbers and their "alert" look dissuaded the Indians from launching a major attack west of the Mississippi River.[26]

Certainly, Boone's rangers gave the frontier people and residents of St. Louis a sense of security that exceeded their ability to guarantee. Although fifty hard-riding, tough marksmen wielded a considerable collective punch, they would not have been a match against a large, organized Indian attack on the settlements. Still, the rangers provided an important mobile defense, and in July 1812, the editor of the *Louisiana Gazette* hailed Boone's rangers as "Spartan Warriors," who deserved well of their country. However, had an Indian army moved into Missouri, Boone's rangers would have needed to be Spartans to stop them, because as late as June 6, only 241 regular soldiers were stationed west of the Mississippi: 134 at Fort Belle Fontaine, 63 at Fort Osage, and 44 at Fort Madison.[27]

By early September, the general sense of security in Missouri began to wane, and the war had seriously affected business in St. Louis. Christian Wilt, a merchant who furnished supplies on credit to Boone's rangers, complained that trade had declined to almost nothing, and he attributed that misfortune to so many farmers being away in the militia. He wrote, "some people are alarmed here—indeed our frontier is not too well guarded." When rumors of a general Indian war swept across the frontier, the residents of St. Louis asked Governor Howard to send the Osages against the other tribes, but Howard and Clark did not trust them to strike only other Indians. By mid-December the people of St. Charles also told the governor that they considered their lives and property "neglected and measurably forgotten" by the federal government, and they appealed to him to seek more troops. Governor Howard agreed that the Missouri frontier needed more military strength, and the year ended with him appealing to the War Department for additional regulars.[28]

While Governor Howard waited for a response from Washington, Boone's rangers continued their patrols and blockhouse construction through 1812. Rumors also circulated constantly about a major Indian uprising on the frontier, but little seemed to come of them west of the Mississippi. In January 1813, however, the scouts for Boone's company of rangers killed a Sac "without hesitation," whom they found in their patrol area. Nathan assumed full responsibility for the killing and justified it by his orders to consider all Indians hostile who were found within the lines of settlement, that is, within the perimeter patrolled by his rangers. Acting Governor Frederick Bates, however, worried that this action would cause the Sacs and Foxes to become even more hostile, and wrote to Benjamin Howard that "it is to be feared that we may not be able early in the spring, to resist that combination which may be brought against us." The situation seemed perilous indeed because Bates also reported that British troops had been spotted consorting with the Indians.[29]

In February 1813, the editor of the *Missouri Gazette* urged his readers to consider the conflict a "second struggle for independence" with the British. Then, switching from patriotic to practical, he also told the settlers: "Let those who live on frontier positions build and repair their forts, have a good supply of ammunition and their arms in good order, let the planting be conducted by numbers in each . . . with centinels." The crisis, he said, called for "extraordinary men." A week later the "trustees of the corporation of St. Louis" informed the governor that the town could not withstand a combined British and Indian attack of five hundred men, especially if they had artillery. They asked him to assign to them militia and regulars that were not needed elsewhere for defense. Secretary Bates responded by telling the residents of St. Louis that they were not in immediate danger but if an attack came, "the enemy must be met at the threshold." Everyone expected a great deal from Boone's rangers.[30]

In early March, a Potawatomi killed a farmer searching for his cattle near Portage des Sioux, and Missourians learned that Boone and his rangers were pursuing Indians who had killed a family along the Kaskaskia River in Illinois. The frontier people were also alarmed by a report that the army would move a considerable number of regulars to the east, and many believed that the frontier settlers should be temporarily relocated near St. Charles, where they could be protected by the soldiers at Fort Belle Fontaine. Armed boats could also patrol the Missouri and, in the words of the editor of the *Missouri Gazette,* "watch the motions of the savages, who are now very numerous on our borders." In late March, however, the frontier people received some good news when they learned that Congress had authorized three additional ranger companies for Missouri. Still, the arrival of spring did not bode well for the settlers or Boone's rangers.[31]

Despite the fears of an Indian attack, however, the peace held on the Missouri frontier. Still, the army decided to abandon Fort Osage because it was too isolated to be defended if a major attack came from a combined force of the Indians and British. The order arrived in early April, and Sibley hurriedly packed his goods and left for St. Louis on April 13. He would not return to reestablish the trading post until the autumn of 1815. In early June the soldiers evacuated Fort Osage. The Little Osages resented this decision because the government violated the treaty by closing the fort. Also, they believed that if the federal government established another trading post below the fort on the Missouri, it would further encourage their enemies to encroach on Osage lands and make war against them. Their fears were partially realized in mid-October, when Sibley established a trading house at Arrow Rock.[32]

In addition to constricting the perimeter for territorial defense by withdrawing from Fort Osage, the War Department also divided the nation into nine military districts. Missouri became a part of the eighth district under General William Henry Harrison. In addition, President Madison made Governor Howard a brigadier general in the army, making him responsible for all military forces in the Missouri and Illinois Territories. Howard accepted the position, resigned as governor, and assumed command of the First Regiment of the U.S. Infantry and the Mounted Rangers. Madison then appointed William Clark as territorial governor.[33]

In June 1813, soon after General Howard received his commission, the terms of enlistment expired for the rangers. Boone's company disbanded and the men went home—with the exception of Nathan. Technically, Boone served as an officer in the army, and the War Department had not notified him that his service had ended. As a result, General Howard gave him command of three companies of mounted rangers and promoted him to major, although he continued to receive the pay of a captain until the War Department approved his promotion.[34]

The lull in the early summer of 1813 did not last. On July 4, eleven rangers were attacked by an equivalent force of Winnebagos near Fort Mason. The rangers rode off when the skirmish ended, but the Winnebagos followed their trail and attacked them again the next day. By the time the rangers reached Fort Mason one man had been killed and three fatally wounded. The rangers counted two Indians left in the dirt, but no one could be sure of Winnebago casualties. A month later an unidentified war party attacked four men and two boys who were planting turnips about seven miles above Fort Howard near the Cuivre River. Apparently these farmers thought that the six Indians, who had painted themselves white, were friendly when they approached. However, the Indians, probably Sacs, fired on them, killing one and wounding another. General Howard learned of the attack on the night of August 3 while he was in St. Charles, and he immediately sent a rider to Camp Defiance with orders for Boone's rangers to break camp and pursue the enemy. By the time Boone's men arrived in the vicinity, the Indians had escaped in their canoes across the Mississippi.[35]

On August 7, General Howard learned that two thousand Winnebagos, Potawatomis, Kickapoos, Chippewas, and Otos had crossed the Mississippi at Cap au Gris about eight miles above Fort Mason. Although this report soon proved false, Howard believed that an attack against the Indians who lived along the Illinois River would curtail their threat to the Missouri frontier. In order to base his plans on the most reliable information, General Howard sent Boone and sixteen rangers across the Mississippi to reconnoiter the area to the north between that river and the Illinois. Boone and his men crossed the Mississippi in boats and headed toward the Illinois River. During the first two days, the rangers did not see any signs of Indians. On the second day out, however, Boone sensed that the rangers had been discovered. He could not say precisely why he believed that they were being watched, but he could feel it. By now they should have seen a few friendly Indians who customarily visited army camps and asked for tobacco. Instead, the rangers saw nothing. Boone had an uneasy feeling learned from experience, and it did not go away.[36]

When the rangers camped for the night, Boone became particularly apprehensive. When a sentry reported that he believed a group of Indians was nearby, Nathan decided that they were attempting to surround his camp. He then doubled the sentries and ordered his men to sleep away from the fire with their backs to the trees, facing into the darkness. Near midnight gunfire and screams broke the silence and the tranquillity of the night. One of the sentries, a man named White, had been hit in the hands and lost both thumbs, while a bullet struck another ranger in the shoulder. Instantly, approximately sixty Sacs and Foxes, who had been following Boone's rangers for some thirty or forty miles, shouted and fired from the woods as they attacked the camp. The rangers fell back, firing across the campsite into the darkness, where they saw muzzle flashes and heard the voices of their enemies.[37]

Boone crouched behind a tree and sensed from the rifle fire that his rangers were outnumbered, and he remembered his father had taught him that flight was sometimes the better part of valor. As the rifle fire increased and as the rangers scrambled for cover, frantically shooting, reloading, and trying to see their enemy in the darkness, Boone called for everyone to retreat as quickly as possible and try to keep together. The rangers needed no encouragement and ran off into the brush. Nathan also turned to run, but in the darkness he fell into a sinkhole and landed flat on his face—just as a volley of rifle fire crashed into the trees and bushes above him. He knew instantly that had he not fallen he would have been dead.[38]

While the Indians who had fired at him stopped to reload, Boone picked himself up, scrambled out of the sinkhole, and ran about fifty yards. He called to his men to rally in a circle behind some trees, and they would make a stand. Although the Indians fired a few more shots in the direction of the rangers, the war party now became more interested in stealing the horses, and the fighting died away. In time the woods became quiet; the rangers spent a long night waiting for the dawn. At sunrise, Boone sent his men to hunt for their horses, but they could only find about half of the mounts. Now short of horses and with the knowledge that at least some Indians in the region were hostile, he ordered the rangers back to Cap au Gris. When Nathan reported the attack, General Howard became even more convinced that a major thrust eastward across the Mississippi was essential to prevent the Sacs and Foxes from further terrorizing the frontier, and he planned accordingly.[39]

General Howard decided to strike the Indians in the Illinois country with a two-pronged attack. In September he sent the Second Regiment of his army, some fourteen hundred men under Colonel Benjamin Stephenson, across the Mississippi about three miles above the mouth of the Illinois River. These troops were to scout the country between those two rivers as far north as Fort Madison. Howard ordered Stephenson to drive away any Indians that he found in this area.[40]

While Stephenson's force scattered the Indian villagers before it, General Howard sent the First Regiment up the west side of the Mississippi as far as Christy's Creek, where it rendezvoused with Boone's rangers who had come from Portage des Sioux on September 10. Six days later this force prepared to cross the Mississippi and link with Stephenson's regiment. In the meantime, Howard ordered gunboats under a Lieutenant Colonel Nichols of the Twenty-fourth Infantry up the Illinois River to block any Indians fleeing to the southeast. General Howard also sent riders to warn the settlements between Cap au Gris and Loutre Island and between Sugar and Shoal Creeks in Illinois to be alert for Indian activity now that he had the villagers stirred up and on the move.[41]

On August 28, after a twelve-day march to the southeast, Howard's infantry and Boone's rangers reached the Illinois River, where they met Nichols and his gunboats a few miles below present-day Peoria. Nichols reported that the day before, he had been attacked by a Sac war party of approximately 150 men, but his soldiers, using the swivel guns on their boats, repelled the assault. Some of the Indians, Nichols reported, wore the hats that Boone's men had lost when they were attacked a few weeks before. This report further convinced Howard that the army had to make its presence known in this region. Accordingly, he took his force above Peoria in search of Indian towns. He found several, which his troops burned; they also took the corn the villagers had left behind. Howard also began building Fort Clark on Peoria Lake. While the regulars, with "infinite labor," wielded saws and axes to construct the blockhouses, General Howard sent Boone north with about a hundred men to scout the Rock River area and report the best route for the army's strike against the Sacs and Foxes.[42]

As Boone led his men toward the Rock River, they encountered a host of abandoned Indian villages. In many cases the Indians had fled quickly, fearing a surprise attack, and they had left many of their belongings behind. When Boone returned to the army's camp about a week later, during which his men traveled some two hundred miles, he informed General Howard that the Indians had fled the area. Nathan's report, together with the onset of bitterly cold and snowy weather, gave General Howard reasons to withdraw his army across the Mississippi. His men had not been equipped for winter weather this early in the autumn, and they suffered severely. Some of the men wore out their shoes and killed their horses to have strips of rawhide to wrap around their feet in the freezing weather. Howard withdrew from Fort Clark on October 15, and his army returned to Missouri four days later.[43]

While General Howard threatened and then withdrew from the Illinois country, Governor William Clark and federal Indian agents arranged for the peaceful Sacs and Foxes, some fifteen hundred in all, to move west of the Mississippi and locate on the south side of the Missouri in present-day Moniteau County near Jefferson City, where the federal government would provide them with a trading post and a blacksmith. They would also share the hunting grounds of the Osages. Here they would live beyond the influence of British traders and the reach of their hostile brothers who had not yet laid down their rifles. These friendly Sacs and Foxes crossed the Mississippi in 155 canoes and rendezvoused at Portage des Sioux, where Clark met them for a grand council on September 28. Two days later, after receiving supplies of pork, salt, and flour and after pledging to remain at peace with the Osages, they headed up the Missouri for St. Charles to receive a ration of corn before continuing to the site of their new home. These Sacs occasionally annoyed territorial officials by hoisting the British flag when they held a tribal council, even though they professed peace with the United States. Even so, Clark had successfully divided the Sacs and Foxes. Now the war would proceed against those who could be clearly identified as hostile.[44]

With the early onset of winter in 1813, the settlers on the Missouri frontier began to feel a sense of peace and security that they had not enjoyed for several years. The hostile Sacs and Foxes had been put on the run, and the tribes had been divided into peaceful and warring bands. Boone and the rangers had performed their duty "in a manner highly honorable to themselves and the army." When Nathan finally received word that the War Department had approved his commission as major on December 10, the conflict seemed over for the Missouri country. The only thing that needed to be done was for the army to clean up the hostile villages east of the Mississippi and give the British a good drubbing. Then, the tribes could be forced to sign treaties that would secure the peace on the frontier. Yet, by late 1813, while many of the frontier people in Missouri thought that the war had essentially come to an end, Boone knew that it had not been settled at all. The hostile Sacs and Foxes had not been defeated, the British still encouraged their resistance, and many of the tribes that had allied in Tecumseh's Indian confederacy still counseled and practiced war. Indeed, after a year and a half of conflict, which translated into isolated attacks and the creation of general fear on the Missouri frontier, nothing had changed. Boone also knew that whether there would be peace or continued war with the western tribes would only be determined when the Indians left their winter camps with the onset of spring. In the meantime, the patrols along the frontier would continue, and while the settlers hoped for the best, he was not optimistic.[45]

Without a major defeat of the Indians, Boone had good reason to worry about the continuation of attacks on the Missouri frontier. When the weather warmed in 1814, his worst fears were soon realized as small bands harassed the settlers. In late March, Indians killed, scalped, and mutilated two people in the Boonslick area. On April 14, an unidentified Indian, who may have been part of a larger war party, shot through a hole in the chinking between the logs at Cooper's Fort and killed Sharsall Cooper. Twelve days later a Sac and Fox war party struck a settlement on the Little Moniteau, taking scalps and horses. Word also came from Lincoln County about an attack near Wood's Fort and another in the Cap au Gris area. Other war parties stole horses and cattle and made working in the fields dangerous. Occasionally, local militia or rangers pursued and caught them, with losses to both sides.[46]

Indeed, through the spring and summer and into the autumn of 1814, Indian war parties made the Missouri River country more dangerous than ever, and the rangers could not prevent the isolated, hit-and-run attacks. Boone's men maintained their patrols but neither they nor the other ranger companies could be everywhere at once, and the Sacs, Foxes, and Miamis struck with care. In late July, Governor Clark learned that the Sacs and Foxes had stolen 300 cattle and 150 horses from the Boonslick settlers. Boone also received reports of an attack near present-day New Franklin, a killing near Fayette, a scalping on the Chariton River, a scalping and mutilation near Moniteau Creek, an attack on Cox's Fort above Arrow Rock with the capture and recovery of a girl, and another raid near present-day Boonville, where settlers fled to the blockhouse of Hanna Cole.[47]

In September 1814, with the frontier people in the Missouri River country in a state of terror, General Henry Dodge, commandant of the territorial militia, took 350 rangers, including Boone's company, to relieve the western settlements. Dodge and the rangers rode to Boonslick country and crossed the Missouri at the same ford that Nathan had used when he led Clark to Fire Prairie six years earlier. Now the Missouri ran swift, and Dodge flanked the rangers with canoes in order to rescue anyone who fell from their mounts. When the last ranger of the column reached the other side of the river at Arrow Rock, Nathan noted that the crossing had taken two hours.[48]

Dodge led the rangers north, skirting the south or right bank of the river. Soon his scouts came in riding hard to report that a band of Miamis had camped a few miles ahead. Dodge then deployed his rangers in a wide arc that swept to the west in order to cut off any possibility of escape except across the Missouri. By the time the Indian pickets discovered the rangers, the camp had been effectively surrounded, and Boone and the other men restlessly sat on their horses and awaited Dodge's command to attack. The Miamis, however, saw that they were outnumbered and signaled to Dodge's Shawnee scouts that they wanted to surrender. Dodge then held a council with his staff, at which time Boone and the other officers advised him to accept the Miami offer. Dodge and Nathan, however, suspected that the men from the Boonslick area wanted revenge rather than a surrender, and Dodge told these militiamen that he would hold them responsible for their conduct; he asked every officer to pledge that they would keep their rangers under control.[49]

The Miami camp included 31 men and 122 women and children, all of whom the Boonslick troops thought had been responsible for the recent attacks in their area. The next day, when Dodge and his officers were trying to decide what to do with the Miamis, Benjamin Cooper, who had lost a brother and a cousin to Indian attacks, rode up with his men and announced that a rifle belonging to a man recently killed had been found in the Indian camp. They demanded the right to find the Miamis who committed the killing. When General Dodge refused, Cooper's men began cocking their rifles. Dodge then drew his sword and held the point near Cooper's chest, reminded him of his pledge, and told him that if his men began shooting the prisoners he would be among the first to die. At that moment of tension, fear, and uncertainty, Boone stepped forward and told Cooper that he and his men stood with Dodge and advised him not to do anything stupid. Cooper hesitated, then backed down, and the crisis passed.[50]

What became of these Miamis is unclear, but in October a report circulated that four hundred Sacs had appeared in the Boonslick area hunting cattle for the winter's meat supply. On November 19, some three hundred rangers and volunteers rode out of St. Charles in an attempt to cut off the Sacs when they returned to their camps to the north. However, after traveling as far west as the Grand River without seeing an Indian, the force returned home. Rumors of Indian thievery and violence on the frontier caused the editor of the *Missouri Gazette* to complain that the officers of the regular army were incompetents who gave "miserable direction" to their men and who allowed "the rangers to loiter about the country, while the border people [were] massacred by savages."[51]

By late 1814, neither the United States nor the British had been able to gain a decisive victory and both governments sought to end the war on the basis of *status quo antebellum,* that is, their pre-war territorial status. On December 24, 1814, the American ministers in Belgium signed the Treaty of Ghent, which ended the war of 1812. It did not immediately stop the fighting on the Missouri frontier, however. Black Hawk, who gave direction to the hostile tribes in the Upper Midwest and whose influence extended into Missouri, had not surrendered, nor had the western tribes suffered a major defeat.

Unbeaten in war, they did not recognize a peace based on a paper document that individuals far away had signed, and their attacks on white settlements continued.[52]

Boone's rangers were doubly discouraged. Not only had the Indians not been forced to accept peace, but military pay seldom arrived. With their wages in considerable arrears, they all complained about the incompetency of the federal government. Boone counseled patience and told them that they would probably see some money eventually. To make matters worse, before news arrived on the Missouri frontier that the Treaty of Ghent had ended the war, the *Missouri Gazette* reported that an estimated ninety-seven hundred hostile warriors inhabited the country west of St. Louis to about a hundred miles above the mouth of the Platte River. Some Missourians urged an expedition of three thousand mounted men to strike their villages when the weather warmed in April.[53]

So, the war on the frontier continued. Boone, however, did not always arrive with his rangers in time to save the people under attack. In the early spring of 1815, for example, a band of Indians stole horses from the Cole settlement located several miles above Loutre Island. Some half a dozen men pursued the thieves, but they could not catch them. Near nightfall, the settlers gave up the trail, turned back home, and camped for the night near the headwaters of Loutre Creek. Several members of the tracking party urged caution and recommended that they sleep away from the fire, but the other men "ridiculed the idea" because the Indians were many miles away. During the night a war party crept up on the camp and attacked the sleeping men. Quickly the fighting became hand-to-hand, with Temple Cole grappling with an attacker near the fire. Stephen Cole helped his brother by stabbing the Indian with a knife. But he had no sooner saved Temple than two Indians ran up and stabbed him eight or nine times. Despite Stephen Cole's serious wounds, he and a James Moredock escaped, the latter by running away from the fighting and hiding under a branch along the creek bank until the Indians departed. Cole and Moredock then ran south, leaving five companions dead at the campsite.[54]

Sometimes Boone reached the scene of an attack too late to help. Not long after the assault on Stephen Cole and his men, for example, a war party killed Captain James Callaway and four of his rangers on the Prairie Fork of the Loutre. The Indians had stolen fifteen or twenty horses from the Loutre Island settlement, and Callaway and his rangers, who were stationed on the island, quickly followed in pursuit with twenty men. After tracking the Indians about forty miles they discovered an empty camp where they recovered the horses; apparently the Indians had set off to raid another settlement. Callaway then ordered his rangers to head back on the trail that they had followed, herding the horses along the way. Scouts for the Sac and Fox war party, however, had discovered the rangers and approximately forty Indians lay in ambush. Taken by surprise, only three or four of Callaway's men returned fire. Five or six rangers died instantly, while Callaway received three wounds. With his horse shot, he attempted to swing on behind several rangers, but their horses were too skittish, so he ran to the bank of the Prairie Fork for safety while the remainder of the rangers made a wild dash across the countryside. Callaway apparently jumped into the creek in an attempt to reach the other side about twenty yards away, but he landed in a deep hole and could not make his way across before an Indian shot him in the head. When the rangers reached Loutre Island a rider was sent for Boone and his rangers. When Nathan reached the ambush site three days later, he found the bodies of the men, which had been scalped and "greatly mutilated," with their heads cut off. Boone had the rangers buried nearby. Flanders Callaway, James's father and Nathan's brother-in-law, found his son's body a few days later about two hundred yards downstream from the battle site. With the death of James, the hard reality of war touched the Boone family, just as it had in Virginia and Kentucky when Daniel had lost two sons. Now a grandson lay in a forlorn grave on a creek bank in Missouri. The frontier exacted a high price from both Indians and whites who wanted to live there.[55]

In May Nathan also visited the site of the Robert Ramsay killing near Charette on the Femme Osage, about six miles from his own home. There, about fifteen Indians killed and mutilated three children and mortally wounded their father and mother. Boone learned of the attack after a fourth child escaped and spread the alarm. When he reached the farmyard, he saw the three children on the ground and heard the calls for help from the Ramsays, who had barricaded themselves inside their cabin. One of the children moved and Boone knelt by the boy of about five years of age. Scalped and with dried blood covering his face, the boy opened his eyes, looked at Boone, and said, "Daddy, the Indians did scalp me." Before Boone left the Ramsay place, he helped bury the three children. About this same time, he received a report of an intense firefight between soldiers from Forts Howard and Cap au Gris and the Sacs, led by Black Hawk, on the Cuivre River at a place called the "Sink Hole." All things considered, peace on the Missouri frontier seemed as distant as ever, and no one thought the Indian war would soon end.[56]

Although the Treaty of Ghent terminated the fighting between Great Britain and the United States, and while William Henry Harrison had defeated the Shawnees and their allies in the Old Northwest, the far western tribes, particularly the Sacs, Foxes, and Kickapoos, were astounded when they learned of the peace. They had not been defeated by the Americans, and they had no intention of abandoning their goals of restoring their lands and expelling white settlers. Thus, they continued their attacks on isolated settlements where the danger of retribution from the army, rangers, or militia would be minimal. In mid-March, Christian Wilt in St. Louis spoke for most Missourians when he wrote "it is the Opinion of the People here that we shall not have peace with the Indians until we drub them soundly into it." Little more than two months later the *Missouri Gazette* called for "nothing but exemplary chastisement" of the Indians to protect Missouri's borders.[57]

While the tribes continued to make trouble on the frontier, the Treaty of Ghent prevented the Missouri militia and rangers from striking back. Article 9 of the treaty stipulated that upon ratification the federal government would terminate "hostilities" with all tribes with whom it had been at war and restore to the Indians "all the possessions, rights, and privileges which they may have enjoyed or been entitled to in one thousand eight hundred and eleven previous to such hostilities." The frontier people in Missouri disapproved of this article and the treaty in general. Although they were glad the war had ended with Great Britain, for the issues of freedom of the seas and national pride were important to them, they had not supported the War of 1812 to defeat Britain or to conquer Canada. Rather, they supported the war as the only means to bring the Indians under control and protect their homes and lands once and for all. However, diplomats meeting in Europe had concluded the conflict; the Indians remained hostile, dangerous, and free to attack, while the settlers could not strike back. Despite the great losses of life, property, and livestock, nothing had been gained. The newly acquired lands had been rendered too dangerous for habitation. Small wonder, then, that the frontier people, who knew about Andrew Jackson's defeat of the Creeks at Horseshoe Bend in March 1814 and his rout of the British at New Orleans on January 8, 1815, wanted the western tribes to be "Jacksonized."[58]

The federal government, however, wanted the restoration of peace, not a continuation of the conflict, and on April 15 Secretary of War James Monroe appointed three Indian commissioners to treat with the Indians: Governor William Clark of the Missouri Territory, Governor Ninian Edwards of the Illinois Territory, and Auguste Chouteau. Monroe informed them that they should not seek concessions from the undefeated tribes or from those that now professed friendship with the United States. Rather, he said: "It is thought proper to confine this treaty to the sole object of peace. Other arrangements between the United States and the Indian tribes adapted to their mutual interests may be entered into hereafter." In order to make the difficult task of the commissioners easier, Monroe ordered the superintendent of Indian trade to send some twenty thousand dollars' worth of goods such as blankets, knives, flints, powder, mirrors, tobacco, pipes, needles, cotton cloth, and coats, to be given as presents when the tribes signed the treaties. He insisted that "these articles should be equal in quality to those which the Indians have been accustomed to receive from the British agents."[59]

The commissioners were less than optimistic, but they went about the task of notifying the tribes in the upper Mississippi valley that a major council would be held at Portage des Sioux on the Missouri River for the purpose of establishing the peace by treaty. The western tribes, however, did not respond with speed or enthusiasm. The Sacs and Foxes especially remained hostile. In late May the commissioners reported to the secretary of war that one of their emissaries to these tribes had been killed and that the Sacs and Foxes treated their communications for negotiations with "cold indifference." When a Sac delegation arrived at Portage des Sioux in June, they did nothing but "frown and strut around with the most insufferable impudence" before hurrying back to their villages on the Rock River. On July 11, the commissioners informed General Bissell at Fort Belle Fontaine that among the Sacs and Foxes the "principal chiefs and warriors continue to cherish the most inveterate and deadly hostility towards the American people and government." Perhaps they did so because Clark lectured them with threatening speeches and they did not trust him. The Kickapoos also remained "sullen and uncooperative." The commissioners believed that "it is the intention of those tribes to continue the war, and that nothing less than a vigorous display of military force can change their disposition."[60]

Despite this gloomy outlook, the commissioners continued their efforts to hold a general treaty-making council with the Sacs, Foxes, and other tribes at Portage des Sioux on July 6, and they urged Missourians to help them by refraining from attacking the Indians. This appeal did not set well with the frontier people such as a correspondent to the *Missouri Gazette* on June 10 who wrote that "we are not permitted to kill the enemy but on condition he first kills us. . . . Shall we allow so sacred a thing as a treaty to be a passport to conduct the murderers into our houses and towns?" Despite the skepticism of the frontier people, however, the commissioners continued their efforts to lure the tribes to Portage des Sioux. In order to ensure tranquillity during the treaty negotiations, the commissioners requested troops from Fort Belle Fontaine, and General Bissell sent 275 regulars under the command of Colonel John Miller. Bissell also sent two gunboats, the *Governor Clark* and the *Commodore Perry,* to anchor in the Missouri with their guns trained on the Indian encampments.[61]

By July 1, the tribes began to arrive. Although these Indians were inclined to make peace with the United States, General Bissell reported that "they attach much consequence to themselves, and hold the Americans in great contempt as warriors, little better than squaws." Bissell did not believe that any peace conducted here would long endure and that a lasting settlement would not come until the Indians were "well chastised." Despite this pessimism, the soldiers erected one hundred tents and went about their duties designed to keep the peace in the encampment, but they did not trust the Indians and they made their contempt for them clearly known.[62]

Despite their posturing, these tribes had little choice but to sign a treaty. They knew that the British had forsaken them and that they stood alone against the army, rangers, and militia units that the U.S. government might soon send against them. Cut off from supplies of food, powder, and lead, and with the game gone from their hunting grounds and the increasing encroachment of white farmers, they could do little else than to make peace and sort out their lives and their relationship with the federal government and the frontier people.[63]

When the council began on July 10, neither the Sacs from the Rock River area in Illinois nor the Foxes, Ioways, Kickapoos, or Winnebagos had arrived. Governor Clark once again sent runners to their villages with a warning that they had thirty days to reach Portage des Sioux for the purposes of making a peace treaty, or the federal government would from that date levy war against them. While the commissioners waited for the Sacs, they began to treat with the host of tribes encamped at Portage des Sioux. Clark reminded the other tribes of the "benevolent intentions of the President, his wish to bury the tomahawk and forget past transactions," while he took a "luminous view" of their conduct during the war. The tribes listened and between July 18 and September 16, the commissioners signed treaties with the Potawatomis, Piankashaws, Teton Sioux, Sioux of the Lakes, Sioux of St. Peter's River, Yankton Sioux, Omahas, Kickapoos, Osages, Sacs of Missouri, Foxes, and Ioways. These treaties were brief and essentially the same. Each asserted "perpetual peace and friendship" between the United States and the respective nation and provided that every "injury or act of hostility" by either would be "mutually forgiven and forgot." In order to keep the Sacs divided, the commissioners signed a treaty with those who lived along the Missouri River that required them to "remain distinct and separate" from the Rock River Sacs and to forgo giving them any assistance until the federal government could negotiate a peace treaty with those bands of the tribe.[64]

When the Ioway chiefs made their mark and thereby brought the treaty council to a close, the Rock River Sacs still had not arrived, and the commissioners again sent Indian agent Nicholas Boilvin and an interpreter to get them. When the tribe finally reached Portage des Sioux, the treaty council had been disbanded for two weeks. Only the trampled ground where some two thousand Indians had made their lodges and campfires remained. The commissioners then sent them word to arrive in St. Louis during the following spring. In the meantime, the Senate approved the treaties on December 21, 1815, which the president signed on December 26.[65]

The next spring, the Rock River Sacs arrived in St. Louis and signed a treaty on May 13, 1816. The commissioners, however, were in little mood to issue mere platitudes to the Indians about the benefits of a reestablished peace. Instead, they rubbed peace in their noses because the Sacs had not come to Portage des Sioux for the great council in 1815. The commissioners told the chiefs that the conduct of their people merited the "infliction of the severest chastisement," but because they had "earnestly repented of their conduct, now imploring mercy, and being anxious to return to the habits of peace and friendship with the United States," they would be forgiven. Even so, the commissioners still required the Sacs to return all property that they had stolen since they were notified that the Treaty of Ghent had ended the war. If they did not do so before July 1, they would lose their annuities. When the Sacs stepped forward to sign their mark before the commissioners and other witnesses, the war on the Missouri frontier officially came to an end.[66]

Many frontier people in Missouri resented the treaties, and disparagingly called the commissioners the "Indian Treaty men," and they still clung to the belief that only after the tribes had been soundly defeated by the army could peace be assured. Although Clark suffered considerable public criticism, the combined work of the army, rangers, militia, and commissioners had brought peace to the Missouri frontier. Thereafter, the federal government entered into a flurry of treaty-making activities to gain land concessions from the tribes in the Mississippi and Missouri River country. Indeed, between 1815 and the election of Andrew Jackson to the presidency in 1828, twenty-four tribes signed thirty-nine treaties (excluding the special treaties in 1825 with the Indians who lived along the Missouri River). William Clark, who became Superintendent of Indian Affairs in 1821, negotiated many of these land cession treaties. As a result, settlers began moving west in greater numbers and speed than ever before. Few settlers feared the Indians on the Missouri frontier any longer.[67]

For Nathan Boone the end of the War of 1812 meant the return to his farm on the Femme Osage; he did not relish the thought, even though he cherished Olive and his children. Planting corn and raising hogs had never appealed to him any more than it had to his father. Although pleased that the killing and terror on the frontier had ended, he felt a sense of emptiness. When Boone received his discharge in June 1815, he could not help but feel both relief and regret. He had played an instrumental role in ensuring the peace on the frontier and in ending the Indian menace. During his terms of service he had faced danger from both rifle-wielding Indians and whites alike and endured the hardships of long rides, cold camps, monotonous fare of salt pork, beans, and coffee, and the drudgery of uneventful routine. Yet he had performed his duty honorably and well. He had confronted the problems of supply when contractors refused to make deliveries because he could only offer the promissory notes of the federal government, and he had tolerated the annoyance of delays in pay. William Clark believed that, all things considered, the Indians did "little mischief" on the Missouri frontier because of the "diligence of the Rangers" and officers like Nathan Boone.[68]

Still, Boone's rangers and others like them did not ride proverbial white horses for all of the frontier people in Missouri. Sometime in 1813, the residents of Peruque, a village near the Mississippi River in St. Charles County, received orders—from whom, it remains unclear—to abandon their homes and take refuge in St. Charles, but they blamed the rangers for it. Although a troop passed through the village regularly, the residents considered them as "troublesome" as the Indians. When the rangers forced them to leave their homes because the village invited attack, they complained that their houses were damaged as they were used for barracks and that their stores of wheat and corn were fed to the horses. Moreover, the stockade and fences were torn down for firewood. When the villagers returned after the war, they found nearly total destruction of their homes, fields, and livestock, and they cursed the rangers as much as the Indians.[69]

Despite the rough and swaggering nature of the rangers, Boone liked the discipline, comfort, and certainty of military routine, the companionship of his men, and the excitement of chasing Indians as much as he had enjoyed hunting deer and trapping beaver. But he had little opportunity to remain in the army, because the War Department quickly sent most of its officers and men home after the return of peace. A peacetime army required few soldiers, even seasoned veterans like Boone, who understood the frontier better than organized society and who had the experience and the wisdom to deal with Indian peoples as both fighters and peacemakers. These veterans would find opportunity upon new Indian threats.

5

INTERLUDE

BOONE RETURNED home to the Femme Osage after his discharge from the Missouri Rangers in June 1815. Much needed to be done about the farm, and he was not keen on the work. But Nathan received good news in 1816 when he learned that the Board of Land Commissioners had reversed its decision, once again, and granted his land claims. On February 2, Frederick Bates submitted a report to Congress in which the board confirmed Nathan's claims to 800 arpents along the Femme Osage and the 420 arpents along Loutre Creek. As a result, sometime during 1816, with title to his lands finally secured and with the war behind him, Nathan began construction of the house that reflected his wealth and status in St. Charles County. Daniel, now eighty-two years of age, could not help much manually but he still had a keen mind and no doubt offered useful advice. Nathan built his new home not far from his log house. He took blue limestone from a nearby quarry, dragged it back with oxen, and laid the stone walls about three feet thick. He also crafted black walnut beams and oak floorboards and laid up large stone chimneys at each end. Upon completion, the house extended forty-six feet long and twenty-six feet wide. With a height of twenty-two feet, it easily accommodated a second floor. With seven large, comfortable rooms, three on the first floor and two each on the second floor and attic level, and with a double veranda on the south, along with a full basement, Nathan's home was a mansion by frontier standards and a sign of wealth

In 1816, Nathan began the construction of this house near the Femme Osage. His father helped him build it by providing advice and assisting with minor tasks. Nathan completed his home about 1819, and it quickly became recognized as one of the most luxurious residences on the frontier. Today, it is known as the Daniel Boone home, but Nathan did most of the work, and it was his house. *Photographer, Mary Ellen Hurt.*

and success. Indeed, this handsome federal-style stone house by all accounts offered the "conveniences of an urban dwelling," and in 1819 the assessor gave it a considerable valuation of three thousand dollars for tax purposes.[1]

After several years of construction, the house was completed and Boone, once again, took up the business of surveying for the federal government. Many of the land claims in eastern Missouri remained contested before the Board of Land Commissioners, which was responsible for determining who owned which tracts of land. Disputes arose as a result of incomplete and overlapping grants made by Spanish authorities to American settlers prior to the Louisiana Purchase. Boone had earned a reputation as a surveyor who was as good as any and better than most before the war, and he did not lack assignments. As a result, during the spring of 1819, the St. Charles

County Court, the governing body of the county, appointed Boone, James H. Audrain, and Joseph Evans to report on the feasibility of surveying a road from St. Charles to Franklin in Howard County. This committee, however, never found time to meet, and in November the county court appointed a five-man delegation, including Boone, to view and mark the road and report back in the spring. By 1821, this committee still had not laid out what eventually would become known as the Boonslick Road, and the county court appointed another committee on February 28, but Boone was not part of it. Local interests, however, could not agree precisely where the road should begin or the route that it should follow out of the county, and nothing was accomplished until January 6, 1827, when the state legislature provided that the Boonslick Road would be a state road. As a result, the county court appointed another committee to determine the best route and authorized Boone to survey it. In February, however, for reasons that are unknown, the court replaced Boone with Prospect K. Robbins, who surveyed the road.[2]

Apparently Boone was too busy surveying for the federal government to complete the work on the Boonslick Road. Indeed, surveying would occupy most of his time for the next sixteen years, and it brought a reliable and comfortable income into the Boone household. By late August 1823, Boone served as a deputy surveyor in St. Charles County. Three years later, in mid-May 1826, he worked the area of the Dardenne River, which drained into the Mississippi to the north. His surveying work in the St. Charles vicinity meant that he remained relatively close to home, and he often returned for the night or made a stop on the way between assignments to see Olive and the children and to eat a home-cooked meal. Yet he was away from home so much that letters went uncollected at the post offices in St. Charles and St. Louis, and his name appeared in the *Missouri Gazette* as one among many who had mail to pick up. In between survey work and dabbling at farming, Boone also served as the administrator of the estates of several friends. This responsibility proved his mark as a trusted and respected man of good character and honor. When leisure time prevailed, he attended local estate sales, like most farmers in the area, and he made small purchases, buying a hogshead here and a few sheep there. Compared to his time as a hunter, trapper, and ranger, his life had become routine and little different from most men who lived on a farm in a region that had become less frontier and more settled community.[3]

Given Boone's experience and past responsibilities and achievements, the people in St. Charles County liked him and considered him to be a "very honest man." With 680 acres of land, Boone was hardly a small-scale frontier farmer. Like many large-scale landowners, he held some of this acreage for later sale when the price went up, and he rented some of his land to gain income and increase its value when his tenants cleared the trees for fields, built fences, and erected buildings. On October 2, 1818, he sold 357 acres on Loutre Creek that bordered his brother Morgan's property for $1,200. A year later, on November 4, 1819, he paid $1,025 for property measuring 150 by 300 feet, including a horse mill on Second Street in St. Charles.[4]

Boone's wealth proved sufficiently large and well known that people asked him for loans and to help them post bond for public office. In October 1815, for example, Boone, along with John B. Callaway and David Bailey, guaranteed a $5,000 bond for Nathaniel Simons to hold the position of St. Charles County sheriff. Unfortunately for Boone and his colleagues, Simons neither repaid the loan nor faithfully discharged his duties, and he forfeited the bond. This default hurt, but it would not be Boone's last bad monetary investment in human nature. On September 13, 1824, Boone needed money, and he used a twenty-six-year-old male slave by the name of Harry to secure a loan from an acquaintance for $372. Boone planned to pay it back quickly because the note was due on January 15 and bore 10 percent interest, but the necessity for the loan indicates financial difficulty of some sort. Failure in the world of business would strike him periodically just as it had smitten his father time and again over land claims.[5]

Periodically, then, Nathan needed more money to take care of his family and farm. Although surveying work gave him a steady income, he did not receive pay for his "services rendered" as a ranger in 1813 until June 26, 1817. However, in 1828, he, Morgan, and two other men received two thousand dollars from William Clark for building a house, corn crib, and poultry house and plowing and planting fifteen acres of corn and pumpkins on Kansa lands about seven miles west of present-day Lawrence. There, on the north bank of the Kansas River, Morgan served as a government farmer employed to teach agriculture to the tribe, and Nathan helped him get started. Periodic financial difficulties, however, together with Boone's long absences from home, began to wear on Olive. Still, she endured and kept their home a refuge; after a few years a visitor noted that she was a "well preserved person" and that she and her "pretty daughters were engaged in making very artistic blankets."[6]

Boone's prominence as a frontiersman, ranger, and surveyor made him a natural candidate for political office among the people in St. Charles County at the time that Missourians advocated statehood. After the War of 1812, migration to Missouri increased rapidly, as settlers, particularly from the upper South, claimed the rich lands along the Missouri River as far west as the Boonslick country. Although many inhabitants had championed statehood since the creation of the Missouri Territory in 1812, Congress now recognized its growing population and permitted its voters to elect a legislative council in the last stage of territorial government before admittance to statehood.[7]

In November 1818, the territorial legislature asked Congress for admission to the Union, but the bill was derailed in the approval process when James Tallmadge, congressman from New York, attached an amendment that restricted the admission of slaves and provided that all bondsmen born in Missouri would receive their freedom at twenty-five years of age. The Senate refused to support this amendment, and Missouri remained a territory where most residents supported slavery. With the number of slave and free states at eleven each, the two sides of the slavery issue were balanced in the Senate. Southerners did not want to lose their voting power nor did they want to lose their constitutional right to own property in the form of slaves. Consequently, the admittance of Missouri to the Union became a political issue of national importance. When Maine applied for statehood, reconciliation between northerners and southerners became possible, and Speaker of the House Henry Clay helped devise a compromise that provided, in part, for the admission of Missouri as a slave state and Maine as a free state.[8]

The Missouri Compromise, as it became known, cleared the way for Congress to pass the Missouri Enabling Act, which President James Monroe signed on March 6, 1820. This legislation defined the boundaries of Missouri and authorized residents to elect delegates to a constitutional convention. These delegates would write a constitution, which Congress would approve, and Missouri would then pass from territorial status to statehood. Thomas Hempstead brought the news of the Enabling Act to St. Louis on March 21, and it quickly spread along with celebrations throughout the territory. In St. Charles, Boone learned of Missouri's impending statehood, and the talk about electing delegates to the constitutional convention began almost immediately.[9]

Soon, sharp debate began in several counties over whether restrictionists or antirestrictionists—those who favored limiting slavery in Missouri or those who fully supported the institution—should be elected to the convention. Thomas Hart Benton and other political leaders in St. Louis quickly foiled the "emancipators" by choosing a county ticket of proslavery candidates for election to the constitutional convention. The antirestrictionist or pro-slavery voters, who far outnumbered the restrictionists, supported this maneuver. In the end the restriction of slavery became a campaign issue in only five of Missouri's fifteen counties. When officials counted the ballots, no restrictionists had been elected delegates to the constitutional convention.[10]

During the first week in May, white males who had lived in the territory for three months and who had reached twenty-one years of age went to the polls and chose forty-one delegates, apportioned by population, from fifteen counties. Among the most prominent men chosen to draft the constitution were David Barton, John Rice Jones, Duff Green, Edward Bates, and Henry Dodge. In St. Charles, the voters elected Nathan Boone as one of their three allotted delegates to the constitutional convention. Although Boone had virtually no experience in politics and had been elected solely on his reputation earned in the field rather than the political arena, he felt some comfort knowing that his old acquaintance and superior officer Henry Dodge would be part of the convention as well as twenty-one men who had seen military service in past wars and Indian engagements. Of this group, Boone and Dodge had earned the greatest military distinction.[11]

However, it was primarily the lawyers, not the military men, who would be responsible for drafting Missouri's first constitution. They had the best educations, knew the nuances of legal terminology, and drew on political experience. Boone could not compete with the lawyers although his large landholding made him their equal in wealth, while his age of thirty-nine placed him two years younger than the average age of the delegates. In short, Boone was among an elite group of men who were of young age and high economic position. Yet, they were all essentially representatives of the frontier people who elected them, and they had more similarities than differences in terms of birth, upbringing, and work.[12]

Boone and the other delegates to the constitutional convention met on June 12, 1820, in the dining room of the Mansion House Hotel in St. Louis. For the next thirty-eight days until July 19, they convened daily except on Sundays and the Fourth of July. When the convention met, the delegates, led by the conservative business- and slavery-oriented attorneys from St. Louis, elected David Barton president and went about the business of drafting the state constitution. Barton in turn appointed lawyers friendly to the St. Louis political faction to the chairmanships of the convention committees. The committees would write the sections of the constitution, which a select committee would revise and consolidate for consideration by the convention delegates.[13]

No one can determine precisely what they discussed, because Secretary William G. Pettus did not record the speeches of the delegates, although their interests can be roughly traced. Barton, for example, appointed Boone to the committee charged with overseeing the convention's printing. Boone and the committee, however, did not exercise caution when they solicited competitive bids for the printing of the constitution and the journal of the convention's proceedings. For reasons that were no doubt politically motivated, they granted the contract to the Isaac N. Henry Company, of which Thomas Hart Benton served as a principal investor.[14]

Boone and the other delegates turned their attention to guaranteeing the institution of slavery, determining the necessary offices, and discussing the taxation of land. They also concerned themselves with the regulation of river navigation, requirements for holding office in the state legislature, and the size of counties. During these deliberations the delegates generally used southern state constitutions, especially Kentucky's, as their guide. In all, the convention considered thirty-three measures for which the secretary did not record the votes. On Monday, July 10, for example,

Boone introduced a measure that would have moved the seat of government to St. Charles until October 1, 1826, but it failed to pass, and the names of those who opposed him are unknown, because the secretary merely noted that the motion was "negatived." Essentially, however, Boone lost because the St. Louis delegation and its supporters were determined to keep the seat of government in the city.[15]

No matter what the reason, Boone proved ineffectual in introducing important measures for inclusion in the constitution, mobilizing support, and winning causes. He was also generally uninterested and did not vote on every consideration, in part, due to an absence of several days. On Friday, June 30, the convention granted him leave, the reason for which remains unknown, until the following Wednesday, but he did not cast his next vote until Friday, July 7. Boone and the delegates, however, considered sixty-nine constitutional measures for which Pettus recorded the votes by name. In this tally Boone joined a group of seventeen delegates, including David Barton, Edward Bates, and Henry Dodge, that cast 48.5 percent of the successful votes and only 25 percent of the unsuccessful ballots for the forty-eight most important measures, including approval of Section 35, which guaranteed the institution of slavery. Boone, however, missed voting on seventeen significant issues. These matters involved the qualifications for governor, the duties of the lieutenant governor, the organization of the judiciary, and the provision of a minimum salary for judges. Essentially, Boone joined his colleagues, especially the conservatives, in supporting the reports of the various committees, and the principal authors—Barton, Bates, John Cook, John Rice Jones, J. S. Findlay, and John Scott.[16]

The delegates to the forty-one-member constitutional convention loosely separated themselves into three factions—liberal, moderate, and conservative—and Boone's sentiments favored the latter group. In the convention, the liberals advocated frequent elections and the popular election of judges and sheriffs as well as the removal of all property qualifications from voting and limits on executive power. The St. Louis "caucus" represented the conservatives at the convention and largely dominated the proceedings, while the moderates brokered compromise between the conservatives and the liberals.[17]

On Wednesday, July 19, 1820, the delegates finished their work and adopted the first state constitution of Missouri. At that time, the Committee of Enrollment, chaired by Jonathan S. Findlay, reported that the constitution was correct as approved, and Edward Bates, who served on the committee, ordered that it be printed and sent to Congress. The delegates then thanked David Barton for his leadership as president of the convention as well as the secretary and the "St. Louis Guards." Barton signed the document and Boone and the other delegates filed by to affix their names to Missouri's first constitution. The convention then "dissolved" and the representatives went home. When the convention ended, Boone was among the five delegates who collectively introduced a mere seven of the important measures considered by the convention, of which none were adopted.[18]

Overall, Boone and the other delegates approved a brief, conservative constitution. Although they provided universal, white manhood suffrage, permitted the legislature to override the governor's veto, and authorized a strong independent judiciary, the delegates also protected slavery. The constitution, moreover, provided that amendments would be proposed and approved by a two-thirds vote of each house, rather than by the direct vote of the people. Most important, the constitution prohibited the legislature from permitting emancipation without the slaveowner's consent and from restricting people from bringing their property in the form of slaves into Missouri. The constitution also included a provision that required the legislature to prohibit freed slaves and mulattos from settling in the state.[19]

With the constitution written, potential candidates for office, who would be elected on August 28, began scrambling for supporters. Boone reluctantly became one of them. He had neither enjoyed the daily meetings sitting behind tables and talking about matters of finance, river regulation, and governmental structure, nor dressing in waistcoat, white shirt, and tie. His world was not that of politics, conference rooms, and secret maneuvering, but rather fresh air, saddlebags, and horses. When the gavel banged adjournment for the constitutional convention, Boone could not have been happier to flee St. Louis for his home on the Femme Osage and the comfort of Olive and his children, at least until another surveying job took him into the open, isolated country where he belonged. He had done his duty and met the expectations of his friends and supporters in St. Charles County.[20]

Yet Boone's participation in the constitutional convention reinforced his sense of responsibility. The people of St. Charles County had sent him to St. Louis, and he now felt an obligation to continue the work of creating a viable new state from a sprawling territory. Boone, however, did not campaign much or well. He took the attitude that the voters would select him as one of the county's three delegates to the state legislature if they wanted him in St. Louis. When the election was finally held, Boone finished behind Uriah Devore, William Smith, and Joseph Evans. Two years later on August 5, 1822, Boone again entered the race for one of three positions in the state legislature for St. Charles County, but he finished fourth in a twelve-man race. Following these two defeats, Boone never again sought or held public office. Instead he took tripod, circumferentor, and surveyor's chain in hand and went back to the open country that he knew best.[21]

Nathan did not have much time to recover from the drudgery of meetings, the tedium of negotiations, and the stale air of conference rooms at the constitutional convention. Two months after he returned home, his father became seriously ill. Nathan's mother, Rebecca, had died on March 18, 1813, and he had expected the death of Daniel three years earlier when he went hunting with James, Nathan's oldest son, during the winter of 1817. At that time, Nathan had tried to talk him out of going, because Daniel had become frail and sickness had bothered him the past few winters. He belonged at home by the fire—not on the ground under a snow-covered blanket or standing in icy water checking his trapline. But Daniel would not listen; he felt as healthy and as strong as ever. Nathan did not need to worry—the fresh air would do him good. Besides, James would be along to help out. Nathan could not talk his father out of going, but he told his son to keep a close eye on his grandfather and to come home quickly if anything went wrong.[22]

It did. James and his grandfather had been gone only two days, when the snow and cold gave Daniel an uncontrollable chill, and they took refuge at the cabin of Isaac Vanbibber near Loutre Lick. James then rode hard for home and informed his father that Daniel was "alarmingly ill," and "thought to be dying." Nathan prepared to depart for his cousin's cabin, but ordered (perhaps one of his slaves) that a coffin be built for his father. He would bury Daniel as soon as he brought him home. But Daniel recovered and returned to Nathan's house where Olive tended his needs.

As Daniel grew stronger, he examined the coffin that Nathan had had made for him, and he told his son that it was "too rough and uncouth," and that he preferred to be buried in one he had purchased when Rebecca died in 1813. At that time, Daniel had two identical coffins made from black walnut. He kept his coffin in the attic and periodically pulled it down for examination, and, as Nathan's daughter Delinda recalled, he would "rub and polish it up, and coolly whistle while doing so." Daniel's preparation for death became frightening to the children in the Boone home, but Nathan saw no harm in his father's eccentricities, such as lying down in the coffin to "show how well it fit him" and to take a nap, although his father's actions, frailness, and lack of "plump cheer" made Nathan a bit melancholy. Still, Daniel amused Nathan's children with stories of his exploits and songs that he had learned over the years, and they soon forgot his preoccupation with dying.

In late September 1820, however, those stories and songs came to an end. Daniel was stricken with fever; Olive helped him into bed and sent for a local doctor. But Daniel would not take any medication, despite the urging of Nathan. Instead, Daniel asked his family to prepare him for burial and for Olive to sing to him. On September 26, "when the sun was half an hour high," Daniel died, with Nathan and his daughter Jemima holding his hands. "I am going," he said, "my time has come"; Nathan felt his father's grip relax and, as he stood by the side of the bed, Daniel's body grew cold.

Nathan grieved for his father. He had been closer than any son to Daniel, and they had many good times together in the woods since his father first took him across the Ohio River into Indian country to hunt deer when he was a small boy. Now Nathan pulled out the black walnut coffin from underneath his father's bed and lifted him into it. The family then carried him by wagon back to Jemima's house, where two days later Delinda's husband, who was an "ordinary" Baptist preacher, conducted the funeral service "pretty well," before Nathan helped lower his father into a grave beside Rebecca. Daniel's life had ended and with it a bond between a father and a son that could be broken only by death.

Nathan worked with a small surveying crew of chain and ax men in an attempt to help settlers and government officials locate legal property boundaries and give system and order to the mess of overlapping land claims that had been perpetuated by a host of Spanish grants. Nevertheless, he remained close enough to civilization to hear about the increasing hostility of the Indians, particularly the Rock River Sacs in the Illinois Territory. Although the Treaty of Ghent had officially ended the War of 1812 and provided the opportunity to establish peace with the western tribes and bring the confrontation between whites and Indians to an end, it did neither. Within a year of signing the peace treaty dictated by William Clark at St. Louis, the Rock River Sacs had become increasingly hostile and reluctant to vacate lands that they had previously ceded for settlement in northwestern Illinois. This earlier "Treaty with the Sauk and Foxes," signed on November 4, in St. Louis, had ceded 50 million acres of Sac and Fox lands that covered the eastern third of Missouri and the area between the Wisconsin River to the north, the Fox and Illinois Rivers on the east and south, and the Mississippi River on the west. Saukenuk, the principal Sac village with approximately five hundred families, extended three miles on either side of the mouth of the Rock River. As the years passed the federal government did not force the Sacs to move, and in time they became increasingly belligerent in affirming their right to the Rock River country. The Winnebagos and Potawatomis gave the Sacs sympathy and support, and many frontier people began to fear another Indian war.[23]

On February 27, 1817, Julia H. Clark, wife of William Clark wrote in St. Louis, "I am afraid we shall have troubles in the spring with the Indians." The term of service of the last rangers who still patrolled the frontier would expire in May and the soldiers in the First Regiment of the army anticipated orders that would send them east to help protect the Canadian border and prevent a British attack. Clark despaired about the safety of the Missourians, saying "god only knows what our fate is to be." Four years later, a volunteer company of one hundred men organized to help protect the counties of Cooper, Cole, Saline, Lillard, Ray, Chariton, Boone, and

Howard from Indian attacks. In 1829, one thousand militiamen in central Missouri mobilized in response to several hostile encounters between settlers and Indians.[24]

Boone knew the great migration of whites to the Missouri frontier that began immediately after the war had made life worse for the tribes. As settlers encroached on Indian lands, the game became scarce, and the treaties forced many tribes to live closer together than ever before. The Sacs and Foxes who lived along the Missouri and Rock Rivers now began to range far to the north and west in search of deer and buffalo. By doing so, however, they crossed onto Sioux lands, and bloody confrontations became the order of the day as these traditional enemies struck and retaliated against each other.[25]

During the early 1820s, Sac, Fox, Winnebago, and Sioux war parties continued to raid and take scalps, and the Sacs and Foxes even struck south to the Missouri and fought with the Osages, Otos, and Ioways. Indian commissioner William Clark threatened the Sacs and Foxes with war if they did not stop their raids against the Sioux and the other tribes, but Secretary of War John C. Calhoun would only permit him to withhold presents and annuities if they did not behave. Clark, however, succeeded in cultivating the friendship of Keokuk, a Sac leader, who spoke for the peaceful bands of the tribe. But he could never gain the confidence of Black Hawk, who continued to hate Americans with a passion and who worked and yearned for British aid that would enable him to renew his war against the ever westering white settlers.[26]

To make matters worse, the Sacs and Foxes disputed the boundary lines between tribal lands and the United States. In 1821, they claimed their southern boundary began at the mouth of the Des Moines River, while the northern line ran west from the mouth of the Two Rivers opposite Prairie du Chien. In July 1824, Keokuk traveled with a delegation of Sacs and Foxes to Washington, D.C., and told Secretary of War Calhoun that they claimed this land by right of conquest, since they had taken it from the Osages, and that the federal government had no right to sell it to settlers. With whites infringing on these boundaries and often crossing onto Sac and Fox lands, the Indians demanded both restraint and restitution. Specifically, Keokuk and other leaders urged the federal government to hold a grand peace council with the upper Mississippi River tribes in order to clearly define and establish tribal boundaries and promote peace.[27]

Congress agreed and authorized James Barbour, who succeeded Calhoun as secretary of war, and Lewis Cass, governor of the Michigan Territory, to join Clark at Prairie du Chien for a treaty council in August 1825, where they would again attempt to make peace with the Sacs, Foxes, Ioways, Chippewas, Winnebagos, Ottawas, Menominees, Potawatomis, and Sioux. When Clark opened the council on August 5, he suggested that fixed boundaries be established between the hunting grounds of the tribes which, if honored, would keep the peace among them. The Sacs and Foxes, however, did not trust the Sioux; Keokuk, who usually spoke with reason concerning Indian and white relations, shook his lance at the Sioux delegation when Clark tried to discuss the subject of a mutually recognized boundary across which neither would cross. Clark and the other officials could clearly see that "he wanted but an opportunity to make their blood flow like water."[28]

Still, Clark remained persuasive, and on August 19 the tribes agreed to sign a peace treaty that essentially noted the boundary for the tribal lands of each nation and proclaimed peace between the tribes. Articles 1 and 13 of this "Treaty with the Sioux" or "Treaty of Prairie du Chien" contained the most important provisions for the tribes and eventually for Nathan Boone. Article 1 provided, "There shall be a firm and perpetual peace between the Sioux and the Chippewas; between the Sioux and the confederated tribes of Sacs and Foxes; and between the Ioways and the Sioux." Article 13 said, "It is understood by all the tribes, parties, hereto, that no tribe shall hunt within the acknowledged limits of any other without their assent." After considerable speech making, smoking of the peace pipe, and feasting, the council broke up. Both Indian and white leaders wondered how long the peace would last. Few believed that it had been established once and for all.[29]

To Black Hawk the Treaty of Prairie du Chien did not apply to him because he had not attended the peace council and he did not agree with the settlement. Now sixty years of age, he intended to live as he had in the past, hunting the same lands and striking his traditional enemies. In May 1827, he planned to send a war party against the Sioux, but he recanted after Keokuk brought him the Sac agent's threat of imprisonment if he picked up the tomahawk. Although

Black Hawk backed down, he refused to leave his homeland in the Rock River area when Governor Ninian Edwards demanded the federal government use the army to remove all the Indians from the lands that they had ceded in the Illinois territory. Edwards particularly wanted the Rock River Sacs moved west of the Mississippi River.[30]

Governor Edwards even proposed to take matters into his own hands. On May 25, 1828, he wrote to Indian Commissioner William Clark that unless the War Department acted quickly, "Those Indians will be removed, and that very promptly." Secretary of War Peter B. Porter tried to calm the governor by assuring him that all of the Indians, except for a few Kickapoos, would be removed from the Illinois Territory by May 25, 1829. He did not, however, take the intransigence of Black Hawk and his followers into his calculations. The Rock River Sacs argued that they had never sold land north of the Rock River and that it contained the bones of their ancestors. The Sacs did not intend to leave their lands for a new home west of the Mississippi along the Iowa River, and they would defend their Rock River lands with all their might.[31]

If Black Hawk's unwillingness to abide by the Treaty of Prairie du Chien threatened the peace in theory, the raid against the Sioux by half-blood Fox Chief Morgan in 1828 destroyed it in practice. When a Sioux war party killed a Sac chief and his wife in retaliation, the three-year-old peace collapsed. While the Sacs and Foxes eagerly went about the business of making war against their traditional Sioux enemies along the upper Mississippi River valley, white settlers continued to claim Sac lands, plow their cornfields, steal their property, and assault their people. Even Black Hawk lost his lodge to an aggressive white squatter.[32]

To the south, Boone, who was still busily at work surveying lands in the St. Charles vicinity, learned of these difficulties, and he knew that a new Indian war was inevitable. Whether it would reach the Missouri frontier, he could not be certain, but the situation between the Sacs and Foxes and whites appeared to be deteriorating rapidly, and the Missouri settlements remained within easy reach of Indian war parties. So he listened and asked questions whenever he visited with anyone whom he thought might know something about the affairs to the north and, like the other frontier people, he waited to see what would happen next. In June 1829, when the secretary of war announced that Sac lands would be sold to white settlers, Boone knew that a new Indian war would soon spread across the frontier.[33]

By the summer of 1829, the encroachment of white settlers on Indian hunting territory forced the Sacs and Foxes to invade Sioux lands in search of game, and mutual attacks and reprisals became common. War parties of these nations roamed the upper Mississippi River country with impunity, and they did not always discriminate among friends and foes when they wielded their knives. By the onset of winter, the white traders, who contributed to the problem of tribal disintegration by exchanging whiskey for pelts and skins, predicted a general Indian war, perhaps as early as spring.[34]

Clark hoped to avert a new war by talking the Sacs, Foxes, and Winnebagos out of it. In March 1830, he met with a delegation from these tribes in St. Louis, and reminded them that they had ceded the territory north of the Rock River in the treaty of 1804, which William Henry Harrison had made with them. Clark also told the chiefs that they could best live in peace with the whites if they would move west of the Mississippi River and sell their lands along the Fever River where important deposits of lead had been discovered and where miners were staking their claims. Keokuk, however, disagreed. Speaking for the delegation he told Clark that the peace was threatened because the boundary line between the Sacs and Foxes and their enemy the Sioux did not prevent the Sioux from attacking his people. He also said that the Sacs were upset because the federal government had purchased land from the Kansa Indians that rightfully belonged to them. Since Clark could not prevent the Sioux from striking the Sacs and Foxes or return their lands, the conference broke up and the danger of war remained, although Clark attempted to buy their friendship with additional gifts to "cover the Dead" killed by Sioux war parties.[35]

In the summer of 1830, the battles between the Sacs and Foxes and Sioux came increasingly closer to involving Boone. On July 15, United States commissioners, William Clark, and Colonel Willough-by Morgan, commandant at Fort Crawford, met with tribes of the upper Mississippi River valley at Prairie du Chien. There, aided by lavish gifts, the commissioners reached a peace agreement, known as the "Treaty with the Sauk and Foxes," which also included the Ioways, Winnebagos, Omahas, Otos, Menominees, and Sioux.

According to the treaty, each nation agreed to keep the peace and cede a large area between the Missouri and Mississippi Rivers to the United States. Specifically, the Sioux, Sacs, and Foxes ceded a tract of land twenty miles wide on each side of a line that ran from the mouth of the Upper Iowa River on the Mississippi to the upper forks of the Des Moines River, a line that had been established by the treaty of 1825. The forty-mile-wide strip extended about two hundred miles southwest, and it became known as the "Neutral Ground" for the purpose of effectively preventing further tribal wars.[36]

In this treaty, Clark pledged that the federal government would provide each tribe with as much as three thousand dollars' worth of goods annually for ten years and to send them blacksmiths, teachers, and farm implements to help them transform their way of life to that of the small-scale white farmers. The federal government would also divide this area into hunting lands that would be reserved for these tribes. Neither other Indians nor whites would be permitted to hunt on specific tribal lands. With clearly defined and mapped boundaries, Clark believed that the animosity, tension, and attacks could be reduced to an inconsequential minimum, if not eliminated entirely. In October 1830, the Dakota Sioux also approved this agreement at a council in St. Louis.[37]

Clark intended to survey the cession boundary of the Neutral Ground as soon as possible. On March 2, 1831, Congress aided his plans by appropriating nine thousand dollars to pay for the surveying and mapping of the boundaries. Apparently Clark wanted Andrew S. Hughes, the Sac, Fox, and Ioway subagent, and Jonathan L. Bean, the subagent for the upper Missouri Sioux, to run the boundary because they were familiar with the country and because they could negotiate any differences that might arise between the hostile tribes who were subject to this cession. Hughes and Bean, however, requested payment of six dollars per mile, and the government refused to employ them.[38]

At the same time, Clark, however, had not considered Black Hawk's opinion about the Neutral Ground cession nor informed him that Sac lands north of the Rock River would be opened for sale and settlement. When Black Hawk learned about the latter plan, he adamantly refused to give up tribal lands, and the governor of the Illinois Territory and the Sac agent alike began to threaten military action to force the Rock River Sacs to vacate their homes and move west of the Mississippi. These threats did not intimidate Black Hawk, but Keokuk believed that war against the U.S. Army would be suicidal, and he counseled peace and accommodation. Black Hawk later reflected, "We were a divided people," but he had a "sacred reverence" for Sac lands east of the Mississippi and north of the Rock River, and he did not intend to give up that area without a fight. By the autumn of 1830, Black Hawk was working to establish an Indian confederacy that would stop white encroachment on tribal lands, and he hoped for British support from Canada.[39]

When spring came, Black Hawk's band crossed back over the Mississippi after their winter hunt onto the prairies to the west, and settlers fled to the safety of Fort Armstrong or back to central Illinois. Governor John Reynolds responded by asking the Illinois General Assembly to call out the militia to drive the Indians from the territory. In May 1831, when the legislators balked, preferring to request help from the federal government, Reynolds dispatched seven hundred militia to remove the Indians "dead or alive." When Clark learned about Reynolds's plan, he sent General Edmund P. Gaines, commander of the Western Department of the Army, along with troops, from St. Louis to the Rock River. Gaines had a reputation for irascibility and toughness, and he quickly arranged a meeting with Black Hawk, Keokuk, and other Sac and Fox chiefs at Fort Armstrong on Rock Island in early June. When they met on June 4, both Black Hawk and Gaines were in foul moods, and neither intended to back down. Gaines told Black Hawk that his people had agreed to cede lands north of the Rock River and that they must now move west of the Mississippi. Black Hawk responded that the Sacs intended to stay and "lay their bones with those of their ancestors." Gaines then threatened to remove them by force, but the old Sac chief replied that "Black Hawk is satisfied with the lands the Great Spirit has given him. Why then should he leave them?" With that exchange, the conference broke up. Although Keokuk counseled patience, war seemed closer than ever before.[40]

Gaines now decided to remove the Sacs and Foxes by force, but he waited for the arrival of fourteen hundred militia that Governor Reynolds had now called out. These men, Reynolds wrote, possessed "all the qualities except discipline, that were necessary in any army." From the time of their muster, the Illinois militia men were difficult to control, and they "entertained rather an excess of *Indian ill-will,* so that it required much gentle persuasion to restrain them from killing, indiscriminately, all the Indians they met." For the moment, however, a military confrontation was avoided, because Keokuk convinced Black Hawk to meet once again with Gaines and to agree not to return to his village of Saukenuk, the lands around which white settlers had claimed.[41]

On June 30, 1831, when Black Hawk met with Gaines on Rock Island, he was presented with "Articles of Agreement and Capitulation." This document called for Black Hawk and his band to submit to Keokuk's authority, move west of the Mississippi, and end all communication with the British. In return, the federal government would guarantee Sac lands west of the river and their right to hunt on the Neutral Ground. After the articles had been translated, Gaines invited Black Hawk to sign the document along with the other chiefs in attendance. Angry and humiliated, Black Hawk knew that he did not have an alternative, at least not until he left the council house. Reluctantly, he stepped forward before the hushed delegates and drew "a large, bold cross with a force which rendered *that* pen forever unfit for further use." Later he said, "I touched the goose quill to this treaty, and was determined to live in peace." Gaines then promised to provide the Sacs with the equivalent amount of corn that they would have harvested from their fields that autumn, an action that caused the frontier people, who clearly preferred the forced removal and even the bloodshed of the Sacs, to dub this agreement the "corn treaty." Still, most Sacs and Foxes as well as white settlers and militiamen were pleased that the confrontation had ended peacefully. The militia then went home and the Sacs prepared for their winter hunt. When spring came government officials and frontier people alike expected that the Sacs would remain west of the Mississippi River.[42]

But not Black Hawk. He had signed the Articles of Agreement under compulsion, and he continued to communicate with the British operating out of Canada. He also counseled the formation of a confederacy with the tribes in the region of the upper Mississippi River valley and Great Lakes. By the end of July, the agreement unraveled after Sac and Fox war parties struck the Sioux and Menominees to pay them back for past attacks, and the Sioux and Menominees planned retribution. When the government contractors failed to deliver the corn that Gaines had promised, some

Sacs attempted to return to Saukenuk to harvest their green corn, but whites shot at them. When Sacs and Foxes again invaded Sioux hunting grounds, they again invited retaliation. By the autumn of 1831, nothing seemed to have changed in the upper Mississippi River valley. Hatred, violence, and revenge remained the operating principles for both Indians and whites.[43]

Keokuk tried to explain the attacks by the Sacs and Foxes as mere retribution that the Sioux and Menominees richly deserved. Besides, neither he nor Black Hawk nor the other chiefs could control all of their young men. He argued that the problems between tribal groups should be solved by the Indians themselves. Since the whites seemed to be constantly fighting, the Sacs and Foxes believed that they should be free to settle their own affairs in the time-honored and traditional way of war. When federal officials demanded that the Sacs and Foxes who had committed the murders against the Menominees be turned over for punishment, many peaceful Sacs and Foxes cast their lots with Black Hawk. Soon thereafter, Black Hawk received a report that the British would help him resist the pressure of the United States and that the Potawatomis, Chippewas, Ottawas, Winnebagos, and Kickapoos had agreed to join the Sacs in any fight against the Americans. If Black Hawk failed, the British implied, his confederation could retreat to Canada and live in peace and safety.[44]

During the winter of 1831–1832, then, Black Hawk gathered his force of five hundred fighting men and planned to strike the frontier in the spring and reclaim Sac lands along the Rock River. In St. Louis, Clark knew none of this, and instead of preparing for a new Indian war, he planned to protect the Sacs and Foxes from Sioux attacks. Thus, he proceeded with the Neutral Ground provisions of the treaties at Prairie du Chien in 1825 and 1830, surveying, mapping, and marking the boundary line between the hunting territory of each tribe west of the Mississippi River. Clark hoped that a boundary marked with surveyor's posts would help the Sioux and Sacs and Foxes keep themselves apart, because they had blatantly disregarded the imaginary treaty lines. In order to locate the lines, Clark needed the help of someone who not only knew how to survey but also could endure the hardship of living in the open for weeks and months at a time; this person also needed experience in dealing with Indians both diplomatically and militarily.[45]

Clark recommended that a skillful surveyor be employed. This surveyor would hire his own men and provide them with supplies. Agents for the Sacs, Foxes, and Sioux would accompany him, along with a number of Indians to ensure his safety and to help solve problems. The secretary of war agreed to these terms and in February 1832, Clark asked Boone to proceed as quickly as possible to the Neutral Ground. Boone had a reputation as a "meritorious and deserving man" who had the ability to run the line of 1825 and the outer boundaries of the Neutral Ground with speed and accuracy. During the course of the survey work, Boone would blaze every tree near the lines and mark every half mile with the distance from his beginning point. He should use stakes or mounds of earth as well as note the nature of the land, "whether level, rolling, or hilly, and fit or unfit for cultivation," and all mineral deposits. For this work the War Department would pay him $1,871 to acquire men, horses, and provisions as well as $5 per day for his services.[46]

Boone understood the importance of the survey. He also clearly recognized the danger. Clark was asking him to take his circumferentor and tripod and ride north near the vicinity of the present-day border of Iowa and Minnesota. First, he would mark the boundary line of 1825. Then, Boone would survey the northern and southern borders of the Neutral Ground. He would hold the office of U.S. Deputy Surveyor to give legal authority to his work. Boone would have a chainman and perhaps an ax man, but by any count his group would be small and unable to defend itself from a war party of any nation bent on blood and revenge and not particular about who it killed and scalped.

He and Olive no doubt talked it over. She understood the danger and worried whether he would be all right. Boone had traipsed long and far from home as a hunter and trapper and as a Missouri ranger, so it was not so much the length of separation that concerned her. Although she knew that no one could tell how long Nathan would be gone, Olive knew that a white man alone in hostile Indian country was asking for trouble. No matter what mission or policy he was trying to execute for the government of the United States, she was not certain that Nathan should accept Clark's call.

Although Nathan and Olive surely discussed whether he should go, she knew that he always preferred to range far beyond white civilization on the frontier, and that he had considerable experience

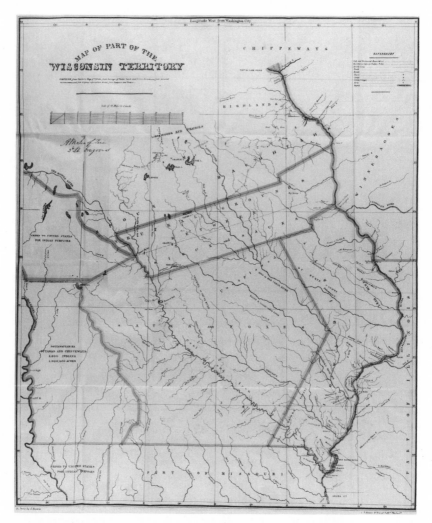

In 1832, Nathan Boone, at William Clark's request, surveyed the center line of the Neutral Ground. The federal government hoped this line would keep the Sacs and Foxes and Sioux apart while permitting them to hunt on neutral territory and thereby end the warfare between them. Boone did not survey the outer boundary, because the Black Hawk War intervened, and he returned home to raise a company of Missouri rangers. *Author's Collection.*

and self-confidence. Both probably knew from the time that Clark made the request that he would go. Still, they likely followed the necessary ritual of talking it through. In the end, Nathan said he would accept. His work would take him far to the west of the warring Sioux, Sacs, and Foxes. Once he began to run the boundary line out of the Mississippi River valley he would be putting time and distance between himself, the hostile tribes, and the pressing whites. He would be careful. It would be all right.

Boone left home for the Iowa country in mid-April and on April 19 began his survey, following the treaty provisions of 1825. First, he ran the line from the mouth of the Upper Iowa River to its left fork. Then, he proceeded south up that fork to its source then turned southwest and crossed the Cedar River on the way to the second or upper fork of the Des Moines River. After 133 miles and 43 chains, Boone stopped at the junction of the east and west forks of the Des Moines River, about three miles below present-day Dakota City. There he set a corner post in the prairie at the high-water mark of the river junction and notched two elms for "witness" trees. Today, this line passes through Allamakee, Winneshiek, Chickasaw, Floyd, Franklin, Wright, and Humbolt Counties. Two months after he had begun surveying the line of 1825, Boone completed that work.[47]

Boone's line would provide the boundary along which the tribes had agreed to establish a forty-mile-wide neutral strip when they met at Prairie du Chien in July 1830. After running the boundary line from the mouth of the Upper Iowa to the forks of the Des Moines River, Boone returned to the Mississippi River and began to survey the southern border of the Neutral Ground. On June 19, 1832, he started at Painted Rock on the Mississippi River about a half-mile north of present-day Waukon Junction in Allamakee County. Boone, however, had proceeded only two miles west of Painted Rock when he received word from St. Louis to return home because the warring tribes made his work too dangerous. The survey of the southern boundary of the Neutral Ground would begin again on September 8 by James Craig, but Boone would not be part of it. When he returned home, however, Boone billed the federal government $2,107.87 for expenses in addition to his daily fee. He used this money to pay his son James Boone, who served as his assistant surveyor; Leander G. Robinson and W. T. McHutcheon, chainmen;

Lorenzo D. Holmes, packhorseman; Benjamin Howland, camp-keeper; Daniel Gillis, ax man; and William Dodson, flagman.[48]

While Nathan and Olive visited about his journey to the Iowa country, the tribes in the upper Mississippi River valley greeted spring with talk of war. Black Hawk had been actively seeking British support and Sac allies for his band, which still refused to relinquish its lands along the Rock River. In early April 1832, Black Hawk had crossed to the east side of the Mississippi below Rock Island with some five hundred mounted fighting men in a band of approximately one thousand, with the intent to reclaim Saukenuk and Sac lands. At the same time, the Sioux and Menominees prepared to attack the Sacs and Foxes to gain revenge for their losses during the past autumn. As a result, from Jefferson Barracks in St. Louis to Fort Armstrong at the mouth of the Rock River and on to Fort Crawford at Prairie du Chien, the officers and officials of the War Department expected nothing less than a new Indian war.[49]

On April 8, 1832, Brigadier General Henry Atkinson, who had relieved General Gaines as commander of the Western Department, and 220 soldiers boarded the steamboats *Enterprise* and *Chieftain* at Jefferson Barracks for a trip upriver to prevent Black Hawk from crossing the Mississippi and to drive him back if he attempted to re-occupy Saukenuk. Three days later Atkinson received word near the mouth of the Des Moines River that Black Hawk had already crossed the Mississippi with his people and had camped two miles below Fort Armstrong. On April 13, Atkinson held a conference with Keokuk and offered him the protection of the army against the Sioux and Menominees. Atkinson also demanded the men who had killed the Menominees, and Keokuk delivered them to federal custody.[50]

In addition, Atkinson told Keokuk and the other friendly Sac and Fox chiefs that Black Hawk's band "can be as easily crushed as a piece of dirt—If they do not recross the river measures will soon be taken to compel them." Atkinson said that until Black Hawk and his people crossed west over the Mississippi River, he would "treat them like dogs." Keokuk and the other chiefs were taken aback by Atkinson's threats because they knew he could deliver his promise of retribution, and they asked for time to think about the situation. When the chiefs met again on April 19, Black Hawk already had departed up the Rock River and, in a fit of anger, Atkinson told Keokuk

Black Hawk led the Sacs who lived along the Rock River in Illinois. He did not recognize the treaties, signed between other bands of Sacs and the federal government, that required his people to move west of the Mississippi River. When he refused to leave, the army destroyed his band during what became known as the Black Hawk War. Boone raised a company of rangers in Missouri to fight, but he arrived at Fort Armstrong after the war had ended. *State Historical Society of Iowa–Des Moines.*

that "If Black Hawk's band strikes one white man in a short time they will cease to exist." Keokuk again counseled patience and sent messengers to Black Hawk asking him to return, but Black Hawk merely reported that he was prepared to die within twenty days.[51]

Governor Reynolds also believed that the time had arrived to stop Black Hawk's Sacs once and for all and, on April 16, he mobilized sixteen hundred militia to aid Atkinson. Twelve days later the militia marched for the Mississippi. Reynolds sent a courier to Atkinson informing him that the expedition would arrive at Fort Armstrong about May 10. Atkinson estimated that Black Hawk's band now approximated six hundred fighting men, including a few Kickapoos and Potawatomis. He also knew that Black Hawk had asked the Winnebagos to support him. Confronted with a strong Indian force, while he had only a few hundred trained regulars and a host of undisciplined and undependable militiamen under his command, Atkinson sent word to St. Louis that he needed help.[52]

Keokuk was a Sac leader who opposed Black Hawk and who sought conciliation with the federal government. He recognized that the Sacs could not defeat the U.S. Army, and he attempted to gain as much as possible for his people through negotiations. After the Black Hawk War, Keokuk emerged as the principal spokesman for the Sacs. *State Historical Society of Iowa–Des Moines.*

Given the tense and seemingly deteriorating conditions along the Rock River as Black Hawk's band moved farther into the interior, as well as the danger posed to anyone who traveled onto Indian lands west of the Mississippi, both Clark and Nathan's family had begun to worry about Boone. If Black Hawk turned and fought, as everyone expected him to do, and if the Sioux and Menominees struck the Sacs and Foxes from the north and west, lone white surveyors would be quickly and easily dispensed with by a war party, and Boone's scalp would soon dangle from a pole. Olive, then, was more than a little relieved when Clark sent a rider to find Boone and tell him to come home.

When Boone returned home in late June he learned that General Atkinson had called for the muster of five hundred mounted men and two hundred infantrymen. Nathan could not say no. Indeed, this seemed to be the opportunity to return to military service that he had long desired. Although his service as a Missouri ranger now lay seventeen years in the past, he had not forgotten his sense of pride and honor as he led his men during the War of 1812. When he rode at the head of his column of rangers, he felt confident that he was doing his duty. He had not expected that feeling of exhilaration to come again. But now, the adrenaline burned the pit of his stomach and the yearning for the companionship of the rangers, the excitement of danger, and a desire for a sense of accomplishment gained from knowing that he had done his duty honorably and well proved too hard to resist.[53]

Atkinson soon asked Missouri to muster one company of rangers, and Boone and everyone else knew the company would be his. He alone had the experience and reputation to lead a company into battle. Still, while Congress had considered an act since December to authorize the president to raise mounted volunteers to help defend the frontier, it did not pass that legislation until June 15, 1832. This act provided for the formation of six mounted companies under the command of a major with the men to serve for one year. The volunteers, like the rangers of the past, were to furnish their own horses and weapons, and the federal government would pay them one dollar per day. Each company would be composed of one hundred men and four commissioned and fourteen noncommissioned officers. The War Department assigned the commander of each company a specific district for recruitment. On June 16, 1832, Boone became the captain of the Mounted Rangers, with his recruitment area the St. Charles vicinity. Boone went to work at once but he had little difficulty raising the company, which mustered at St. Charles, where his men were sworn into service on August 11.[54]

President Andrew Jackson appointed Henry Dodge as the major of the Rangers. Nathan had supported Dodge against the unruly militia from Boonslick at the Miami camp on the Missouri during the last war, and Dodge welcomed Boone's desire to return to military duty. Consequently, he supported Nathan's commission as captain of a mounted company. Because the army did not designate letters or numerals for the ranger companies, each quickly became known by the name of its commanding officer. The Missourians, then, became designated as Boone's Mounted Rangers.[55]

These men who volunteered to serve with Boone had been little more than boys when he led other rangers on patrol along the Missouri frontier during the War of 1812. They had heard about his toughness and endurance, his expedition with Clark to Fire Prairie, his reconnaissance into the Rock River country, and his flight from the Osages who caught him and Vanbibber trapping along the Grand River. For these rangers, Boone was a bit larger than life, nearly a legend in his own time, not to mention his being the son of Daniel Boone. They trusted him and they were proud to serve under him. Although most were apprehensive about what might happen in the days ahead, they were confident that whatever trouble came their way, Boone would see them through. These young rangers, then, like those who followed Boone nearly twenty years before, rode behind him with the confidence and easy manner of those convinced of their superiority. They would ride with Boone and put Black Hawk and his defiant Sacs in their places, whether west of the Mississippi or in their graves.

Almost immediately Boone and his rangers rode north to join Dodge at Fort Armstrong, located on Rock Island where the Rock River joins the Mississippi. There, the army had established its base of operations against Black Hawk. Boone's rangers probably crossed the Mississippi at Yellow Banks, located a few miles below Fort Armstrong, and soon learned that the Black Hawk War was over. Once at Fort Armstrong Boone discovered that while he had been busy recruiting his ranger company, Illinois Governor Reynolds, at the request of General Atkinson, had called out another thousand militia to join the two thousand that he had sought on May 25. One observer noted that: "They were a hard-looking set of men, unkempt and unshaved." He did not need to add that they yearned to kill Indians and that the authority of their officers meant little to them. Atkinson's command had also been reinforced by two infantry companies from Fort Leavenworth. With four hundred regulars and three thousand militia, Atkinson planned to sweep up both banks of the Rock River, catch Black Hawk's band, and defeat it. The general had great confidence, and on June 15 wrote: "I cannot fail to put an end in a short time, to the perplexed state of Indian hostilities in this quarter."[56]

President Andrew Jackson, however, believed that Atkinson moved too slowly and in June, he gave Major General Winfield Scott command of the campaign against Black Hawk. On June 15, Jackson ordered Scott to strike Black Hawk's band and not to stop fighting until he had been "effectually subdued." The War Department assigned an additional eight hundred regulars, the recently organized ranger companies (excluding Boone's), and the militia to Scott's command. Scott, however, did not reach Fort Armstrong before the war ended. In the meantime, Atkinson continued to pursue Black Hawk. By late June, he had not yet caught Black Hawk and the militia under his command grew tired and began to go home. While his army unraveled, Atkinson wrote that as long as Black Hawk's band could "subsist on roots and fish taken from the swamps and lakes," the army could never defeat his people.[57]

Atkinson, however, gave too much credit to the Sacs' ability to live off the land. As Black Hawk's band fled from the soldiers, they lived on roots and bark because they could not fish or hunt in the best areas. By early July, starvation became another enemy of the Sacs. Black Hawk now realized that he could only save his people from entrapment and starvation by fleeing west to the Wisconsin River and descending it to the Mississippi, cross it, and either link with Keokuk's band or flee to the Great Plains. Before Black Hawk could move his people far from their camp near present-day Hustisford, Wisconsin, a band of Winnebagos reported his location to Major Dodge, who conveyed the information to Atkinson. Dodge's troops were the nearest, and they moved out fast on July 15, but they did not make contact with Black Hawk's band until they reached the area of Four Lakes, near present-day Madison, on July 21. A running fight began that lasted all day. When darkness fell about seventy Sacs had been killed. Dodge had lost only one man.[58]

While Dodge rested his men, Black Hawk moved his band across the Wisconsin River under the cover of darkness. When dawn came Dodge decided not to pursue until he could replenish his supplies, and he did not cross the river until July 28, after Atkinson joined him with more soldiers. On August 1, the army finally made contact with Black Hawk and his five hundred remaining Sacs when they reached the Mississippi at the mouth of the Bad Axe River. There, the steamboat *Warrior* blocked their crossing of the Mississippi with cannon fire. When the *Warrior* withdrew for fuel, many Sacs crossed the Mississippi during the night while Black Hawk prepared to take the remainder of his band over the next morning. Atkinson's force, however, struck Black Hawk's camp during the early morning of August 2. Less of a battle than a massacre, the fighting lasted about three hours. The action was one-sided, with an estimated 150 Sacs killed to Atkinson's 7 men. Although Black Hawk escaped and fled northeast into Winnebago territory, where he would be captured a few days later, the Black Hawk War had ended on the killing fields at the mouth of the Bad Axe River.[59]

While the army ran Black Hawk's band to the ground, Boone knew nothing of that campaign. On the day of the final battle, he was at work recruiting his ranger company. Although word of the fighting reached Jefferson Barracks at St. Louis a few days later, Boone must have just missed learning about Black Hawk's defeat. If Boone had heard about the battle, however, it would not have mattered, because he still had orders to report to the fort; still, had they known the fighting was over, their excitement would have been tempered and their disappointment less keen when they reached Fort Armstrong about mid-August.

Instead of preparing to ride against Black Hawk and his Sacs, Boone's rangers confronted overcrowded conditions and poor sanitation, which brought Asiatic cholera to the camp. Men were dying and morale had plummeted among the troops waiting to be sent against the Indians. Faced with these disappointing and frightening circumstances, Boone's rangers quickly lost their ardor for fighting Indians. Boone, however, did not remain long at Fort Armstrong, because soon after he arrived with his company, Dodge ordered a general evacuation of the camp beginning on August 31. Nathan received orders to proceed immediately to Fort Gibson in the Indian Territory, where his command would serve the Western Department of the U.S. Army. Before his men drew their provisions and prepared to cross back over the Mississippi and ride to Fort Gibson, however, the ranger captains drew lots to determine their seniority. Boone drew the second piece of paper behind James D. Henry. Because Henry was assigned to Fort Winnebago in order to patrol the frontier between the Wabash, Chicago, and the Wisconsin Rivers, Boone became the senior ranger captain assigned to Fort Gibson.[60]

Dodge, however, did not want Boone's company to take the cholera with them, and on September 3, ordered them to remain at Fort Armstrong until the epidemic had ended. Thus, Boone remained at the post but could do nothing more than look out across the Mississippi at the place where Davenport, Iowa, now stands, where, on September 21, General Scott, Governor John Reynolds, and the Sacs signed the Treaty of Fort Armstrong. The site was chosen because they did not want to expose the Indians to any more cholera. Soon thereafter Boone learned that this treaty, known as the "Black Hawk Purchase" ceded all Sac lands east of the Mississippi River, as well as 6 million acres of Sac and Fox lands in eastern Iowa, to the United States, with the requirement that those tribes settle on a four-hundred-square-mile reserve along the Iowa River by June 1, 1833. With this land cession and tribal removal, Boone believed that the Indian threat to Missouri and the upper Mississippi River valleys had finally ended.[61]

On September 23, Dodge ordered Boone to proceed to Fort Gibson by the "nearest practicable route," and he left Fort Armstrong the next day with his rangers. Apparently Boone crossed the Mississippi near Fort Armstrong, because he led his company southwest on a route that took him through present-day Boonville and his old trapping grounds among the Osages in Missouri. He may have stopped along the way, because given his reputation for traveling a considerable distance during a day, he did not arrive at Fort Gibson until November 22. In any event, his men began building their winter quarters on the opposite bank of the Neosho River about a half-mile below Fort Gibson at a site called Camp Arbuckle. For Boone, the Black Hawk War proved a disappointment, because his service had been all too brief and routine. Even so, Boone knew that it also had brought opportunity, and he took it.[62]

6

THE DRAGOON EXPEDITION

B Y LATE AUTUMN 1832, when Boone arrived at Fort Gibson in the present-day state of Oklahoma, the Indian policy of the federal government had been long established if not well executed. Since the end of the War of 1812, government officials, most notably Andrew Jackson, who now served as president, had advocated moving the eastern tribes west of the Mississippi River. There, in specifically designated Indian Territory, they would be given lands in perpetuity in exchange for their eastern holdings. Government teachers and farmers would provide instruction to help them learn to live like white, small-scale farmers, and, in time, the Indians would be acculturated and assimilated into white civilization.

Although the federal government had used the cession treaty process since the end of the American Revolution to gain Indian lands, it had only recently begun the actual removal of tribal groups from their lands east of the Mississippi River. When Congress passed the Indian removal bill and Jackson signed it into law on May 28, 1830, the legal process had been established for relocating the "Five Civilized Tribes"—the Cherokee, Creek, Chickasaw, Choctaw, and Seminole nations—west of the Mississippi River. Government officials also knew that they would need to negotiate a host of treaties with the tribes already claiming much of present-day Oklahoma before they could settle the displaced eastern tribes there. Boundary surveys would be required and the military would be needed to protect both whites and Indians and to keep the peace. As a result of this policy and the conclusion of the Black Hawk War, Major Henry Dodge sent Boone and the Missouri Rangers to Fort Gibson. Boone would join the Seventh Infantry and the ranger company under the command of Captain Jesse Bean, who had arrived at the fort in October, as well as Lemuel Ford's company, whom Dodge also sent to Fort Gibson from Fort Armstrong at the same time that he ordered Boone to the post. Boone, along with the rangers and infantry, would separate the immigrant and native tribes, keep the peace, and aid the treaty-making process until their enlistments expired in August 1833.[1]

By the time Boone and his rangers arrived at Fort Gibson, Congress had already appointed a commission, composed of Montford Stokes, recently governor of North Carolina, Henry L. Ellsworth of Hartford, Connecticut, and Rev. John Schermerhorn, for the purpose of helping the eastern tribes relocate in the Indian Territory. These commissioners made Fort Gibson their headquarters, arriving at the post several weeks before Boone, and they quickly went about the business of contacting nearby tribes and exploring the area. While the commissioners conducted their business, Boone settled into the routine of daily life at a frontier post.[2]

It was not an easy life, except for rugged men like Boone who accepted hardship as a natural fact of frontier life. Built in 1824, Fort Gibson already showed signs of wear and the log buildings had begun to decay. Even so, the post and army provided a dependable, though hard, daily order that Boone found comforting. Although the rangers had less discipline than the regulars, Boone and his men had experienced some of the ritual and routine that made an army function when they had stayed at Fort Armstrong for a month. They were already accustomed to the bugler sounding reveille at daybreak and to the cannon salute as the flag ran up the pole before the men who stood on the parade ground in the early morning light. At Fort Gibson drill followed breakfast, with officers shouting orders and the bugle announcing changes of camp duties. Evening brought the soldiers and rangers to the parade ground once again, where drums and the bugle called retreat, followed by the lowering of the flag and a cannon salute. At nine o'clock a drum and fife sounded tattoo, which brought the soldiers to their quarters, and Boone rested in his bunk until reveille brought the post to life again. Although Boone's rangers complained about the drudgery of army life and the boredom of camp routine and longed for home, he found that his new assignment gave him a sense of purpose and a feeling of achievement and fulfillment. Boone liked all of the army's ritual and ceremony, and he did not find fault. No doubt he missed Olive and the children, but not enough to forsake this new life that would now become his calling. Boone would remain a soldier and an officer until he resigned from the army on July 15, 1853.[3]

Army life at Fort Gibson quickly became routine for Boone. Certainly, he enjoyed watching the horse races between visiting Indians and the soldiers, although he apparently disapproved of the wagering that went with them, not so much for moral reasons as for the animosity and disruption of good order that gambling brought with it. When Colonel Gustavus Loomis, post commander, issued an order barring civilians from the reservation who came into the area specifically to race horses and gamble, Boone approved without question. He also liked to watch steamboats arrive when the Arkansas River ran high, or keelboats tie up at the landing when it ran low. Whether steam- or keelboats docked, Boone knew that each might bring a letter from Olive with news from home and the children. The arrival of the paymaster always proved a welcome sight to Boone, and he kept most of his money safely hidden in order to give it to Olive when he returned home. Many people kept Fort Gibson busy and noisy despite its isolated and dilapidated condition. There were Indian traders and sutlers, who brought goods to sell to the officers and soldiers; Cherokee men, who visited the post to buy merchandise; Cherokee women, whom the officers often invited to parties and whom the enlisted men usually sought for sex; and the occasional arrival of white women, who were wives or sweethearts of the officers or laundresses and whores for the garrison. One observer likened the garrison to an Arkansas jail.[4]

If the iron bars on the windows, which were intended to keep the men inside after tattoo rather than the Indians out, caused Boone any concern he did not mention it nor did he comment about the customary punishments meted out for the violation of military rules at Fort Gibson, such as hard labor, standing with head and hands in stocks in the old tradition of Puritan New England, or branding deserters with the letter "D" and shaving their heads. Boone also became more accustomed to the sight of death at Fort Gibson. Located near the convergence of the Arkansas, Verdigris, and Neosho

Rivers (the latter of which was then known as the Grand River), Fort Gibson was an unhealthy place where mosquitos brought malaria and the water caused other unknown illnesses commonly and collectively called "miasmas." During the first dozen years of the post's existence, 561 privates and 9 officers died. Little wonder that Fort Gibson became known as the charnel house of the army, that is, the place for receiving the dead. Boone, then, often watched the burial parties go by and hoped that his strong constitution and good health would hold.[5]

During the winter of 1832–1833, Boone settled into the daily military routine at Fort Gibson and army life on the frontier. Although Boone knew that his enlistment would expire in August, he intended to give a good day's service for his pay. But while he accepted the drills, parades, and daily camp chores, he yearned for an assignment that would take him away from the post, the routine, and the waiting, and, if the assignment proved important, he might be able to gain recognition and credit that would serve him well and lead to a permanent commission in the army when his ranger company disbanded.

In the spring of 1833 Boone got the opportunity that he desired. It came with the treaties signed on February 14, 1833, by Commissioners Stokes, Ellsworth, and Schermerhorn with the Creeks and Cherokees. These treaties resulted from a boundary dispute that caused considerable ill-will between the tribes. Animosity had developed and increased between the Creeks and Cherokees since 1828 when Congress signed a treaty with the Cherokees in Arkansas that provided for their removal to lands in Indian Territory. The lands they were assigned by the treaty, however, were already occupied by a group known as the McIntosh Creeks. By 1834, however, the Creeks had selected the rich bottomlands at the junction of the Verdigris and Arkansas Rivers for their new home, as authorized by their removal treaty in 1826. The Creeks cleared this area for crops and built their homes on it. When the Cherokees from Arkansas began to encroach on this land, the Creeks became contentious and petitioned President Jackson to form a commission to adjudicate the boundary between them and the Cherokees. Jackson responded favorably and sent Commissioners Stokes, Ellsworth, and Schermerhorn to investigate the problem and solve it. In response, the commissioners negotiated separate treaties with the Creeks and

Cherokees that adjusted the boundary between the tribes. These treaties called for the line to run from the mouth of the North Fork of the Canadian River to the south bank of the Arkansas opposite the mouth of the Neosho River.[6]

Once the treaties with the Creeks and Cherokees had been signed, the commissioners needed an experienced surveyor to locate and mark the boundary between the tribes. They knew about Boone's experience as a government surveyor in Missouri, and the commissioners also realized that he had more experience than anyone at Fort Gibson in making expeditions into Indian country and living off the land with his skills as a woodsman. Given his experience and ability, Boone was the best available man for the job. When the commissioners approached Boone and asked him whether he would undertake the survey they were relieved to learn that they would not need to ask twice.

The opportunity to survey the Creek-Cherokee boundary offered Boone the chance to leave the dismal quarters at Fort Gibson for the open country to the south. Although he had begun to love army life more with each passing day, the survey would not take long and a brief return to his past craft would enable him to enjoy the sunshine and fresh air on his own time and at his own pace. He accepted the offer at once although he did not receive formal instructions from the Commissioners of Indian Affairs until March 25.[7]

During the month between the signing of the treaties and the receipt of his orders, Boone planned his expedition, selecting a circumferentor, tripod, poles, and chain. He studied the area from the best maps available to learn the lay of the land because his assignment also required him to map the boundary line. Boone also selected two or three men to accompany him to serve as ax men and to hold the poles and move the chain as they worked their way from the North Fork of the Canadian toward the Arkansas. By late March, Boone had completed his plans. He then drew his provisions, packed his horses, and rode south. On March 28, he sighted with his circumferentor from the north bank of the Canadian River at the mouth of its north fork. There, he set a cedar post for the beginning mark of the boundary line. For the next two weeks Boone periodically set rocks to help designate the boundary, made notes about the physical features of the land, and mapped his line. On April 9, after surveying nearly thirty-eight and a half miles of the

Creek-Cherokee boundary, Boone reached the Arkansas River. He then returned to nearby Fort Gibson and put his report in order. Boone submitted it to the commissioners on April 17, and H. S. Stambaugh reported that the survey had been made "agreeably" to the provisions of the treaties.[8]

Boone felt satisfied with his work. It had been good to get back into the field with his surveying equipment after being cooped up at Fort Gibson for the winter. By the time he had finished running the boundary line, warm spring weather had returned to the southern plains and both the army and the Indians began to leave their winter camps, the former to show the flag and keep the peace, and the latter to replenish their food supply with fresh meat from the bison that grazed in uncounted numbers across the greening land.

Less than a month after his return from surveying the Creek-Cherokee boundary, Boone became a part of the army's spring campaign to both intimidate and make peace with the tribes on the southern Great Plains. On May 6, Colonel Matthew Arbuckle, commandant at Fort Gibson, ordered two companies of the Seventh Infantry and three companies of rangers under the command of Lieutenant Colonel James B. Many to ascend the Blue and Washita Rivers to the west and convince the Comanche and Wichita chiefs to come to Fort Gibson for a parley. Arbuckle wanted to impress these tribes with the strength of the army and make them agree to leave the eastern tribes, who would be arriving in large numbers, alone and to refrain from attacking traders and settlers.[9]

Boone's rangers were selected to participate in this expedition, and on May 7, they rode west along the Arkansas River. With the infantry along, the pace proved far slower than Boone preferred to travel, but he could not do anything about it. As the days passed and blended into weeks, the soldiers and rangers saw only buffalo, the distant courses of rivers, and the ever undulating and stretching plain. The sun, heat, and monotony of the march began to make the expedition careless, and the officers failed to keep the men grouped in a tight, disciplined formation. Boone and ranger captains Lemuel Ford and Jesse Bean also let their men ride out from the column. The regulars and rangers did not seem to be in any danger, and after several weeks without seeing any Indians, many of the men ceased to pay any attention to the possibility that hostile tribes occupied the area.[10]

On June 2, however, as the column approached the Washita River north of present-day Ardmore, Oklahoma, a band of Indians, possibly Comanches, who either lived or wintered in the area, shook the lethargy and complacency of the rangers and infantry to the core. Although the circumstances are not clear, apparently Private George B. Abbay, one of Boone's rangers, rode too far astray, and an Indian party that had been secretly following and watching the expedition from a distance captured him. When Abbay yelled for help, Boone quickly saw that his man was in trouble and ordered his rangers to rescue him. With Boone racing his horse in the lead, the other rangers and infantry followed behind. More Indians quickly emerged from the brush and trees along the Washita. Boone estimated their number between 150 and 200, and they quickly crossed the river ahead of his rangers, leaving a trail of buffalo robes, saddles, bows and arrows, and stray horses in their hurry to escape the oncoming soldiers.[11]

Many's command pursued the Indians' trail for twelve days riding west, but they could not catch them, and Boone never recovered his man. By the time the rangers and infantry reached the vicinity where Fort Sill would soon be constructed, Many had exhausted his supplies, and the expedition had left the buffalo range. Exhausted and hungry, the column now turned back toward Fort Gibson. Arbuckle's plan to intimidate the hostile tribes and force them to peacefully accept their new neighbors had been an abject failure. When Many's expedition reached Fort Gibson in early July, Boone was depressed because he had not only lost a man but also because the expedition had failed to achieve its mission. Moreover, he also believed—probably incorrectly—that Abbay could have been rescued if the infantry had not slowed the rangers' pursuit. Still, fifty-four days of campaigning in the sun, heat, and dust of the plains bothered him less than many of the other rangers and regulars, even though the expedition lived entirely on buffalo meat during the last thirty days. They did not have flour for bread or even salt to make their fare more palatable. During the last eight days of their return march, they ate only buffalo meat boiled in tallow.[12]

Still, Boone had made long, futile rides before in both winter and summer, and hardship was no stranger to him. Little did he know, however, that this expedition would be the beginning of many others, with similar circumstances and similar results. Yet, without men like Boone, the Army of the West would not only have ceased to exist but it would not have had the officer corps necessary to execute federal Indian and military policy. Simply put, men like Boone made the army work.[13]

While Boone once again proved that he was a dutiful, reliable soldier who could endure great hardship while executing his orders, the ranger companies that had given him the opportunity to show his military skill proved too undisciplined, undependable, and expensive for long-term army service and planning, and the War Department decided to forgo using the rangers again after their enlistments expired in the summer of 1833. Boone perhaps knew something about the impending disbandment of the rangers and plans for the reorganization of mounted riflemen as troops of dragoons. In fact, as early as March 2, 1833, Congress authorized the replacement of the rangers with a regiment of dragoons more than eighteen hundred strong. The dragoons were to be under the command of Boone's old friend Henry Dodge, now a colonel. The ranger companies that had been organized at Jefferson Barracks during the winter of 1832–1833, which were soon stationed at Fort Gibson, merged into a new regiment. When the enlistment of Boone's ranger company expired in mid-August, the men went home but he remained and accepted a commission as the captain of a company of dragoons, with his rank dating from August 15, 1833. With this appointment Boone officially joined the United States Army and became the captain of a company that still had to be recruited.[14]

Boone felt well pleased with his new commission and the promise of long-term employment in the army. When the paymaster at Fort Gibson settled his account with Boone on September 30, he pocketed the money and headed for Jefferson Barracks and home. Boone managed to save a considerable amount of money while at Fort Gibson. Between October 1, 1832, and September 30, 1833, he received $600 in pay. In addition, the army allowed him $292 for subsistence, that is, food, clothing, and incidentals, and $192 for forage. As an officer, Boone also received $60.93 for servant's pay, $66.80 for servant's subsistence, and $27.50 for his servant's clothing. Beginning on October 1, 1833, Boone received an additional $50 per year in pay for his rank as a captain and an additional $96 to feed his horse as well as a substantial raise to cover the pay, food, and clothing of his servant. With this pay safely packed, then, he began a tradition of arriving home with gold coins jingling in a pouch to be dumped on the kitchen table before his excited children. They would keep the memory of such returns for their entire lives.[15]

Early in October 1833, then, Boone took whatever savings he had managed to accrue from his pay, subsistence, forage, and other allowances and rode to Jefferson Barracks. If Boone traveled at his preferred speed he would have covered the 510 miles in about three weeks. In any event, he reached his home country toward the end of the month. Although Boone gained a brief leave of absence to return home and see Olive and the children, he could not linger on the Femme Osage, because he had the responsibility of recruiting a company of dragoons from Missouri.

The War Department intended the regiment of dragoons to reflect a national commitment to the defense of the frontier. Secretary of War Lewis Cass contended that: "It is deemed indispensable to the peace and security of the frontiers that a respectable force should be displayed in that quarter, and that the wandering and restless tribes who roam through it should be impressed with the power of the United States by the exhibition of a corps so well qualified to excite their respect. These Indians are beyond the reach of a mere infantry force. Without stationary residences, and possessing an abundant supply of horses, and with habits admirably adapted to their use, they can be held in check only by a similar force, and by its occasional display among them." Cass also argued that the eastern tribes needed protection from the plains Indians as well as white settlers, but peace and security could "only be fulfilled by repressing and punishing every attempt to disturb the general tranquility." By so doing, Cass believed "there is reason to hope that the display of this force will itself render unnecessary its hostile employment. The more barbarous tribes will perceive that their own safety is closely connected with the permanent establishment of pacific relations both with the United States and with the other Indians." With this rationale dictating Indian policy in the War Department, Lieutenant Colonel Stephen Watts Kearny, who superintended the recruiting process from Jefferson Barracks, received orders to enlist a regiment of dragoons, and he sent officers as far east as New York on recruiting missions.[16]

Boone had orders from Kearny "to recruit healthy, respectable men, native citizens, not under twenty, nor over thirty-five years of age, whose size, figure and early pursuits may best qualify them for mounted soldiers." Any man who enlisted, Boone noted, would receive food, clothing, horses, forage, and medical care at the expense of the federal government. Privates would also receive $8 per month, or $288, during the course of the three-year enlistment. He also noted, "The officers were authorized to inform candidates for enlistment that they would be well clothed, and kept in comfortable quarters in winter."[17]

Accordingly, Boone was soon off to recruit in Franklin, 165 miles away. Although he made Franklin his base of operations from October 15, 1833, to April 29, 1834, Boone traveled to the major Missouri towns to urge men to enlist in the army. In the late autumn he made a 145-mile ride to St. Charles, but he was quickly back in Franklin, then on again to Independence, 108 miles away. By the end of January 1834, Boone had ridden 1,181 miles recruiting dragoons; the army reimbursed him $141.72 through April for transportation and $61.24 for housing and firewood in Franklin.[18]

Boone used the local newspapers to advertise his recruitment of men for the dragoons. On October 26, 1833, he placed a notice in the *Jeffersonian Republican* in Jefferson City, perhaps while on his way back from Fort Gibson. Young men looking for adventure no doubt felt some excitement when they read,

> The undersigned being anxious to make up his Company of United States Dragoons, *entirely* from the State of Missouri, gives notice to the enterprising and able bodied citizens of Missouri, who may be disposed to enlist in the new Regiment, now about to be organized, "for the more perfect defence of the frontier" that they can have an opportunity of doing so by applying to the under signed at Franklin, Howard County, Mo. or to Lieut. James W. Shaumburgh, in Palmyra.[19]

Despite the secretary of war's optimism, the dragoons got off to a rocky start. With the exception of Boone and a few other men, most of the officers did not have experience in mounted service, and their training went slowly at Jefferson Barracks as they learned to drill their men. Uniforms and weapons had to be designed for this new branch of the army. Horses had to be purchased and colored (matched) to help identify the companies, and equipment had to be secured. Raw recruits had to learn military procedures, and all did not go well. One private described the first drill of Company D as a "ludicrous piece of work," and he observed that the muskets issued were "a lot of condemned pieces that had lain in the arsenal since the last war." The dragoons would eventually wear—as daily attire— handsome uniforms consisting of double-breasted blue jackets, with two rows of gilt buttons and a yellow collar framed with gold lace, and blue-gray pants, with double yellow stripes. They would also be decorated with a gold cord and white horsehair plume, ankle boots, brass spurs, and white gloves. However, when the recruits arrived, they did not receive the promised clothing. As a result, most of the dragoons soon began to grow "threadbare" in their civilian clothes. Moreover, the army failed to provide adequate arms and ammunition for target practice, which caused Colonel Dodge to complain to the War Department that "it is important that the Dragoons should be drilled at Target Shooting as well as to fire with precision on Horseback the season is fast advancing." As a result of these problems, the morale of the recruits plummeted. One dragoon noted that "there is much murmuring and disaffection in our regiment. . . . Desertions are becoming every day more and more numerous." He also noted that: "The guardhouse was kept continually filled to overflowing." At Jefferson Barracks, whippings and brandings were common punishments for transgressions, for the army considered mutiny, cowardice, desertion, stealing, and drunkenness the worst offenses for a soldier. Boone often saw the lash well laid on as both a punishment for some wrongdoing and an incentive to do better. Boone, then, faced a host of leadership challenges once he recruited his company. After he left Franklin in April 1834, Boone returned to Jefferson Barracks where he helped train his men, designated as Company H. After a good month of drill, the War Department ordered him to Fort Gibson, and he left with his company sometime in May.[20]

Boone led Company H along the trail made by other companies that had left as early as November 20, 1833. They angled southwest past the village of Springfield, which was then composed of only fifteen or twenty cabins where many of the inhabitants sold whiskey to the soldiers at the "exorbitant price" of twenty-five cents per pint. Then his column dropped south to Fayetteville in the Arkansas

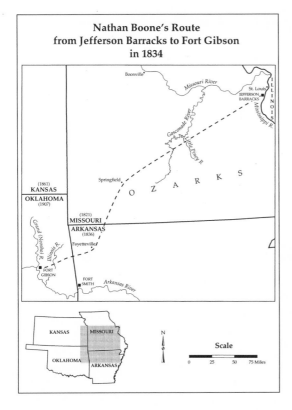

Nathan Boone's Route from Jefferson Barracks to Fort Gibson in 1834

Boone led Company H of the newly organized First U.S. Dragoons from Jefferson Barracks near St. Louis to Fort Gibson in Indian Territory during the spring of 1834. He followed a route that passed Springfield and skirted the area that would soon become his new home in present-day Greene County, Missouri. *Based on a map in the* Chronicles of Oklahoma *31 (Spring 1953). Cartographer, Adrianne Nold.*

Territory before completing its journey to Fort Gibson. Before Boone's dragoons arrived at the post on June 12, they had begun to learn something about riding a horse all day in the heat and sun and over rugged terrain. They also learned to endure the basic fare they prepared for meals over an open fire. Most important, they learned that Boone knew his way on the frontier. They could not help but see that he sat his horse during the twenty-mile-a-day rides better than any of the enlisted men and notice his easy manner about the campsites. Boone was clearly in his element, and even the hardships of the trail gave him the comforting feeling of familiar surroundings.[21]

When Boone led Company H into Fort Gibson, the post was already crowded with the men from companies A through G. Boone now saw that Fort Gibson was busier and noisier than ever before. The constant clang from the blacksmith's shop attested to the army's hurry to shoe a great number of horses in anticipation of a campaign. Tailors worked at making uniforms while saddlers plied their trade. Amidst this scurry of activity, daily military life continued as usual. Each day began with reveille at sunrise, the doctor's call at seven thirty, breakfast at eight, and guard changes at nine, followed by horse and foot drill and tactics, target shooting, wood chopping, water drawing, carbine cleaning, road building, inspections, and tattoo at nine in the evening. Boone also noticed that half of the regiment seemed to be detailed to watch the horses and cattle graze near the fort. With the daytime temperatures reaching 107 degrees, the dragoons paid a heavy physical price, especially from heat exhaustion.[22]

Almost immediately after his arrival at Fort Gibson, Boone learned that his company would join a major expedition led by Colonel Henry Dodge and accompanied by Brigadier General Henry Leavenworth, who had assumed command of the post in May. The War Department had ordered Leavenworth west about 250 miles to the Pawnee Pict (Wichita), Kiowa, and Comanche villages located somewhere along the Red River. These tribes had not yet signed peace treaties with the federal government and their nomadic lifestyle made them difficult for the army and Indian commissioners to find for the purpose of calling a council. In keeping with his earlier belief, Secretary of War Cass wanted the dragoons to ride deep into the southern Great Plains to impress these tribes with the power of the United States. In so doing, he thought, the army would intimidate them into keeping the peace and not attacking white traders and trappers who might venture into the region. They would do what the infantry could not do. The dragoons would serve as a mobile police force and fly the flag along the vast and sprawling frontier. The expedition would also enable the dragoons to rescue the man that Boone had lost the previous summer, if he remained alive, and a boy that the Comanches had captured from a family who lived along the Red River.[23]

Leavenworth had been waiting for Boone's arrival along with companies I and K, and he wanted to begin the expedition on June 12. Dodge particularly wanted Boone along; he had already recommended that the War Department give Boone command of a dragoon company. On February 2, 1834, Dodge had written to

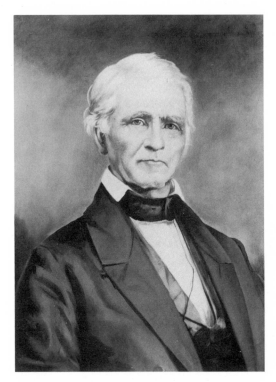

Major General Henry Dodge served in the Missouri militia during the War of 1812. Nathan Boone and his company of rangers rode with Dodge to relieve the Boonslick settlements from Indian attack during the war. Dodge was impressed by Boone's ability to command men and endure hardship on the frontier, and he later recommended Nathan for a commission in the U.S. Dragoons. Dodge commanded the dragoons on the summer campaign in 1834, which included Boone and his company. *State Historical Society of Iowa–Des Moines.*

Colonel R. Jones, adjutant general, from Fort Gibson that "Captain Boone is a first rate officer for the woods service. He commanded a company of U.S. Rangers under my command in 1812. He is a good woodsman and would be valuable on an expedition and has good knowledge of the southwestern frontier." Because Boone's men were exhausted from four weeks' riding over a difficult trail, Leavenworth delayed leaving Fort Gibson for three days. But on the morning of June 15, when the bugler called the dragoons "to horse," eight companies, totaling about five hundred dragoons, including Boone's Company H, assembled in the morning sun of the parade ground at Fort Gibson. Boone and the other officers rode up and down the line, conferring among themselves and with their first sergeants. The young dragoons were restless and anxious to begin a great adventure. When Dodge gave the order to march, the column wheeled and moved away from the post and crossed the Arkansas near the mouth of the Neosho River. The cavalcade was

Stephen Watts Kearny served as the lieutenant colonel of the First Dragoons, organized on March 4, 1833. Kearny led the expedition, accompanied by Boone, that provided the reconnaissance for the construction of a post on the Des Moines River and encouraged the Sioux to keep the peace in the upper Mississippi River valley. *State Historical Society of Iowa–Des Moines.*

an imposing sight with the company horses colored—bays, sorrels, blacks, whites—all forming a long line of two columns. The drawn-out calls from the officers carried over the land, and the creak of the baggage wagons accompanied the men and horses as the expedition moved west under a heavy sun. George Catlin, who went along, observed that the column strung out for more than a mile, and from a hilltop it looked like a "huge black snake, gracefully gliding over a rich carpet of green." He wrote, "I start this morning with the dragoons for the Pawnee country, but God only knows where that is." Neither Boone nor any other officer in the expedition knew, either.[24]

The expedition included not only Leavenworth, Dodge, and Kearny but also First Lieutenant Jefferson Davis along with Count Beyrick, a German botanist from the University of Berlin, who the War Department had authorized to accompany the dragoons to conduct scientific research. Four bands of Indians, including eleven Osages, eight Cherokees, six Delawares, and seven Senecas,

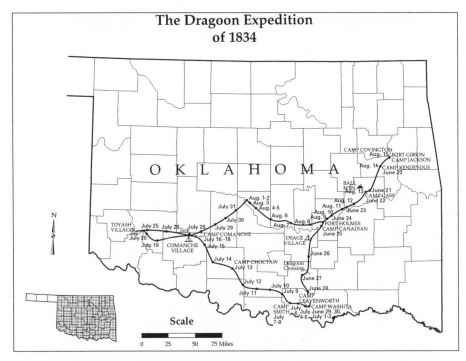

The Dragoon Expedition
of 1834

During the summer of 1834, Henry Dodge led an expedition that included Nathan Boone and other dragoons into southwestern Oklahoma to treat with the plains Indians and encourage them to keep the peace. Boone accompanied Dodge on the entire route, but he returned to Fort Gibson ill from the scorching sun and bad water, which had brought heat exhaustion and dysentery to most of the dragoons on the expedition. *Based on a map in the* Chronicles of Oklahoma *28 (Spring 1930). Cartographer, Adrianne Nold.*

also traveled along to serve as guides, hunters, interpreters, and representatives of their people. A fifteen-year-old Kiowa girl, who had been captured by the Osages in 1833, and an eighteen-year-old Wichita woman, who had been taken prisoner by the Osages several years earlier, also accompanied the expedition to be returned to their tribes as a sign of goodwill by the United States.[25]

This troupe, along with the quickly trained dragoons, baggage wagons, and seventy beef cattle, made its way southwest for eighteen miles where the men rested at Camp Rendezvous for six days before riding toward the Washita River. Not long after the expedition had departed, the dragoons sighted a herd of buffalo, and Boone took six men and joined several hunting parties that Leavenworth sent out

Here, a herd of buffalo broke through the dragoon ranks while being chased by the Indians who accompanied the summer expedition. George Catlin recorded the scene. He wrote that these "affrighted animals, made a bolt through the line of the dragoons, and a complete breach, through which the whole herd passed, upsetting horses and riders in the most amusing manner, and receiving such shots as came from those guns and pistols that were *aimed*, and not fired off into the empty air." *From George Catlin,* North American Indians.

to get fresh meat. Soon, the dragoons had all the buffalo meat that they could eat and transport before it spoiled in the heat. Often, to Boone's dismay because it showed a lack of discipline, Leavenworth, Catlin, and First Lieutenant T. B. Wheelock, the ordnance officer, wore out their horses making mad dashes across the plains to shoot buffalo, which they left to rot in the sun. Leavenworth suffered a bad fall on one of these chases, which no doubt contributed to his death before the expedition returned to Fort Gibson. Yet even with the diversion of a buffalo chase, the column of dragoons moved relentlessly southwest, and both officers and enlisted men hoped they would meet the Indians soon for a council. In the meantime, the sun bore down as the expedition traveled during the heat of the day. Usually the dragoons broke camp about eight or nine each morning and made camp in the late afternoon. Soon, bad water and the excessive eating of buffalo meat by men whose systems were accustomed to neither, added to the hardships of military life far removed from white civilization, began to take a toll on the health of the dragoons. On June 25, the expedition crossed the Canadian below the mouth of the Little River, near present-day Holdenville, Oklahoma.[26]

The dragoons reached the Washita on July 3, and the expedition made a difficult crossing because the narrow, deep stream with steep, muddy banks required considerable work to pull the wagons and ferry the supplies across, and several horses drowned under their heavy loads. Then, the dragoons proceeded west. By now, however, the sun had become "extremely oppressive," and heat exhaustion made many of the men severely ill; others began to die from sunstroke. Leavenworth realized that the baggage wagons slowed their march too much, and he decided to speed his mission by sending Colonel Dodge and the 250 most physically fit dragoons, along with ten days' provisions and eighty rounds of ammunition each, ahead on a forced march. Leavenworth estimated that Dodge would need twenty days to reach the Indian villages and return. Although the dragoons would have rations for only half of that time, Leavenworth believed they could supplement their food supply by living off the land. He also believed that speed was essential because the dragoons had already traveled 180 miles, and 86 men had become ill from the sweltering sun that burned down unmercifully from the clear blue sky. Lieutenant Wheelock, however, noted in his diary that "our horses in general, though thin, are apparently well able, if treated with care, to perform the campaign before us; spirits of the officers and men good; sanguine expectations of a successful march upon the Pawnees." His optimism would not last long.[27]

Boone's command would be one of the six depleted companies of forty-two men each to accompany Dodge and four staff officers to the Indian villages. No one except Leavenworth liked the plan. Indeed, Boone and Dodge, and the dragoons that followed them, felt considerable apprehension about what Leavenworth had ordered them to do. Still, they had little choice but to follow his orders. For two weeks they rode west under the oppressive sun, while the provisions in their packs and saddlebags fell dangerously low. Men dropped from their saddles with heat exhaustion and horses collapsed on the trail and did not get up. As they rode west, the dragoons began to see the "suspicious" signs of pony tracks and cold campfires, and Boone knew they were probably being watched. At night they made camp by forming a square about fifteen to twenty rods across by placing their saddles and packs on the perimeter for protection, and each man staked his horse inside the square close to his bedroll. The country west of the Washita belonged to the Kiowas, Comanches, and other nomadic tribes, who claimed it for their hunting grounds, and Boone and the dragoons rightly expected trouble. Everyone was ill at ease and "worn with fatigue."[28]

One night about midnight the sharp report from a sentinel's carbine startled the camp and brought both fear and confusion to the sleeping men. Horses broke their fastenings and ran in all directions. Boone and the dragoons seized their weapons and positioned themselves on the ground behind their saddles and prepared for an Indian attack as the bugler pierced the night air with the call for assembly. After a few minutes that seemed like hours, word passed through the companies that a nervous dragoon on guard duty had mistakenly shot a horse that had slipped its fastening and wandered out of the encampment. After this fright, Boone and the dragoons spent the remainder of the night rounding up the scattered horses, to keep them from being taken by the Indians and to ensure they would not themselves be afoot on the vastness of the plains. By the time Boone and the command first saw Comanches on July 14, the summer expedition had become a journey into hell.[29]

Soon after the sighting of that band of thirty Comanches, who apparently had been watching the expedition for some time, the expedition reached their village of about two hundred conical skin lodges with approximately four hundred inhabitants. Some one hundred mounted Comanches rode out to meet the dragoons, but they showed neither fear nor hostility. Boone was impressed by the broad-faced, powerfully built, and "copper" colored Comanches. The men rode with such skill that their every movement flowed with ease. Each carried a lance, bow, quiver, and buffalo-hide shield, and they sat good horses. The Comanches carried themselves proudly and acted with boldness and confidence. No doubt Boone agreed with Lieutenant Wheelock, who noted that the Comanche women were "good looking" with short cut hair. He also saw hundreds of horses grazing nearby, and his men quickly began trading blankets

When Nathan and the dragoons approached the Comanche village, they were met by a line of a hundred fighting men. Catlin noted that the Comanches wheeled and dressed their line like "well-disciplined Cavalry." Dragoons and Comanches faced each other for half an hour; then the Comanche leader came forward, shook hands with Dodge, and rode down the columns touching the hands of Boone and the dragoons. *From George Catlin,* North American Indians.

and knives for fresh mounts. The expedition, however, did not linger at the Comanche village; the leaders were away on a hunting trip, and Dodge did not believe that anyone remained with sufficient authority for negotiating or to impress. He then asked whether anyone could lead him to the Wichita camp. A Comanche volunteered, and the dragoons continued west. Dodge remained intent on either making peace or war with the Comanches or Wichitas or both. He did not need to order Boone and the dragoons to keep alert. The senses of Boone and the dragoons were keen, Wheelock wrote, "as if in the atmosphere of war."[30]

The three days' rest at the Comanche village had not been sufficient for Dodge's dragoons to regain their strength and stamina. By July 19, Boone's company had lost several more men to heat exhaustion, and Dodge's command had been reduced to 183 men—

George Catlin accompanied Colonel Henry Dodge, Nathan Boone, and the other dragoons on the summer campaign in 1834. Catlin recorded the events with pen and brush and gave the expedition its only pictorial record. When the dragoons spotted a Comanche war party, Dodge sent a man with a white flag toward it. The Comanche leader then approached with a piece of white buffalo hide dangling from his lance and shook hands with Dodge. Then, all of the Comanches approached and shook hands with Boone and the other dragoons. *From George Catlin,* North American Indians.

75 had been left behind to catch up if they regained their health, to return to Fort Gibson, or to die. Others deserted under the cover of darkness. The dragoons had depleted their rations, and they had passed beyond the buffalo range. Although they killed a few deer, the meat proved scanty, and one dragoon recorded that "game is now divided among the command with great care." Starvation became a present danger and mirages promised water where only heat waves glistened in the sunlight and where the grass waved in the wind. The shoes on the horses now began to wear out, and the mounts "suffered very much" from sore hooves. Wheelock noted that although they had an adequate supply of good water, "Our men seem somewhat discontented on account of the scarcity of

George Catlin used his brushes and canvases to record daily life in the Comanche village. Here the women dried meat and scraped buffalo hides while children played. Catlin recalled that the Comanches treated them "with as much curiosity as if we had come from the moon," and noted that their children and dogs were afraid of the dragoons. *From George Catlin,* North American Indians.

game; they are very improvident." As the command bordered on disintegration, Dodge compensated by increasing the speed of the march, and tempers flared. The newly recruited and poorly trained dragoons now began to question the orders of their commanders. Boone, however, held his men together largely by setting an example through his ability to endure, suffer, and even accept depravation as a natural condition of life and a part of doing one's duty. His men followed him in part because of his leadership and in part because they did not have any place to go. To leave the command meant certain death.[31]

On July 21, the dragoons reached the Wichita village of approximately two hundred grass lodges, some of which measured thirty feet high and forty feet wide, on a branch of the Red River. Dodge feared a surprise attack and ordered Boone and the dragoons to fix bayonets and prepare for a fight, but it did not come. Instead,

The grass lodges of the Wichitas, whom Catlin called Pawnees, proved a stark contrast to the buffalo hide tepees of the Comanches. Catlin was surprised with the size of the village, which he estimated had between five hundred and six hundred wigwams. "To our surprise," he wrote, "we found these people cultivating quite extensive fields of corn (maize), pumpkins, melons, beans, and squashes; so, with these aids, and an abundant supply of buffalo meat, they may be said to be living very well." *From George Catlin,* North American Indians.

sixty Indians met the dragoons and begged the soldiers not to shoot them. After five long weeks of riding, Dodge, Boone, and the dragoons were relieved to discover that they had not only reached the object of their mission but that the Indians proved peaceful and willingly shared their corn, beans, squash, watermelons, plums, and dried meat. Some dragoons were not too exhausted to observe that the Wichita women were "prettier than the Comanche squaws." Boone and his men gladly exchanged tobacco, knives, and clothing for the Wichitas' food, and they prided themselves that they had endured the first leg of their journey.[32]

After the command had rested and other Indian bands arrived, Dodge held a grand council with the Wichita, Comanche, Kiowa, and Waco chiefs. While they talked, Catlin worked hurriedly with pen and brush, and Boone listened to Dodge tell the chiefs: "We are the first American officers who have ever come to see the Pawnees [Wichitas]; we meet you as friends, not as enemies, to make peace with you, to shake hands with you. The great American captain is at peace with all the white men in the world; he wishes to be at peace with all the red men of the world; we have been sent here to view this country, and to invite you to go to Washington, where the great American chief lives, to make a treaty with him, that you may learn how he wishes to send among you traders, who will bring you guns and blankets, and everything that you want."[33]

Dodge then asked for the Comanches to return a nine-year-old white boy whom they had captured on the False Washita earlier that summer as well as for information about Abbay. He offered in return the young Wichita girl, but the Indians balked and denied any knowledge of the white boy. As the demands and denials became stronger, a pistol shot fired accidentally by one of the Cherokees in Dodge's party brought added tension to the negotiations and a flurry of commotion as the women and children fled the camp. One soldier noted that the Indians seemed eager to fight; they did not believe the pistol shot had been an accident, and they could not be "pacified" until "the hand of the Cherokee who had caused the alarm was shown them bloody and considerably injured by the discharge." Dodge then adjourned the council until the next day. Boone no doubt agreed with the dragoon who noted in his diary that "suspicion reigned in the bosom of all."[34]

When the Indians and soldiers met in council the next day, Dodge held firm demanding an exchange of prisoners, and the Comanches eventually brought the white boy forward for a trade, along with a reluctant black youth who had escaped from his master along the Arkansas only to be captured by a Pawnee hunting party. One chief became so moved by the exchange of the boys and the reunion of the Wichita girl with her relatives that he hugged Dodge and each officer. Boone understood the importance of this show of affection as well as the significance of reciprocation. When his turn came, he let the old chief place his left cheek against his and they held each other for several minutes in a "silent and affectionate manner." More than an hour passed before Dodge could resume the negotiations.[35]

The council then reconvened, but now under much more favorable circumstances, because the tribes had gained a sense of trust for Dodge and the dragoons. Then, with Boone and the other officers and the Indians who had accompanied them from Fort Gibson standing by, Dodge told the chiefs that the president of the United States wanted to make a peace treaty with them and to exchange all other prisoners. "Peace cannot be made with all the tribes," he said, "till a large white paper be written and signed by the President and the hands of the chiefs. Will your chiefs go with me now to see the American President?" When Dodge finished with a promise of many presents, Boone could tell that the chiefs were not convinced. They murmured among themselves, and Boone saw that some clearly objected to what Dodge had asked them. Dodge met with his staff and decided to close the council and wait for the answer of the chiefs the next day.[36]

When the council resumed, Dodge again urged the chiefs to accompany him to Fort Gibson where they would make a treaty. The chiefs, however, remained unconvinced except for one, known as We-ter-ra-shah-ro, who said he wished to make peace with the Osages, to see the lands of the Cherokees and Creeks, whom he had only heard about, and "to shake hands with them all." This acknowledgment broke the impasse, and leaders of the Osages, Cherokees, and Delawares, who had accompanied the expedition, stepped forward and testified that they lived with the whites in peace and friendship and that they had nothing to fear from each other. With these speeches of encouragement, the chiefs decided to select some men who would accompany Dodge to Fort Gibson and learn more about the wishes of the white leaders.[37]

Before the expedition had organized for the return march, Boone and the other dragoons were more than a little startled when a band of about thirty Kiowas almost rode into the doorway of Dodge's tent with a speed and force that boded trouble, and the women and children quickly "fled in great alarm." The Kiowas were armed with strung bows and quivers filled with arrows. Boone could see that they were spoiling for a fight, and he ordered his men to grab their rifles and hold ready for firing at his command. Boone saw that the Kiowas were bold, sat fine horses, and rode well. He also noticed that they did not dismount. Trouble seemed inevitable.[38]

When the shouting and dust died down, the Kiowas and dragoons faced each other with weapons drawn. Dodge reacted swiftly and brought an interpreter forward to ask the Kiowa leaders what they wanted. The Kiowas told him that they had learned he held a girl from one of their bands, and they intended to take her back. Dodge, then, in the words of one observer, "immediately addressed them with the assurance of our friendly disposition, and gradually led them into gentleness." Dodge assured the Kiowas that he held the girl strictly for the purpose of returning her to her family. If the Kiowas would bring her father and mother or relatives to him, they could have the girl once he was certain that she would be safe. Dodge's audacity made the Kiowas pause, and they hesitated, unsure whether to fight or negotiate. After a hasty council with several of the Comanche and Wichita chiefs, the Kiowas decided to return the next day for the release of the girl to her family. When they rode away, Boone and the dragoons uncocked their carbines and breathed a sigh of relief. Neither Boone nor his men slept well that night, and when morning came, they all hoped that they would be alive by nightfall.[39]

During the morning of July 24, small and large bands of Kiowas arrived at the Wichita village, and at ten o'clock the chiefs began to assemble for the council. Boone could see that they all came mounted and armed. When the council began, some two thousand Indians surrounded the proceedings. Amidst the growing commotion in the camp, the parents of the Kiowa girl approached Dodge's quarters. They asked for their daughter and Dodge brought the girl forward. When parents and daughter rushed toward each other in an emotional reunion, Dodge was satisfied that she had been returned to the appropriate people. The Kiowa chiefs were also pleased that Dodge had kept his word, and they began to consider him a friend, just as he had planned. Dodge then addressed the assembly, saying, "Kiowa chiefs! I herewith present to you your relation; receive her as the best evidence of the sincere friendship of the Americans." Then the chiefs and officers passed around the peace pipe and pledged lasting friendship. When the council drew to a close, Boone and the dragoons prepared to begin their return trip to Fort Gibson the next morning, but neither Dodge nor Boone knew whether any Indians would go with them.[40]

Soon after sunrise on July 25, however, Dodge summoned Boone and the other officers to his campsite, because fifteen Kiowas along with several Comanches, Wichitas, and a Waco had arrived at their camp. After the Indians told Dodge that they had decided to accompany him to Fort Gibson, he gave them presents of pistols and rifles as symbols of friendship. All of this took time; thus, the Indians were not prepared to leave until mid-afternoon. At that point, the expedition headed east, back across the land of dried grass and little food and water.[41]

Boone and the dragoons rode hard for the next week, covering more than a hundred miles and living on the parched corn and dried buffalo meat that they obtained from the Kiowas. Although each mile they traveled brought them closer to Fort Gibson, the summer sun bore down unmercifully. Heat exhaustion, once again, made men hang from their saddles for fear of falling off and dying or being left behind. Those too sick to ride were placed on litters lashed between two horses. One dragoon, however, found something to enjoy about the return journey when he wrote in his diary, "We are eagerly pursuing our way home with our Indian Ambassadors who seem remarkably jovial & delighted with every thing they see[.] Nightly they amuse us with their wild unintelligible & unaccustomed songs which are far from being displeasing as they all join in seemingly endeavoring to exceed each other in noise, altogether creating a compound of the most unearthly discord."[42]

Despite the amusements of the Kiowas around the campfire at night, the dragoons still carried few provisions and their hunger soon became keen. As a result, when the expedition re-entered the buffalo range on July 29, a shout went out to report the first sighting. Boone no doubt agreed with Lieutenant Wheelock, who wrote that "never was the cheering sound of land better welcomed by wearied mariners, than this by our hungry columns." Dodge halted the command and soon quarters of buffalo roasted over open fires and Boone and the dragoons sliced off chunks with their knives. The next day, even Boone was impressed when he learned that one of the Kiowas had killed three buffalo with three arrows.[43]

With fresh meat now plentiful, the dragoons began to feel that they could make it back to Fort Gibson; only the sun and heat remained their enemies. On August 1, the expedition crossed to the north bank of the Canadian River about twenty miles south of present-day Oklahoma City. Here, Boone saw a "beautiful plain" and "countless numbers" of buffalo grazing into the distance, and he evidently joined the other officers and men who, in the words of George Catlin, "were well enough to sit on their horses" in "killing buffaloes much in excess of any possible demand for their meat." On August 4, Catlin, who was too sick to take part in the killing, also wrote, "the men have dispersed in little squads in all directions, and are dealing death to these poor creatures to a most cruel and wanton extent, merely for the pleasure of *destroying*, generally without stopping to cut out the meat. During yesterday and this day, several hundreds have undoubtedly been killed, and not so much as the flesh of half a dozen used." The dragoons had so stirred up the buffalo in the area of their camp that, Catlin noted: "They have galloped through our encampment, jumping over our fires, upsetting pots and kettles, driving horses from their fastenings, and throwing the whole encampment into the greatest instant consternation and alarm." If Boone did not take part in this freelance killing spree, neither Catlin nor anyone else made a note of it.[44]

After resting five days, the expedition left the Canadian River and continued toward Fort Gibson. Although Boone and the dragoons had plenty of buffalo meat, a lack of water now made the punishing sun even worse, and any sighting of a tree line along a dry streambed gave them a brief but unfulfilled hope of relief in a land of unceasing heat and wind. Catlin wrote: "From day to day we have dragged along, exposed to the hot and burning rays of sun, without a cloud to relieve its intensity or a bush to shade us, or anything to cast a shadow except the bodies of our horses." The grass had turned brown and scarcely provided sufficient nourishment for their horses. Catlin continued, "sometimes for the distance of many miles, the only water we could find, was in stagnant pools, lying on the highest ground, in which the buffaloes have been lying and wallowing, like hogs in a mud-puddle. We frequently came to these dirty lavers, from which we drove the herds of buffaloes, and into which our poor and almost dying horses, irresistibly ran and plunged their noses, sucking up the dirty and poisonous draft, until, in some instances, they fell dead in their tracks—the men also (and oftentimes amongst the number, the writer of these lines) sprang from their horses, and ladled up and drank to almost fatal excess, the disgusting and tepid draft, and with it filled their canteens, which were slung to their sides, and from which they were sucking the bilious contents during the day." The result was dysentery, which made their ride in the heavy sun and sweltering heat the epitome of misery.[45]

On August 10, Lieutenant Wheelock reported a "vast many sick," including three officers, one of whom may have been Boone. Two days later, seventy men suffered heat exhaustion, dehydration, and dysentery. Fewer than ten horses remained in good condition, and Dodge ordered Boone and the other company commanders to alternate walking and riding every hour. As the dragoons slowly moved toward Fort Gibson, they turned their faces from the hot wind as though it were the "keen blasts of winter." Catlin reported that fifteen days were required for the dragoons to travel from their camp on the Canadian to the fort. The expedition traveled slowly because so many horses kept collapsing and the well soldiers stopped to dig graves for the dragoons who died in the litters.[46]

Later, after the expedition had returned safely to Fort Gibson, Dodge reported that: "Perhaps there never has been in America a campaign that operated More Severely on Men & Horses. The excessive Heat of the Sun exceeded any thing I ever experienced[.] I marched from Fort Gibson with 500 Men and when I reached the Pawnee Pict Village I had not more than 190 Men fit for duty they were all left behind sick or were attending on the Sick the Heat of the Weather Operated Severely on the Dragoon Horses there was at Least 100 horses that was Killed or Broke down by the excessive Heat of the Weather the Men were taken with fever and I was obliged to Carry Some of my Men in Litters for Several Hundred Miles." Clearly, Dodge had been worried about his men and the outcome of the expedition, although he did not add that more than one hundred dragoons had died. Boone, however, whose constitution always had been strong, endured better than most of the dragoons. Still, the campaign took a toll on him as well, and he evidently required medical attention.[47]

The smell of unwashed men and sweaty horses announced the arrival of the dragoons when Boone reached Fort Gibson and camped on the west bank of the Arkansas on August 15. After the two-month campaign on the southern Great Plains, he was as weary as any other man in the expedition, and not more than ten dragoons were reported in good physical condition. Catlin observed that many of the sick were carried into Fort Gibson "merely to die and get the privilege of a decent burial." He was appalled by the misery the men had experienced on the expedition, "I have," he wrote, "the mournful sound of 'Roslin Castle,' with muffled drums, passing six or eight times a-day under my window, to the burying ground, which is but a little distance in front of my room, where I can lay in my bed and see every poor fellow lowered down into his silent and peaceful habitation." Those who survived returned with their clothing dirty and tattered and their horses jaded. Colonel Kearny did not arrive with the litters of sick dragoons and with the horses that were too worn out to ride, until August 24. Wheelock reported of the Kiowas, however, that: "Our friends from the prairie are in good health and are apparently contented."[48]

Many of the dragoons no doubt wondered whether they had accomplished anything. Certainly, the War Department questioned the organization and leadership of the expedition, and critics charged that it had left Fort Gibson six weeks too late. As a result, the campaign was carried out during the hottest part of the year. Moreover, Boone and his men, along with the other two newly arrived companies from Jefferson Barracks, had not been given sufficient time to rest before Leavenworth took them onto the southern Great Plains. In the minds of most officers in the War Department and among the dragoons, the expedition had been a disaster from the beginning. While some dragoons began to doubt the success of the campaign, they became convinced of its folly when they learned that the Indians, who had accompanied them back to Fort Gibson, had no intention of going to Washington to meet the President of the United States. As a result, Dodge hurriedly arranged for a grand council with the Kiowas, Comanches, and Wichitas who had returned with him, and the nearby Cherokees, Osages, Choctaws, Creeks, and Senecas.[49]

When some 150 Indian delegates assembled at noon on September 1, 1834, Boone followed the proceedings, possibly from a hospital bed. Dodge and Major Francis W. Armstrong, superintendent of Indian Affairs for the Western Territory, again professed the peaceful intentions of the United States, and they gave the Indians medals and flags as symbols of friendship. They also told the Indians that traders wanted to visit their villages and cross their lands to Santa Fe. They would come in peace and both whites and Indians would profit from this trade. Boone knew that Dodge believed he had laid the foundation for a lasting peace with the tribes of the southern Great Plains, but not everyone agreed. George Catlin contended that the summer expedition had been a "most disastrous campaign," although the officers had conducted themselves well. Boone, who knew about white and Indian relationships as well as any man, was less optimistic than Dodge but less pessimistic than Catlin, and he took a wait-and-see attitude toward the results of the expedition and the proceedings that followed.[50]

Dodge did not have the authority to hold a peace conference and negotiate a treaty at Fort Gibson, but he could offer peace and friendship until formal proceedings could be organized the next year. Still, the conference at the fort provided the first contact between officials of the federal government and the tribes of the southern Great Plains. It also began the process of negotiation that opened the Indian Territory to occupation by more than one hundred thousand members of the Cherokee, Creek, Chickasaw, Choctaw, and Seminole nations, as well as others. The conference also laid the groundwork for providing safe passage for whites to travel through this area. Yet while Dodge believed the expedition and conference would soon lead to a "permanent peace" with these tribes, and although Secretary of War Cass reported that "the efforts to introduce amicable relations were successful," considerable hostility and fighting remained in the future between whites and Indians in the region. The summer expedition of 1834 and the conference at Fort Gibson, along with the Treaty with the Comanche, Wichita, and Associated Bands on August 24, 1835, helped establish an initial peace with the Indians. To a lesser degree the expedition also succeeded because it obtained the release of the white boy, learned that Abbay had been killed by his captors, and most of the dragoons survived. Still, it had been expensive in terms of loss of life and suffering. Catlin called the experience of the dragoons "unexampled" and "almost incredible." Boone agreed, but he knew that he had been a part of a major effort by the federal government to shape Indian policy for the Great Plains, and he felt satisfied that he had done his duty to the best of his ability and survived.[51]

Boone, however, did not question the purpose or results of the summer expedition. He had sought a commission in the regular army, and he had conducted himself well under the most trying circumstances. He had endured the heat, the hunger, and the oppressive sun, and he had stood with Dodge when the Kiowas showed more interest in fighting than talking. He had gazed for the first time at the seemingly endless sweep of grass on a deceptively undulating plain, and he had met nomadic Indian peoples. This country was far different from his childhood home along the Kanawha and Ohio Rivers and from eastern Missouri, and he found everything about it fascinating, luring, and even comforting in a hard, dependable way. The expedition had reached the Wichita village, met with the chiefs of several tribes, and brought back nearly two dozen Indians for the purpose of making a peace treaty. For Boone the summer campaign had been a success. The army gave meaning to his life, and he did not want to be anywhere else. This expedition had been his first experience on the Great Plains. It would not be his last.

Boone did not have long to dwell on these thoughts after he returned to Fort Gibson. Soon after he arrived at the post, he received orders to proceed with two other dragoon companies, under the command of Lieutenant Colonel Kearny, to the Iowa country. There, the dragoons would take up winter quarters "on the right bank of the Mississippi, within the Indian country near the mouth of the Desmoines." But when Kearny's command left Fort Gibson on September 3, Boone did not ride in the lead of Company H. When the time came to leave, Boone could not go on. Apparently, he had suffered prolonged heat exhaustion, dehydration, and dysentery, and his body remained too weak to endure another long, hard ride. The post's doctor evidently ordered him to rest and stay behind. Although Boone wanted to remain with his men, he knew that he did not have the strength to push himself as he had in the past. At the age of fifty-three, he no longer had the resilience of his youth. While his dragoons were either in their late teens or early twenties and could recover from physical hardships relatively easily, Boone recognized that he needed time to regain his strength. Like it or not, he had little choice but to convalesce at Fort Gibson. He would see his company as soon as possible in Iowa. With that, he bid his men goodbye and watched as Captain E. V. Sumner took his place before Company H and rode out of Fort Gibson toward Missouri and the country that he knew so well. Still, Boone realized that his orders to rest and restore his health might give him the opportunity to return to the Femme Osage before he rejoined his company, and the thought of home lifted his spirits.[52]

7

FULL STRIDE

BOONE RESTED at Fort Gibson for little more than two months before returning to active duty in the autumn of 1834 following the summer campaign. Sometime in September he regained his health, or at least felt well enough to receive clearance to join his company in Iowa. Evidently, he pushed his recovery and suffered a setback, because he traveled only about two weeks through southwestern Missouri before he stopped at Franklin for further convalescence. Whether Boone returned home during this time remains unclear, as his army records do not indicate a furlough or leave of absence. Apparently, he just kept going toward the dragoon camp on the Des Moines River as quickly as his health permitted after he received his release from medical care at Fort Gibson. In any event, he rejoined Company H and Colonel Kearny's command in October.[1]

The dragoons' encampment on the Des Moines River no doubt disheartened Boone when he arrived. To a man still in the process of regaining his health, the site was dismal. Neither the quarters for the officers and soldiers nor the stables for the horses had been completed. Although the dragoons labored with axes, saws, planes, and hammers and hurried in the late autumn to provide protection from the oncoming winter weather, they lacked the skills of master carpenters, and their work proved makeshift at best. The dragoons were grousing, and their spirits declined further when Lieutenant Benjamin S. Roberts, the acting commissary of the post, who was not only in charge of the construction but also fresh out of West Point, ordered Company I to tear down its barracks because the dragoons had not provided for doors. Although the dragoons explained that they had left notches in the logs through which a crosscut saw would be inserted to make the cut when they had finished, in the frontier building tradition, Roberts stood firm. Only after considerable argument and commotion did Captain Jesse B. Browne overrule his junior officer.[2]

Despite problems such as these, Colonel Stephen W. Kearny, who commanded the encampment, hoped to complete the buildings by the end of October, but he recognized that they would be "less comfortable and of meaner appearance, than those occupied by any other portion of the Army." The dragoons lived in tents while they built the post on the site of present-day Montrose, Iowa. Although lumber arrived by steamboat from Pittsburgh, the log barracks offered only slight protection during the winter of 1834–1835, which proved bitterly cold. One visitor remarked that the dragoons had "pale and sickly countenances." While the men shivered in their cabins, many complained that the recruiting officers had duped them into joining the army by telling them they "would have nothing to do but to take care of their horses and perform military duties." The dragoons were to be an elite group—thus, mundane work details like carpentry were beneath them.[3]

On October 20, Colonel Henry Dodge complained to Adjutant General Roger Jones that "there has been much discontent evinced among the men on that subject and I have no doubt it has been the cause of many desertions." When the dragoons balked at orders to build stables, Dodge asserted, "The first duty of a soldier is to obey his orders, and I am determined this work shall be done for the preservation of the horses." Boone no doubt agreed with Dodge, because he knew as well as anyone that strong, well-built horses were essential for any man who traveled across the frontier and put his life in danger, particularly from Indian attacks. The success of the dragoons depended on the quality and care of their horses, because both could be asked on a moment's notice to traverse any kind of country, and the value of "light troops" relied on their mobility and ability to strike quickly and hard. So building corrals and taking care of the horses made sense to Boone, and he likely reminded his young charges that the work had to be done.[4]

Despite these problems, Dodge remained optimistic in his headquarters at Fort Leavenworth that the dragoons would become good soldiers. "I shall pursue a steady and determined course," he wrote, "with the insubordinate men until they are brought to a proper sense of duty." Dodge's plan, of course, meant that officers, such as Boone, had the responsibility of ensuring discipline for the execution of all orders and the maintenance of good morale. It would not be an easy task to take young men, who had been promised an easy and exciting life as dragoons, and make disciplined, reliable soldiers out of them. Boone understood the problems. Although he loved the army with its regimented life, he still remained a loner and wanderer; still, he also understood duty and responsibility and the need for the army's activities. He would lead by example, enduring the same hardships as his men, complimenting them when necessary, and encouraging their sense of unity. While the men shivered in their cabins, the quartermaster did his best to improve their situation. He struggled to stretch his already inadequate provisions and complained bitterly about the supply line from St. Louis.[5]

Boone could tell that the army did not have a clear purpose for their encampment nor a plan for a permanent fort on the Des Moines River. Colonel Kearny said so as well and complained to his superior officers in the War Department. "I should like to know," he wrote, "if it is contemplated that we are to occupy this post, after the ensuing winter, and I wish to know whether I am authorized to keep away settlers from here, and how far I may proceed in doing so; also what is required of this command, while stationed here[?]" In reality, the War Department could not precisely answer Kearny's question. It had not intended the post, which it called "Detachment Headquarters of the Regiment of Dragoons at Camp Des Moines, Michigan Territory," to be a permanent fort. Rather, Camp Des Moines would only serve as a temporary winter quarters for the dragoons, who would move northwest into the Sioux country in the spring and locate a site for building a permanent post. Kearny's constant complaining about the conditions and temporary nature of the camp, however, finally brought results in February 1835, when Secretary of War Lewis Cass designated the site "Fort Des Moines," and ordered that it be designated a "double-ration post," that is, a hardship assignment for anyone stationed there.[6]

Life at Fort Des Moines proved especially difficult for Boone because of its everyday boredom. Army life at Fort Gibson, where the dragoons contributed five hundred men to the post, was also routine, but he liked its structure and reliability. Opportunities often arose for a break in the monotony, including occasional assignments for surveying, buffalo hunting, or expeditions to Indian camps. At Fort Des Moines, all of the food supplies arrived by steamboat. Moreover, the major survey of Indian lands in Iowa had already been completed, and he had been a part of it. With only seventy-eight dragoons in camp, daily military life with its drills and camp assignments became a drudgery as the days of winter passed into weeks and months. Lieutenant Albert Lea, who was stationed at Fort Des Moines, and who returned from Fort Gibson late in the winter with seventy-nine dragoons to reinforce Kearny's command, later said of Boone that he was a "good honest man, a brave and skillful frontiersman and Indian fighter, but was inexperienced in the duties of a dragoon officer in garrison." Simply put, Boone was a man of action. Garrison life, especially duty at an isolated post during the winter, proved too confining. Boone grew tired and bored with the daily orders to drill his company in parade maneuvers and tactical fighting—not to mention the paperwork involved with assigning guard, mess, and clean-up details. Although Boone completely regained his health during the winter, when spring came he grew increasingly restless. He needed a campaign and the opportunity to break free from the confinement of the fort and its ties to civilization.

Colonel Kearny also thought that the dragoons needed to do something to shake off the winter doldrums and boredom of camp duties and improve their discipline, which had suffered during the winter. He believed that an expedition into the field would help restore their morale. The War Department, however, planned for Kearny to do more than practice marching and maneuvering away from the fort. By the early spring, the War Department reasserted its original plan to use the dragoons to make the presence of the army known among the Sioux in present-day northern Iowa and southern Minnesota. In doing so, they hoped to encourage the Indians to keep the peace and refrain from attacking settlers who were moving into the prairie region in increasing numbers.[7]

On March 9, 1835, Kearny received orders to take three companies up the Des Moines River to the Raccoon Fork, reconnoiter the area, and select a site for a permanent post. Kearny would then ride to the Sioux villages "near the highlands on the Mississippi" and proceed west as far as he thought best before returning to Fort Des Moines. Kearny welcomed the orders and made plans to begin the expedition on June 7 with 150 men, including Boone and companies B, H, and I. Boone would be the only captain and the second in rank to Colonel Kearny. When he learned about the expedition and his part in it, Boone could not have been happier. Kearny planned to remain in the field until mid-August, and Boone welcomed the opportunity to spend two months on his horse exploring the countryside and making the presence and power of the army known to potential enemies.[8]

As winter faded into the warmth of spring with budding trees and greening grass, the ice broke up on the Des Moines and Mississippi Rivers, and the dragoons busily went about the task of preparing for the summer expedition. Horses had to be shod and leather packs and gear mended or replaced. The dragoons now took target practice from horseback and on foot with greater seriousness, and they made certain that their carbines were in perfect condition. Provisions had to be acquired and packed, and the dragoons were relieved to learn that the army did not expect them to live off the land as they had done with Dodge the previous summer. Although they would travel though country where buffalo, elk, and deer still remained plentiful, the summer expedition in 1834 had taught the army a lesson, and it reverted to its old policy of acquiring cattle to be driven along with the dragoons to provide fresh meat. Boone no doubt relished all of this activity, and he drove his men hard with a seriousness that showed both experience and a respect for the unknown.

When Boone rode out of Fort Des Moines with Kearny and the dragoons on the morning of June 7, his spirits could not have been higher, although persistent heavy spring rains had turned the trail to mud and made traveling "very bad." The dragoons, however, were anxious to leave the post and the drudgeries of the winter behind. Most of them expected the expedition to be a vacation, a pleasant ride in the summertime during which neither danger nor want would trouble them. Boone knew better, and although he did not expect the worst, he knew about the unpredictable and cranky, if not war-like, nature of the Sioux. He also had enough experience as both a ranger and a dragoon to know that the best-made plans of quartermasters never provided adequately for the needs of the men in the field. The expedition would not be a lark, but the coming hardships should be manageable, nothing worse than living out of a pack while on a long hunt.[9]

The expedition traveled only seven miles the first day. That night, careless pickets let many horses run back to their corral at Fort Des Moines, and the dragoons had to wait until their mounts were returned before they could begin again. By the end of the first week, however, they had reached Keokuk's village at the present-day town of Agency in Wapello County, Iowa. There, they secured the services of six Indians for guides and a half-blood by the name of Frank Labashure for their interpreter. Although the health of the dragoons remained good, in contrast to the early days of the summer expedition in 1834, the "disagreeable wet weather" of the spring lingered and soon dampened their spirits, but not enough to make them want to return to Fort Des Moines. On June 15, one man in Company I, who left an unsigned diary, reported that "So much rain renders marching unpleasant we have to encamp each night in mud & water but still I am better contented than when in quarters."[10]

Despite the frequent rains and camps in the mud, Boone enjoyed riding across the Iowa prairie in the early summer of 1835. The deep grass waved in the breeze and wild strawberries gave a red tint to the undulating land, providing a delicious luxury for their meals. Deer ran from the timbered areas along watercourses as they approached; as Boone and the dragoons made their way northwest along the north bank of the Des Moines River, turkeys, grouse, and prairie chickens flushed before their horses. Boone liked the lay of the land. No farmer had turned a furrow in the native sod, and this open country gave him a badly needed sense of freedom after months of idleness at Fort Des Moines. Yet as much as Boone relished the return of the dragoons to the field, the expedition began to experience more difficulties as each day passed. By June 23, they had exhausted their pork, and their salt and sugar supplies were nearly gone. Still, they had their beef cattle and plenty of flour as well as the bounty of the land.[11]

After the expedition missed the Raccoon Fork of the Des Moines River, Kearny turned northeast for the Dakota Sioux village under the leadership of Wabashaw. On June 25, they camped on the banks of the Iowa River and killed a half dozen buffalo. Boone probably laughed at the excitement of many young dragoons, who had enlisted from the eastern states, when they saw their first buffalos and rode out to chase and shoot them. Afterwards, they ate roasted buffalo and rested. The next day, after some difficulty, they located a place to ford the rain-swollen river, but the crossing took three hours and Boone and the dragoons were wet and cold by the time the last man made it safely through the swift water. One dragoon reported that the summer weather was "Remarkably cold with some frost," and the men hunkered deep in their jackets and tried to stay warm. All things considered, however, Boone likely preferred the cold and damp to the blazing sun and oppressive heat that he had experienced the year before, and he met each day in his own quiet but contented way.[12]

By the last week of June the expedition had passed into present-day Minnesota and crossed back into country where settlers were beginning to plow fields. The dragoons continued north to the vicinity of present-day Winona, Minnesota, where they finally made contact with about thirty Sioux, who were eager to trade with them. Boone knew that the Sioux were shrewd traders and viewed theft as a badge of honor that showed skill and bravery when dealing with an enemy. The young dragoons, however, who had little understanding of cultural differences and no inclination to learn them, soon considered the Sioux to be "mostly a dirty thieving race living in the most abominably filthy manner." Although the Sioux wanted many things that the dragoons had to offer—guns, knives, clothing—they could provide little in return, and one dragoon complained, "Trade is poor with these Indians on account of their poverty."[13]

Boone and the dragoons lingered along the Mississippi River for nearly two weeks while they waited for the Sioux to come to their camp for a council. Finally, on July 19, Wabashaw arrived with a band and Boone and the other officers watched and listened as Kearny told him that the United States wanted peace and trade with his people. Wabashaw and his people were impressed by the dragoons and their uniforms as well as by their horses and fine saddles and leather bags, and they were eager to profess their intent to keep the peace and refrain from attacking settlers in the area and travelers crossing their lands. After Kearny gave the chief some presents, the council broke up with everyone in good spirits, and the dragoons began their preparations to ride south toward the Raccoon Fork of the Des Moines River to locate a site for a permanent fort and thereby complete their mission.[14]

On July 21, Kearny and Boone led the expedition west, turning south near present-day Albert Lea. Now, however, their supplies began to run dangerously low. After a march of thirty-five miles on July 31, which took the dragoons through present-day Kossuth County, Iowa, an area that they found "without wood or good water," one dragoon reported, "We are wandering about like half-starved wolves & no person appears to know in what direction we ought to steer." The weather remained cold for July, and morale plummeted, causing "Much murmuring by the men." Boone, how-ever, whom one dragoon described as "a rather ordinary looking man, small of stature, and with little of the military about him," probably kept the complaining to a minimum in his company as well as among the other dragoons. His reputation gave him credence. They had watched him many times confer with Kearny about their course of travel. When horses were lost, they had seen Boone swing his leg over the saddle and dismount, adjust his glasses and get down on his hands and knees to examine the ground, and eventually locate their trail. He had enjoyed poking fun at his men by reminding them that Company H rode sorrels and to catch those horses when they found them. The dragoons, then, particularly those in Company H, trusted Boone, and even if they had not been soldiers, they would have followed his lead in making their way across the frontier. As a result, during the next eight days, Kearny and Boone not only kept the expedition together but also led it across two hundred miles of prairie. On August 8, the dragoons encamped near the junction of the Raccoon and Des Moines Rivers, in present-day West Des Moines.[15]

Kearny, Boone, and Lieutenant Albert Lea scouted the area to locate a fort site. Kearny did not like the location, however, because steamboats could not reach it at all times for resupply, and because the Sacs opposed the construction of a post on the Raccoon River, arguing that it would attract whites who "would drive off the little game that is left in their country." Kearny did not believe a fort at this location was "necessary or advisable" because the army could impose sufficient "restraints" on the Sioux from Fort Des Moines which remained in "striking distance" of their villages. All things considered, Kearny decided that if the War Department still believed it necessary to separate the Sacs and Sioux, a permanent fort would be best located on the upper fork of the Des Moines River on the

Neutral Ground, and with that decision, the expedition headed home on August 10. By that time the men were on half rations of meat and flour, and they were more than happy to turn toward Fort Des Moines.[16]

Kearny and Boone led the dragoons down the right bank of the Des Moines River and arrived at the fort about 2:00 P.M. on August 19. Boone was well satisfied with the expedition. Although they had suffered from the rain and cold as well as scanty provisions, this reconnaissance had been easy compared to the previous summer. The dragoons had not lost a man during the ten-week march that covered eleven hundred miles. One dragoon best summarized the expedition when he wrote: "Sickness and all Disease has been a stranger to the camps and all have enjoyed good spirits except [for] that stupidity caused by the want of food & upon the whole I can say we have had a pleasant campaign."[17]

Back at Fort Des Moines, Boone, once again, resumed the daily military routine of drills, parades, and paperwork. It also involved waiting—for the next order, detail, or expedition—and Boone did not do that well or with ease. The summer campaign had been invigorating. It had given him the opportunity to do what he did best, that is, scout new terrain, lead men during difficult days when duty gave them the only reason to keep going, and help make the army an instrument of national policy. Compared to the green beauty of the rolling prairie, even under brooding rain clouds, Fort Des Moines was a forlorn and depressing outpost where the morale of the men never seemed to rise above rock-bottom. One English passenger on a steamboat that docked at the landing on the Mississippi River learned that "The number of desertions from this post was said to be greater than from any other in the United States."[18]

In the autumn of 1835, approximately 184 men, including 49 in Boone's company, called Fort Des Moines their home, and they primarily occupied their free time by gambling. Frequently, they took boats across the river to Nauvoo in order to gamble away from post grounds. Boone did not gamble, and he spent most of the coming winter engaged in routine army activities, such as building repair, because several roofs remained "bad and leaky," distributing seventy-one new carbines that arrived for his company, and he longed for another assignment that would put him back on his horse and in pursuit of an objective.[19]

On June 6, 1836, his wish came true when he received orders to accompany Captain Edwin V. Sumner and companies B, H, and I on another summer campaign. This time, however, the dragoons would not be riding into the wilds of the northern prairies or the desolate southern Great Plains. Rather, they had orders to fly the flag and make the military presence and power of the United States felt among the Menominees, Winnebagos, and Kickapoos, who had been showing hostile dispositions toward federal authorities after the abandonment of Fort Armstrong on May 4. Boone and the dragoons would verify whether these tribes were making plans for war or endangering white settlers. If so, they were to snuff out any thoughts of insurrection by these tribes.[20]

The dragoons crossed the Mississippi at Fort Madison, located about fifteen miles north of Fort Des Moines, and rode northeast across Illinois to Peoria and through country that Boone had seen during the War of 1812, nearly twenty-five years earlier. One observer at Peoria recalled hearing the sound of a bugle as the dragoons approached, and people went outside to see what it meant. "In a few moments," he wrote, "a lengthened troop of cavalry, with baggage-cars and military paraphernalia, was beheld winding over a distant roll of the prairie, their arms glittering gayly in the horizontal beams of the sinking sun as the ranks appeared, were lost, reappeared, and then, by an inequality of the route, were concealed from view." Boone and the dragoons impressed the residents of Peoria when they camped nearby with their white tents, carbines stacked near the campfires or hung from trees, and their easy-going, friendly nature.[21]

The dragoons did not linger at any place long, and they were soon on their way to Chicago, then a town of about six thousand, where they veered north toward the settlements of Milwaukee and Green Bay. Then, the expedition ascended the Fox River to Fort Winnebago before following the Wisconsin River downstream before dropping south to Galena and Fort Armstrong at Rock Island. From there they followed the east bank of the Mississippi and crossed over opposite Fort Madison and returned to Fort Des Moines. This expedition proved uneventful, but Boone preferred a peaceful, long ride and camping under the stars to living in the barracks with leaky roofs at Fort Des Moines.[22]

Boone knew as well as any officer or enlisted man that the site for Fort Des Moines had not been chosen well, and he welcomed the order for the abandonment of the fort. Boone considered the post nothing less than a sickly pest hole. Located on the bank of a muddy creek that turned stagnant during the summer, the fort was plagued with mosquitoes, and the men usually suffered "a good deal of sickness," probably malaria. The hospital was too small by half and the storehouses and barracks remained "full of chinks and unsafe" and in a general bad state of repair. Moreover, with the dragoons expected to scout the Sioux country far to the north, long and often difficult rides would be necessary to maintain a military presence for the federal government on the northern prairie frontier.

While the authorities in the War Department contemplated moving the post farther up the Des Moines River, speculators began to encroach on the garrison's lands, even laying out a town site and selling lots within sight of the fort. Whiskey sellers arrived to relieve the soldiers of their pay and to trade with the Indians for the furs and deerskins that could still be taken from the streams and woodlands. At the same time, freight charges for the shipment of supplies from St. Louis to the fort were becoming prohibitively expensive because of the post's location at the upper end of fourteen miles of rapids on the Mississippi. Had the fort been located at the base of those rapids, the army could have avoided "immense and useless expense." One observer noted that rates for the shipment of freight via steamboat from St. Louis to Keokuk, a distance of 170 miles, cost twenty-five cents per hundredweight, but the rate doubled between St. Louis and Fort Des Moines, even though the trip was little more than a dozen miles longer. These and other problems began to mount for the officers and men at Fort Des Moines.[23]

On September 18, Lieutenant Colonel Richard B. Mason, who had assumed command of the fort from Colonel Kearny, complained to the War Department about the ever-pressing settlers near the post and asked for permission to establish a reserve two miles wide on each side of the fort. "This reserve," he wrote, "is absolutely necessary to the convenience and well being of the garrison." Mason's letter forced the War Department to end its procrastination about moving Fort Des Moines. On October 20, the Adjutant General's Office issued the orders: "The Dragoon post of Fort Des Moines will be broken up without delay, and the squadron immediately proceed to join the Headquarters of the regiment at Fort Leavenworth." Boone would have envied them if he had not already had other assignments to take him away from the post between the end of the Illinois expedition and the first departures for Fort Leavenworth on October 30.[24]

Boone did not settle into garrison life for long after he returned. Soon thereafter he received a brief leave of absence to visit home. In a letter dated St. Charles County, September 19, 1836, to a Jesse Vanbibber, a relative of Olive, he wrote, "Our family begins to scatter about." His eldest daughter, Delinda, lived "high up the Mississippi river." One daughter lived "on the Missouri," while another lived in the "neighborhood." He did not mention his other eleven children except to say that: "We lost a daughter Nancy last Fall. She died on 22 October, with a sickness of four days." Nancy was twenty-two years old when she died. Whether Boone made it home for her burial remains unclear, but he left no further record about the loss of his daughter. The only other glimpse into his family life at this time came with his comment that "Olive has become very fat and can hardly ride."[25]

Although Boone traveled home sometime in September 1836, he may have returned to Fort Des Moines soon after he wrote to Vanbibber, because he was assigned to the post until mid-November. The dragoons from the fort provided a security detail when Henry Dodge met in council with the Sacs and Foxes at Davenport later that month. By summer 1836, the federal government sought the removal of the Sacs and Foxes from Iowa. Keokuk supported the cession of the four-hundred-square-mile Sac and Fox reserve that enclosed his village on the Iowa River to reduce the confrontations between his people and whites who encroached on tribal lands. In September, Dodge, now Governor of the Wisconsin Territory, of which the Sac and Fox reserve was a part, asked Keokuk and the other chiefs to cede the entire reserve and move south of the Missouri. Apparently Boone once again observed his old friend in negotiations, hearing Keokuk's offer to sell only 256,000 acres at $1.25 per acre. Boone, who had speculated in lands himself, understood that Keokuk wanted to keep the remaining lands until settlers drove up the price. He no doubt also observed Black Hawk's reactions to the negotiations as the old warrior watched the proceedings from the perimeter of the meeting.[26]

Certainly Boone appreciated Dodge's shrewd bargaining, ultimately gaining land for the federal government at 75 cents per acre that could be immediately sold for $3.00 per acre, as well as the Sac and Fox agreement to vacate those lands by November 1 and to refrain from hunting, fishing, or planting on them thereafter. With the Sacs and Foxes to receive $30,000 for ten years and $10,000 per year thereafter as well as two hundred horses, Boone surely considered the treaty a fair agreement for both parties, and he no doubt enjoyed seeing his old friend again and watching the proceedings.[27]

Not long after Boone attended the signing of the Sac and Fox Treaty, he received orders to proceed to Jefferson Barracks to assume duty as a road commissioner for the army. He gladly left Fort Des Moines on November 14; he would not rejoin his company until June 19, 1837, at Fort Leavenworth. In the meantime, the War Department had other plans for Boone and his surveying skills. Indeed, by the autumn of 1836, the War Department planned to survey a military road from the upper Mississippi River near present-day St. Paul to the Red River of the South to enable the rapid movement of troops in case of war with the Indians as well as speed communications between the forts already in existence and those the army wanted to build. The department also wanted to move Fort Gibson to a location farther east on the Arkansas.[28]

As a result, the War Department appointed Boone, Colonel Kearny, and Major T. F. Smith to serve as a commission charged to investigate the feasibility of these plans. Boone met with his colleagues in St. Louis to discuss their orders, then traveled with them to Fort Gibson where, in December, they recommended that the location of the fort not be changed because its position remained too important for the protection of the southern Great Plains. Boone and the other commissioners reported: "Having visited Fort Gibson, and considering it, as we do, *the key of the country around it,* and that the government, in removing the Indians from the East to the west side of the Mississippi, has pledged its faith to protect them from each other, and from the wild Indians of the Prairies, we recommend to you [War Department] the erecting of new barracks for the quartering of troops near that point, for the above purposes." The commissioners also reported that "About half a mile northeast from the present fort is an elevated piece of ground, where troops have occasionally been in camp for the benefit of their health; and we are of the opinion that a regiment of infantry and four companies of dragoons, distributed at that point and the site above referred to, will answer the purposes of the law, and preserve peace and quietness among the Indians in that particular section of the country." Moreover, Boone agreed, "The presence of a military force, near Fort Gibson is indispensable for the preservation of peace amongst the Indians themselves." Boone, Kearny, and Smith, however, also recommended the construction of another post, which became Fort Coffee. Winter weather prevented the further investigation of a route for a military road, and Boone returned to St. Louis and home for an extended leave.[29]

Sometime during the winter of 1836, Boone decided to sell his home on the Femme Osage. Whether he decided to sell it and seven hundred acres because of financial need remains uncertain. No evidence of financial difficulty exists, and Boone's regular army pay and income from either crops or rental from his lands should have met the needs of his family. In all probability, Boone chose to sell and move his family west because his work would frequently take him back and forth between Fort Leavenworth and Fort Gibson. During the course of his travel he could easily divert for a brief stop at home, if he located land and built a house on his general route of travel. In any event, Boone may have sent his son Benjamin Howard to purchase and preempt land, eventually totaling three hundred acres, near present-day Ash Grove in Greene County, Missouri, sometime in 1836. Boone knew the region well. Walnut and ash trees covered much of the land and open meadows provided areas for grazing livestock and cropland. In any event, Olive and Nathan sold their property for $6,120 on January 24, 1837. Then, sometime during spring 1837, Boone's sons James, Benjamin Howard, and John Coburn arrived and built a walnut log house, although Nathan no doubt stopped by periodically to lend a hand and give advice. This two-room house with a stone fireplace at each end was far less spacious and elegant than their stone home on the Femme Osage, but another log house for his slaves and a clear-running stream and nearby spring helped meet basic necessities.[30]

Although Boone rejoined the dragoons at Fort Leavenworth in June 1837, he did not resume command of Company H, because he continued to serve as a road commissioner for the army. There, he discussed possible locations for the construction of a military road

In 1837, Boone moved his family from the Femme Osage to southwestern Missouri. There, he and his sons built a log house that had few of the amenities and none of the style of his home in St. Charles County. When Boone's family lived in this house, the logs and chinking could still be seen. Later, other owners covered it with clapboard siding. Boone's house remains standing about one mile north of Ash Grove. *State Historical Society of Missouri–Columbia.*

that would link the forts on the upper Mississippi with those on the Red River of the South with Colonel Kearny. When Captain Charles Dimmock, late of the U.S. Army, whom the War Department appointed chief civil engineer for the road building project, arrived at Fort Leavenworth, Boone left with him, Kearny, and several other officers on September 1, to make a reconnaissance for laying out a road to Fort Gibson. They also blazed timber and built rock mounds to mark the route they thought best. This new commission studied various options for a route until November. Boone and the commissioners then went into winter quarters at Fort Leavenworth. During this time they decided to divide the western frontier into four sections and assigned a surveying team to each area, to facilitate the quickest possible construction of roads for the movement of troops and supplies.[31]

No sooner had spring 1838 arrived, however, than Boone received orders to take a company of dragoons from Fort Leavenworth south to the Osage country. The Osages had been causing trouble for settlers in western Missouri. After two white men and several Indians had been killed, Governor Lilburn W. Boggs had called out the militia to drive them from the state during the previous autumn, but they had returned. Boone and the dragoons reached the area in mid-March and patrolled the region until April, when he returned to Fort Leavenworth and prepared to renew his work on the road commission. During the summer of 1838, Boone and Captain Augustus Canfield of the Topographical Engineers began the survey of the northern section of the military road that would lead from Fort Leavenworth on the Missouri to Fort Snelling at the junction of the Minnesota and Mississippi Rivers. He did not return to Fort Leavenworth until September, when he received a long-awaited furlough that took him home until April 23, 1839.[32]

Each spring when the grass turned green on the prairies and plains to support horses sufficiently on a long march, the army customarily sent troops on reconnaissance missions into Indian country where tribal groups had "known propensities" for "committing depredations upon the property of the whites" or had already made attacks on settlers and traders. These expeditions, of course, were routine for Boone, and he was not surprised when he learned not long after returning from his lengthy leave in the spring of 1839 that the Otos and Missouris had been causing trouble by threatening whites, particularly government employees who had been sent among them to provide educational and agricultural training. With Fort Leavenworth not only the army's headquarters in the West but also the closest post to the problem, the assignment to put down the disturbance came to Kearny and Boone.[33]

Consequently, on September 5, 1839, Colonel Kearny, who was commanding the First Squadron, Boone, and a Captain James Allen, leading the Second Squadron—about two hundred men in all—left Fort Leavenworth and followed the old "Council Bluffs" road north along the west side of the Missouri River. One dragoon reported that "the troops moved leisurely onward, over a country luxuriant, picturesque, and at some points beautiful; the monotony of the march being varied by, at one time, the necessity of cutting down the abrupt banks of some prairie stream, to allow the passage of the wagons, at another, of turning from a direct course to head some hollow whose marshy bottom would bear neither man nor horse." They crossed the Wolf River, the Great and Little Nemahaw Rivers, and Table Creek before striking the wide and shallow-running Platte. Although the dragoons could easily cross on their horses, they knew the river had a reputation for quicksand that would hopelessly mire their wagons. They had brought, however, an experimental inflatable boat made from Indian rubber and capable of supporting fifteen hundred pounds. When the cylinders were inflated and the first wagon towed across, Boone and the dragoons were not only elated with the ease that the rubber boat made of the crossing, but they marveled at this new technology that would change army life forever.

Their excitement from the successful transport of the wagons across the Platte River in the rubber boat, however, was dampened by the discovery of three skeletons in dragoon uniforms on a sandy flat of the riverbed. The company insignia on their clothes, swords, and cartridge boxes identified them as three dragoons reported drowned in the river earlier that year. They had attempted to make a crossing on their way to the Omaha reserve to return several members of that tribe who had been taken prisoner by the Sacs. Boone helped oversee the placing of their remains in a box and an evening burial with the "honors of war."

When the dragoons reached the Oto village, located near present-day Bellevue, Nebraska, they invited the Indians to council with Kearny the next day, September 16. The Otos, however, were in no hurry and treated Kearny, Boone, and their men with contempt. Finally, after a long delay, sentinels called out the approach of a "long string of warriors, boys and women," who halted several hundred yards from the dragoons' camp. Boone thought trouble was coming, and he quickly gave commands to his squadron to be ready for an attack. As soon as he saw the Otos dismount, however, he knew that they had no intention of fighting, but he told his men to keep alert and ready.

Boone stood close by when twenty chiefs and other leaders entered the encampment and approached Kearny's tent. Kearny invited the chiefs to sit on the ground nearby for a council. When Kearny told them that what he had to say should be heard by all of their people, the chiefs signaled for their villagers to come forward and they soon stood behind them. Boone and the other officers stood behind Kearny. Before he spoke, however, Kearny insisted that the Otos lay aside their weapons saying that it was contrary to custom for councils to be held among armed men and that while he did not fear them, he had not come to fight. The Oto chiefs agreed and ordered their people to put down their weapons. Then Kearny addressed the council.

As Boone stood behind Kearny and watched the Oto chiefs and their people, he heard Kearny say that he was glad to see them and that their "Great Father," the President of the United States, had sent him onto the Great Plains to observe their conduct. He also told the chiefs that many reports of their "misconduct" towards their "white brethren" had reached his ears. Kearny knew the names of the Otos who had harmed the whites who had come among them and, although he did not want their entire nation to suffer for the acts of a few people, he had the responsibility to punish the individuals who had caused the most trouble. Kearny then gave the chiefs the names of three young men who had killed a white man and asked one chief by the name of Kanzas Tunga or Big Kaw to deliver the men to him so that they could be punished before the tribe. This punishment, Kearny told the chiefs, would provide a lesson for their nation about the consequences of harming white people. If they did not learn from this lesson and he again received complaints from whites that the Otos had harmed them, he would easily return and punish them again. Kearny then told the chiefs that they should talk to the agent about any problems, because he had been sent to help them adjust to life on their reserve.

The chiefs had expected Kearny to say something like this, and they assumed he would execute their young men—which is why they had come to the council armed. If the dragoons made an attempt to seize any of their people as hostages or to inflict retribution for the attacks that some of their men had made on whites, they would fight. But first, they would talk. Chiefs Kanzas Tunga, Waronisa, and Le Voleur and most of the other leading men generally admitted that "their young men had acted badly, but that they were not able to restrain them." Boone had heard this excuse before, which he knew was in fact true, because tribal chiefs could only lead by persuasion and not everyone, particularly hot-headed young men, listened to their advice. He was somewhat surprised, however, when Waronisa and Le Voleur, who clearly had reached an advanced age, offered themselves for punishment in place of the three men who had been brought forward at Kearny's request. Then Boone saw a young chief rise to speak. His face and actions showed great nervousness as he stepped forward and said to Kearny, "My Father, I place myself among these prisoners, whatever punishment you inflict on them, let me under go first." Then, a murmur spread through the crowd and the tension became worse.

The Oto agent, named Hamilton, could see that if Kearny planned to execute the men for killing a white man, that many people, both Indians and dragoons, would die either before or after any official killing took place. He then rose and asked Kearny to give him the prisoners and not to punish them. Hamilton told the council that he would be responsible for the future good conduct of these men, and that he believed the Otos had already benefited from the proceedings as much as if punishment had actually been inflicted. Nothing would be gained from executing the young men or taking them back to Fort Leavenworth for trial and imprisonment. Boone saw the wisdom of Hamilton's argument, but Kearny had to be convinced that he should accept the agent's offer. Finally, after "some consideration" and with the recognition that the situation was confrontational and the emotions of the Otos and dragoons intense, he again addressed the council. Kearny told them that because Hamilton, their "peace-father," had interceded on behalf of their young men, he would give the prisoners to him. However, he assured the chiefs that he had not intended to execute them. Rather, he had only planned to whip them before the Oto nation so their people would know that the men had been punished. But, he said, if he ever had to come among them again to punish those who misbehaved, his ears would be "closed" to any appeals for leniency from their agent.

When Hamilton translated Kearny's speech and had released the prisoners after advising them to conduct themselves in "good faith" toward the white people whom their "Great Father" had sent among them for their benefit, Boone could see that the chiefs and surrounding Otos were pleased, even happy with the results of the council. It could have ended far worse, and both he and many of the dragoons and Otos had expected a bad outcome. With the prisoners set free and the Otos firmly told to act peacefully and to refrain from harming whites, the council broke up.

The next day, September 17, the dragoons swam their horses across the Missouri River and camped for the night at a Potawatomi village located in present-day southwestern Iowa. The following morning Kearny invited the Potawatomi chiefs to a council. When the proceedings began, about a dozen headmen sat before Boone and the other officers and heard Kearny tell them that the federal government wanted to make a new treaty in which they would exchange their present lands for other lands located south and west of the Missouri River. Kearny also invited the chiefs to accompany their agent on an inspection of those lands, and he explained the advantages of living in a *"territory"* under the laws of the United States in contrast to living within a *"State,"* which would tax their lands and make them abide by the laws of that jurisdiction. If they remained in their village, the surrounding lands would soon be part of a new state, and they would be subject to its authority. Boone listened as Kearny urged the Potawatomis as their friend to "accede to the wishes of their Great Father," at least to examine the country that he proposed to exchange for their land.

The Potawatomi chiefs listened but remained unconvinced and noncommittal. One chief, who spoke for the group, told Kearny and his staff that their ears had been "deaf" to any suggestions that they cede lands again and move elsewhere, because the previous cession and removal treaty that they had signed had not been fulfilled by the federal government. However, they thanked Kearny for his advice as a friend and told him that they were glad to see him and that he was welcome in the Potawatomi towns. With that exchange, the council broke up and Boone and the dragoons recrossed the Missouri River and headed for Fort Leavenworth, where they arrived on September 25.

Boone did not have long to rest after the expedition to the Otos along the Platte River. On October 27, he left with Kearny and 250 men of the first regiment of dragoons for the Indian Territory, present-day Oklahoma. Kearny had received a letter, dated September 28, sent by General Matthew Arbuckle, commandant at Fort Gibson, to the honorable Archibald Yell, Congressman of

Arkansas, that he expected trouble from the John Ross faction of the Cherokees, which had quarreled with the group led by John Ridge (who had agreed to the removal treaty in 1835), over the political control of the tribe. A council between the two groups in June 1839 failed to resolve their differences and soon thereafter Ridge and two other chiefs from his faction were murdered. Arbuckle expected armed resistance from the Ross faction when he sent soldiers to find and arrest the murderers. He also feared the outbreak of civil war among the Cherokees, and he worried about the safety of the other tribes that had been located near them. After seeing the letter, Kearny rode south with Boone and the dragoons in late October to Fort Wayne on the Illinois River about sixty miles from Fort Gibson, with the intent of protecting the peaceful tribes from the Cherokees if war broke out.[34]

When Kearny, Boone, and the dragoons arrived, however, they found the Cherokees preparing to flee because they believed the army had been sent to attack them. Kearny soon learned at Fort Wayne that the reports of intended hostilities by the Cherokees were "utterly groundless," that the "whole country" remained peaceful; the Cherokees had no intention of going to war with the United States. Kearny also learned that if the authorities at Forts Gibson and Wayne ever found the murderers, there would not be organized tribal resistance to their arrest. Given the peaceful situation, Kearny kept the dragoons at Fort Wayne only three days, and then they returned to Fort Leavenworth. Boone liked the way Kearny traveled. They covered the three hundred miles back to their headquarters in nine days. By now, however, the seasoned dragoons that followed Boone and the other officers had become accustomed to long rides and forced marches. They had become hard men who could sit in a saddle for hours, sleep on the ground, and endure the punishment of the weather. When they returned to Fort Leavenworth on November 20, none were the worse for the twenty-four-day, six-hundred-mile round-trip, and their horses were reported to be in "fine condition."[35]

By the end of the decade, Boone surely felt satisfied that he had helped the army fly the flag in hostile territory and enforce the Indian policy of the United States. He had led his men into one hostile Indian camp and to another friendly, but distrustful, nation.

He had clung to his saddle horn twice as his horse swam across the Missouri, and he had helped make an experimental crossing of the Platte with an inflatable rubber boat. Once again, he had stood close to his commander as an officer in the army and a representative of the power of the United States on the frontier, as Kearny and the Oto and Potawatomi chiefs met and shaped the course of Indian-white relations. He and the dragoons had patrolled much of the country along a line between the Arkansas and the Platte Rivers west of the Missouri. Their rapid movement encouraged the tribes to keep the peace. The dragoons also protected the newly arrived eastern Indians whom the removal policy of the federal government had located on these lands. Boone had done his duty in the face of danger, and he accepted, even relished, it in a way that many men love the comforts of the routine and familiar.[36]

During the 1830s, the army had become Boone's career as well as his home. Between the Black Hawk War in 1832 and 1840, when Fort Leavenworth served as his base of operations, Boone hit full stride in his chosen profession. Respected for his craft as a woodsman, recognized for his ability to lead men, admired for his capacity to endure excruciating hardship, and sought after for his skill as a surveyor, Boone earned a reputation as a man who not only had good judgment but who also could be relied on to get the job done in difficult circumstances. He did not conduct himself with flair and bravado, but rather with quiet competence. Without men like Boone, the army would have failed the test of leadership, and without question, Boone helped make it an important instrument of national policy on the frontier.

8

THE FINAL YEARS

URING THE WINTER of 1839–1840, Boone engaged in road planning and garrison duties at Fort Leavenworth. Meanwhile, in February two bands of Otos left their villages along the Platte, crossed the Missouri, and struck south. The raiders proved little more than renegade young men bent on the intimidation of white settlers rather than a war party intent on ravaging the Missouri frontier. Even so, by entering homes and demanding food and whiskey and killing hogs and cattle, they brought fear to the whites who had begun to claim lands in the northwestern corner of the state. The Oto chiefs, once again, could not control their young men. To make matters worse two Ioway bands also were reported to be encamped along the Nishnabotna River, where they too went about armed and painted, all the while "levying contributions on the whites, under threats of death." These Ioways, along with the Otos, were reported to be awaiting the arrival of the Sacs, at which time they would "commence direct hostilities."[1]

The news about the bullying by the Otos and Ioways reached Fort Leavenworth in March 1840. Kearny knew that further "admonition" with these Indians would not make them leave settlers alone and keep the peace. Only a "strong and visible" force would appeal to "their fears and not their reason." Consequently, on March 25, Kearny sent Boone and two companies of dragoons across the Missouri to the Nishnabotna. When Boone and his men reached the Indian camp along the river, the Otos and Ioways had not expected to see such a large force nor had they anticipated that the dragoons would come ready for war. They, of course, knew that the army would send some soldiers to find them, but they expected another council with threats. The young men could handle mere words, but more than a few of them arrogantly believed they could successfully stand against the dragoons in a fight.[2]

The sight of some one hundred dragoons, riding stripped for action without the hinderance of lumbering supply wagons and with their carbines clearly cleaned and oiled gave the Otos and Ioways pause. When Boone rode into their camp and swung down from the saddle, the young leaders saw an experienced soldier with a hard face who spoke directly and forcefully. "Where are your leaders?" he no doubt asked. The answer was silence and nervous eyes that shifted across the dragoons who remained mounted, watchful, and ready for action. Then, several men stepped forward as the leaders. What did Boone want? Boone did not want much at all; he got right to the point. The army had learned, he said, that they had been robbing and threatening settlers. The whites had a right to the land that they farmed. The Otos and Ioways did not have any claim to this land. They had other lands, and they could neither hunt nor live in Missouri, nor could they stay. Then Boone told the leaders, as their followers crowded around, that they had to leave Missouri, and they had to leave now. If they did not break camp and return to their villages, the dragoons would force them to leave. If they threatened or harmed other settlers or returned to Missouri he would find them and punish them. The time for talking was over. The army would speak to them no more about keeping the peace. If they were wise, they would not cause him to order the dragoons to use their guns against them or to destroy their camp.

The young Oto and Ioway men could see that they were outnumbered and that the dragoons had superior weapons and a plentiful supply of ammunition. Moreover, Boone and his men clearly were ready for a fight, and they were not prepared to stand against them. Cowed by the military strength of the dragoons and intimidated by Boone's forceful admonishment for them to leave Missouri, the Otos and Ioways broke camp and trailed away toward their villages. Boone and the dragoons patrolled the area for several days to make certain that all bands had departed and that the settlers were safe. Then, he led them back across the Missouri to Fort Leavenworth.

By now councils with various tribes had become routine for Boone. He was one of the few officers that had broad diplomatic experience with the Indians, and his superior officers also knew that he had the military experience and confidence to exercise force if the occasion required it.

Upon his return to Fort Leavenworth, Boone once again conducted routine patrols to the south toward Fort Gibson and engaged in training exercises with his men. Inspections, reviews, and paperwork occupied much of his time as well as the supervision of woodcutting, cleanup details, and building repairs. Every day proved much the same as the one before. Reveille sounded at dawn. A stable call came fifteen minutes later. The bugler blew the sick call at 7:30 A.M., and the men assembled for breakfast twenty minutes later. Then came fatigue, guard, and orderly calls. The dragoons lined up for dinner at noon. Another fatigue call sounded at 1:00, followed by a stable call thirty minutes later. Retreat came at sunset, and tattoo at 9:00. During the course of these daily activities, Boone waited for orders that would take him on another assignment far more exciting and challenging than daily duties at the fort.[3]

He had to wait until the autumn of 1841, however, before he received orders that took him away from Fort Leavenworth for a period of time. Once again, his assignment involved surveying in Indian Territory. In September, Pierce M. Butler became the government agent for the Cherokees, and he opened his office at Fort Gibson in the quarters formerly occupied by General Matthew Arbuckle. The officers at the post, however, resented the presence of an agent among them, because they considered such officials to be little more than Indian lovers who did not understand the real problems between the army and the tribes on the frontier and who constantly meddled in army business, particularly regarding the pacification of the Indians. Their complaints became so numerous and annoying that the army sent Boone to survey a section of land immediately south of the military reservation for the Cherokee Agency. This work did not take much time and Boone soon returned to Fort Leavenworth.[4]

Nathan, however, did not remain there for long. In April 1842, he left the post for Fort Wayne in the Arkansas Territory, where he arrived on April 28. The next day, he departed for Fort Gibson, where he assumed command of Companies D and H as well as a detachment of Company B. There, he continued training activities and made routine patrols in the area, and in early November 1842, Boone and Company H of the dragoons provided the escort for the funeral of Montford Stokes, who had recently been appointed subagent for the Senecas, Shawnees, and Quapaws at Fort Gibson.[5]

Boone did not have another major assignment until the spring of 1843, when General Zachary Taylor, commander of the Second Military Department, informed Adjutant General Roger Jones that Boone had been ordered to embark on another expedition to the west and into the general region that had nearly defeated the dragoons in 1834. Boone had orders to provide protection for white traders on route to Santa Fe. His instructions required him to remain on the left bank of the Arkansas River until he reached the Santa Fe Trail. There, he would meet with traders who passed by and assure them that the army would provide protection and keep the Indians peaceful. After several days he would then proceed south toward the Canadian River and learn about the precise location of the Big Salt Plains, near present-day Freedom, in Wood County, Oklahoma, a five-thousand-acre area of red sand that extended south from the confluence of Buffalo Creek and the Cimarron River. There, groundwater mixed with rock salt and produced a brine that reached the surface, evaporated, and left a white, snow-like crust of salt.[6]

Boone looked forward to the expedition with eagerness, although he keenly remembered the heat and thirst and lack of food that had plagued the summer campaign eight years before. Still, he would leave a month earlier than Dodge in 1834, and when his column of sixty noncommissioned officers and privates rode out of Fort Gibson at 11 A.M. on May 14, 1843, he felt confident that he could once again fly the flag and gain the respect of the tribes who showed a inclination to cause trouble for the traders bound for Santa Fe. Boone led the dragoons across the Verdigris River at Unswatoy's Ferry. Then, after striking northwest through heavy timber for about a dozen miles, the dragoons made camp.[7]

The next morning Boone broke camp about half past seven, which was his preferred time to get on with the day, and the dragoons traveled about twenty-two miles, a distance that still remained an agreeable ride for Boone. As they traveled, he kept a diary and noted the lay of the land, the varieties of trees and the kinds of

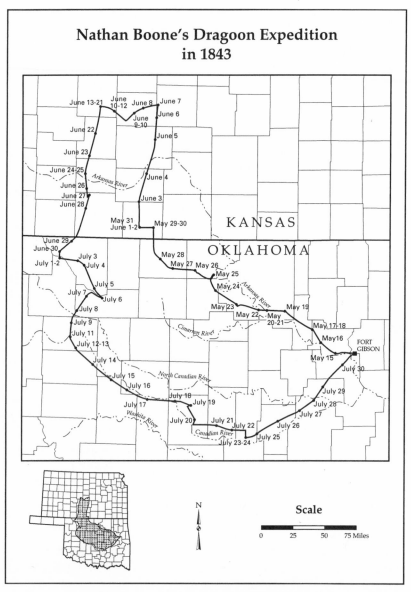

Nathan Boone's Dragoon Expedition in 1843

In 1843, Nathan Boone again led dragoons into the southern Great Plains in the present-day states of Oklahoma and Kansas. His assignment involved assuring travelers on the Santa Fe Trail that the army would protect them and meeting with any tribes in the area to encourage them to keep the peace. Boone kept a journal on this expedition, making many observations about the salt plains in western Oklahoma and providing new information about the environment of the region. *Based on a map in the* Chronicles of Oklahoma *7 (March 1929). Cartographer, Adrianne Nold.*

animals—post oak, blackjack oak, and deer, antelope, and buffalo. On Thursday, May 25, Boone wrote: "Our march to day was principally over the short buffalo grass, the prairie grass having almost entirely disappeared, the timber was getting scarcer, and on leaving one creek it was like putting out to the open sea until we rose the ridge, when a narrow skirt of trees would point out the position of the next." The open, rolling plains still fascinated Boone, and he could not help but marvel at the differences between this land and the country around his home in western Missouri, as well as the land of his childhood along the Ohio River.

On Saturday, May 27, Boone prophetically remarked about the eventual destruction of the buffalo. He wrote: "Passed more recent sign of Buffalo, and what was at no distant day the stamping grounds, of countless hordes of them. The destruction of these animals yearly and their falling off so rapidly makes it certain, almost, that in a few years they will only be known as a rare species." Boone believed that the extensive killing of buffalo by white hunters for shipment of their hides to the east would surely drive them into extinction. "More than 30,000 robes for Commerce come down the Missouri annually, these added to those which go elsewhere, must make the tax on the buffalo robes annually come to exceed 100,000." Boone also added that "Taking into consideration the fact that the animals destroyed for food are taken in the summer while the hair is almost all off, and, of course, the robe useless, we can readily account for this disappearance from the grounds we have been traveling over, and make it certain that the buffalo must soon cease on these plains altogether."

Two days later they had crossed into present-day Kansas, and Boone and the dragoons sighted a band of approximately forty Osages who had just killed twenty-five buffalo. Boone asked them about the location of the Salt Plains and learned that they were within twenty miles of that area. The dragoons camped that night near the Osages and one agreed to go along with them the next day as a guide. When morning dawned, however, Boone received a report that several horses were missing; because their lariats had been cut, it was clearly a case of "foul play." Not long after learning about the stolen horses, Boone reported that the soldiers heard a "great disturbance" coming from the Osage camp, and he soon learned that Pawnee raiders had stolen some of the Osages' horses as well.

Boone responded by sending thirty men and two officers in pursuit. After following the trail at a fast pace for thirty miles, however, the dragoons lost it in a sandy plain filled with buffalo. They returned to camp and reported losing the trail, but they also told Boone that they suspected the Osages were the real thieves and that they had used the Pawnees as a ploy to deflect attention from themselves.

That night Boone had the horses picketed in another bottom along the creek, but so near the Osage camp that no Pawnees would dare come near them. The next morning Boone informed the Osages that he believed that they had stolen the dragoons' horses, and they had to return them before he would allow them to continue their buffalo hunt. The Osages still pleaded innocence and agreed to lead the dragoons on the trail after the Pawnees. Boone, however, knew as much as the Osages about following a trail, and he soon detected their attempt to lead the dragoons in the wrong direction. After the Osages had taken him along the same route that they had led the detachment of dragoons on the previous day, he discovered a second set of tracks that diverged, which the Osages had not wanted him to see. Boone confronted them with the evidence, but they still pleaded ignorance about the theft and professed to know nothing about the second trail.

Boone knew that he had little reason to expect the return of his horses and turned his column ten miles south where he saw a salt plain that looked "like a large lake of white water in an extensive level country" from a distance. Looking down at the plain from the crest of some sand hills, probably in present-day Alfalfa County, Oklahoma, he considered the view "really magnificent." From the appearance of the plain, he wrote, "one might expect to find salt in a solid mass for the whole extent of the plain, of several feet in thickness." After crossing a stream, which he called the Little or Upper Fork of the Arkansas River, the dragoons reached the plain, which they found covered with the "slightest possible film of crystallized Salt on the surface, enough to make it white." Boone always marveled at the workings of nature, whether in the forests or on the prairies and plains; "Such was the effect of Mirage on the plain that we could not see across it, and the buffalo bones whitening in the sun looked like large, white animals in the distance. Buffalo appeared to be standing in water, and, in fact, the whole plain appeared as if surrounded by water." Boone could not determine the source of the salt, but he noted that "This plain is called the Pawsa Salt plain by the Osages—or big Salt." Today, it is known as the Great Salt Plains near Cherokee, Oklahoma.

On June 7, after twenty-five days of reconnaissance, Boone and the dragoons camped in a grove of timber about four miles from the Santa Fe Trail, where they shot an elk, the meat of which Boone called "very delicate," and which his men roasted for their evening meal. The next day they rode toward the Little Arkansas in a "cold, sleety rain" with a north wind, which followed the dragoons all day. That night Boone noted "the rain increased and made our night very uncomfortable." Despite the hardships of heat interrupted with rain and cold, the dragoons, once again, admired Boone's strong constitution. He seemed not to know weariness, and at the age of sixty-two he appeared to be in a constant state of motion when conducting an expedition. Long, hard rides bothered him not at all. On Sunday, June 11, twenty-nine days out of Fort Gibson, for example, Boone took two lieutenants and twelve men on an early morning buffalo hunt. After twenty miles, they located a herd, made their kill, and loaded their packhorses for the return ride to camp, where they arrived at 2:00 A.M.

On June 13, a column of dragoons from Fort Leavenworth, under Captain Philip St. George Cooke, joined Boone and his men on Cabin Creek. That evening Boone reported, "our camp was surrounded by thousands of buffalo, and the grass very much eaten off by them." The next day, Boone sent a hunting party after buffalo. By now Boone was an expert buffalo hunter, and he instructed them to use a short-barreled shotgun with a large ball, and to shoot the buffalo that were thick through the hump because "they will be the fattest that are broadest through there, and plump." Then, the dragoons spent the day butchering and drying buffalo meat to sustain them for the remainder of the expedition. Boone had the men cut the meat in long strips and place it on a low scaffold of poles stretched across a "brisk fire," which, together with the sun, dried it sufficiently in one day to permit it to be packed away for later use.

All in all, the day was uneventful and routine until a "terrible thunderstorm with a great quantity of wind and hail," blew down the tents during the night, and Boone went about the camp in the rain giving orders and encouragement as the wet and cold dragoons re-set their tents as best they could. He also instructed his men about using buffalo dung for their campfires, noting that "it burns like peat" and that it made an "excellent fuel."

Certainly Boone and the dragoons did not want for either meat or fuel. On June 23, he reported that from an elevation of about twenty feet on the plains, they saw a "grand sight of perhaps 10,000 Buffalo feeding on the plain below as far as the eye could reach." They also saw a herd of a dozen wild horses that ran through the buffalo after spotting the dragoons.

Boone and Cooke made camp together for ten days, before Nathan headed south across the Cimarron to explore the Big Salt Plain, near present-day Freedom, Oklahoma, because Cooke believed that his force was sufficiently strong to protect the traders along the Santa Fe Trail. Boone agreed, and he was anxious to execute the remainder of his orders, which involved exploring the Salt Plains. As a result, on June 30, forty-eight days out of Fort Gibson, Boone reached the vicinity of the Big Salt Plain. At this place, he noted, springs periodically boiled up and covered the ground with brine. In time, the salt had crystallized on the surface. To the old salt maker, the plain proved nothing less than fascinating. Boone thoroughly explored the plain and wrote that "a crust of chrystals is now on the plain in many places an inch in thickness, and is easily obtained, perfectly clean and as white as anything can be." Boone and the dragoons dipped their hands and arms into the springs that dotted the plain and marveled when the air evaporated the water and left salt crystals on their skin. The mineral appeared so abundant that its supply seemed to be "unlimited." Talle, an Osage chief whose people camped with the dragoons at that time, told Boone that the Indians boiled water for salt here and that the salt on the ground disappeared after each rain, but the sun brought it back again.

On July 7, Boone buried one of his men by the name of Bean on the bank of a stream that he named Dragoon Creek. Then, he and his men continued to explore the country. Eleven days later and sixty-six days out of Fort Gibson, Boone led the dragoons south and east of the Canadian. He now skirted the south bank of the river "with the view of crossing it," in order to travel on the dividing ridge between the Canadian and Little Rivers to make his way back to Fort Gibson. The Canadian ran dry and lush red plum thickets, which the dragoons "found ripe and very palatable," crowded its banks. Now the heat "parched" the grass and danced in waves before them, and the buffalo had disappeared. By July 20, Boone's men had only enough dried buffalo meat for supper and breakfast the next morning, the latter of which would be the last meal they would eat for two days.

Hungry, they now pressed eastward, striking a road that would take them through the Cross Timber and to a Shawnee encampment where they hoped to acquire beef and corn. On Sunday, July 23, Boone met a party of Creeks who lived nearby and who had sufficient food to meet the needs of the dragoons. "Measures," Boone wrote, "were immediately taken to supply our wants, and the men were soon engaged in preparing their meals with an eagerness which plainly showed their gratification in once more having the means of gratifying their appetites." Although this expedition had not degenerated into the life-threatening campaign of 1834, Boone and the dragoons clearly were tired and hungry, and the sight of the Creeks and the opportunity to acquire needed food supplies lifted their morale. "More merriment and hilarity in Camp to day," Boone reported, "than I have witnessed for some time past." He also noted that "our Creek friends lived on the Canadian; had good farms, an abundance of stock of every description, and seemed to understand the art of living and surrounding themselves with comforts."[8]

The next day, Boone had the dragoons remain in camp to rest and dry the beef from the cattle that they had purchased from the Creeks. Soon word spread through the neighborhood that hungry dragoons had camped nearby and were eager to purchase food. "Indians visited us throughout the course of the day," Boone recorded in his diary, "bringing in marketing of various kinds—Seemed to regard our presence as a kindly visitation of providence in supplying them with means of disposing some of their produce and the means of getting a little money." Boone did not linger long at the camp near the Creeks. By Thursday July 27, he led the dragoons to a road that ran from old Fort Holmes to Fort Gibson, at a point "about four miles from the Canadian where Fort Holmes is located."[9]

Now the dragoons were close to Fort Gibson, and Boone and his men eagerly pressed forward. On July 31, after seventy-nine days in the field, Boone had the dragoons on the trail at 5:00 A.M. Soon they saw the timber that skirted the Arkansas River, together with the elevated hills that surrounded Fort Gibson and a series of ridges that Boone called the Devil's Card Table. They struck the Arkansas at 10:00 and followed it down to Fort Gibson, where at 1:00 P.M. Boone had his men form for inspection on the parade ground. However, Boone did not submit his report to Brigadier General Zachary Taylor until August 11, because he immediately came down with a severe cold, perhaps brought on by riding in a "constant drizzling rain" the day before he arrived back at the fort. General Taylor read Boone's report with great interest and informed headquarters at Fort Smith that Boone's journal provided "much valuable and curious information, particularly in relation to the Salt region on the Red Forks of the Arkansas." Taylor also reported that "the instructions given to Captain Boone were faithfully carried out, and much credit is due to him and his officers for the good management of the expedition." By so doing, Boone provided valuable geographical information about the southern Great Plains to the soldiers, traders, and settlers who ventured into the region.[10]

After the summer expedition of 1843, Boone remained at Fort Gibson, participating in several other expeditions. For example, a year later, on August 31, 1844, Commissioner of Indian Affairs T. Hartley Crawford wrote to Boone that he had learned that officials from the Republic of Texas planned to hold a council with the Comanche and other Plains Indians on Tawakoni Creek near the Brazos River on September 15. The Texans wanted a representative of the United States present to empower those treaties with the force of its government, and Crawford wanted Boone to attend the proceedings and conduct the negotiations for the federal government. For some reason, however, Crawford did not expect the Indians to arrive at the council site before the end of September. Crawford instructed Boone to take a company of dragoons with him "not from any apprehension of Danger to yourself or the Texan Commissioner, but to make an impression upon the Indians." Because the council would be held soon, Crawford asked Boone to leave as quickly as possible. Clearly, Boone had gained a good reputation for establishing the presence of the federal government during his career in the army, and when either the Office of Indian Affairs or the War Department needed someone to undertake a mission of this kind, officials immediately thought of Boone.[11]

Crawford prepared a rough draft of a treaty for Boone to take with him and gave him instructions to insert other provisions or articles if he thought it expedient to do so. The Commissioner of Indian Affairs and the War Department trusted Boone's experience in dealing with the Indians and his ability to think on his feet and represent the best interests of the United States. Crawford's instructions and draft treaty, however, did not arrive at Fort Gibson until late September and, although Boone departed for Texas and a rendezvous with the Comanches on September 25, time was against him. On the twelfth, the Department of State had informed the Texas legation in Washington, D.C., that Boone would probably arrive at the council site about October 1, and that they "hoped the Indians will be detained until his arrival." However, by the time Boone had traveled the four hundred miles to the council site on Tawakoni Creek, the Comanches either had already left or had never arrived, and he had no alternative but to return to Fort Gibson, which he reached after a round-trip march that lasted six weeks.[12]

Boone's next assignment came in February 1845, after some Creeks, whose village, Took-paf-ka Town, was located on their reservation on the north bank of Little River, about five miles from present-day Holdenville, Oklahoma, began fleeing to Fort Gibson because they feared an attack by the Osages and Wichitas. On February 15, members of a Creek hunting party had discovered the trail of a band of Pawnees on their land. Convinced that the Pawnees had come onto their reservation to steal horses, the Creeks followed the trail and found the camp of Pawnees, who showered the Creeks with arrows but inflicted little injury. This assault infuriated the Creeks, who had not meant to harm the Pawnees. In response, the Creeks fired guns at the Pawnees and killed four of them. When the Creek hunting party reported what they had done, fear of reprisals on the isolated Creek settlements spread through the tribe and the neighboring Chickasaws. This fear was not unfounded. On March 1, 1845, the Creek agent, James Logan, reported, "A band of four or five hundred Pawnee Maha came into the neighborhood to avenge the death of their people."[13]

The commander at Fort Gibson, General Arbuckle, was uncertain about the identity of the intruders on Creek lands but he did not think that they were Pawnee Mahaws. Rather, he suspected "some bands of Kiowas, Comanches or Wichitas," and he ordered two companies of dragoons to proceed to the Little River settlement to ensure the safety of the Creeks. In the meantime, rumors reached the Creek settlement on the Verdigris River that the Osages had combined with the Pawnees and other hostile plains tribes and that they had attacked and destroyed the Creek settlement at the mouth of the Red Fork of the Cimarron River. After killing the inhabitants, this war party allegedly moved toward the Creek agency and the Verdigris settlements. With most of the Creek fighting men on their way to relieve the Little River settlement, the women and children along the Verdigris remained unprotected. Creek agent James Logan reported their state of near panic, saying, "I should not previously have believed the Creeks to be so excitable a people." But, he noted, "In extenuation, however, it may be said that they knew no mercy would be shown by the invaders. Everything was in the greatest possible confusion. Here was to be seen a crowd of the poorer class of women on foot, loaded down with their children and bundles containing their valuables; here a line of wagons laden with the property of the richer class with their negro drivers . . . and their owners and their families on horseback; there a warrior begrimed with paint, rifle and tomahawk in hand, making the welkin ring with the discordant war whoop!" Logan also observed: "The rivers were literally covered with canoes, laden with women, children . . . all wending their way to Fort Gibson; here they all congregated, conceiving themselves secure under its protection." As the frightened Creeks fled to the safety of Fort Gibson, they were not alone. Logan and several white traders left with them for the protection of the fort.[14]

The chiefs from the Verdigris settlements demanded that General Arbuckle provide them with more protection, and he agreed to send a company of dragoons up the Canadian and ordered two companies of infantry to ascend the Arkansas. When the chiefs, however, called upon their people to march against the invading Indian army, they were met with resistance. Arbuckle reported that "at this emergency . . . many absolutely refused to budge a foot, asserting as a reason that as *they* kept all their money, they might likewise do the fighting." This objection stemmed from the custom of the federal government of paying the tribal annuities to the chiefs for distribution to their people. The chiefs, however, usually kept a large portion of the annuities in the form of goods, food, and cattle, which caused considerable complaint among the "common people." Still, the chiefs raised a force of about two hundred men and left to meet the invaders. After two days of searching, the Creek army could not find the enemy, and it became clear that the alarm was due solely to rumors. In response, Arbuckle wrote, "They had however a serious effect in disturbing the quietude of the country, and many were and still continue to be alarmed for the safety of the frontier settlements."[15]

Boone was involved in this disturbance; on February 25, General Arbuckle sent him with a company of dragoons to the Little River settlement. They were to provide protection to the Creeks who had not fled the village and to drive away any hostile tribes in the area. After a hard ride for two days, which covered about half the distance between Fort Gibson and the Little River settlement, Boone met a party of Creeks who told him that the threats of an invading Indian army or even retribution by a small war party were nothing more than rumors. Boone proceeded on to the Creek village on Little River, but returned a week later after determining that no danger of an Indian attack existed.[16]

In the late autumn of 1845 General Arbuckle, now commanding the Second Military Department, sent Boone among the Cherokees to keep the peace. Various opposing groups within the Cherokee Nation vied for control of the tribal government, and political relations remained bitter between the Old Settlers, Eastern, and Treaty Cherokees. Personal animosities resulted in a host of killings, and the Cherokee problem in the Indian Territory proved especially complex during the 1840s. At that time the Cherokee Nation numbered approximately eighteen thousand members, with twelve thousand under the leadership of John Ross, who had opposed the removal treaty signed at New Echota in 1835. This group was known as the Eastern Cherokees. The followers of the late Major Ridge numbered four thousand and were known as the Treaty Party, for they supported the Treaty of New Echota; meanwhile, two thousand Cherokees who had immigrated to Arkansas as early as 1794 and whom the federal government moved to northeastern Oklahoma in 1832, called themselves the Old Settlers or the Western Cherokees.[17]

The political divisions were numerous. The Old Settlers organized around a council and three chiefs, but they did not have a written constitution, in contrast to their more populous eastern brethren, who were a majority of the tribe. Although John Ross sought union with the Old Settlers, they rejected his demand for fee simple title to Cherokee lands in the Indian Territory, that is, the right of private rather than tribal or communal ownership of the land. The most serious division, however, occurred between the Eastern Cherokees and the Treaty Party. The hatred between these groups worsened on June 27, 1839, when Major Ridge, his son John, and Elias Boudinot were murdered by members of the Ross faction. Animosities festered; in May 1842, friends of Major Ridge killed a member of the Ross faction in Arkansas who had allegedly been involved with the Ridge murder. In response, the Ross followers armed and prepared for reprisal, and whites who crossed Cherokee lands and conducted business with them now considered their lives in danger.[18]

As a result, Archibald Yell, governor of Arkansas, demanded that the federal government protect whites from the Cherokees along the Arkansas and Oklahoma border. Pierce M. Butler, the Cherokee agent, pleaded for understanding and argued that conflicts between whites and Indians were "eight times out of ten provoked on the part of itinerant persons from all parts of the United States, tempted or induced there by gain. It is not too much the habit abroad," he wrote, "to cry out 'Indian outrage,' without a just knowledge of the facts." Butler also contended, "All persons familiar with that portion of the Cherokees bordering on Crawford and Washington counties, in Arkansas, know that they are industrious, intelligent, and neighborly disposed. The inhabitants of those two populous counties are distinguished as a laboring, intelligent, high-minded, and judicious people. It is not from them the difficulties occur, or complaints are made, but from a plundering predatory class. . . . These are evils of no small import, and of everyday's occurrence, and which produce angry and embittered feelings." Despite Butler's contention that Arkansans stirred up trouble, whites continued to charge that the Indians made the frontier unsafe for settlers.[19]

At the same time, the Cherokees continued to fight among themselves. On August 7, 1843, the tribe conducted its second election under the constitution of September 6, 1839. Violence and the destruction of election papers resulted, but the federal government believed the Cherokees could manage their own affairs. Still, more killings followed, including several whites. In addition, the Old Settlers demanded a separate part of the Cherokee reservation for their own use, where they would be free from the arguing and fighting between the Ross and Ridge factions. The Old Settlers also wanted a revision of their treaties to provide them with a larger share of the Cherokee annuities. The Ross party, however, which controlled tribal government, responded by saying that the Cherokee Nation was represented by a republican form of government and that its officials could not favor factions within the tribe. In addition, the Old Settlers were unhappy because the tribal council declared all salt springs to be tribal property. This edict of October 30, 1843, stripped many Old Settlers of their property and chief source of income from salt making. The Treaty Party also demanded a per capita payment from the tribal government as provided by the treaty of 1835. Thus, relations between the Old Settlers, Treaty Party, and Ross faction had deteriorated so badly by the summer of 1845 that the Old Settlers and Treaty Party discussed leaving the Cherokee Nation for a new settlement in Mexico. They held a conference to discuss removal and even sent a delegation from Evansville, Arkansas, about September 1, to explore lands in Texas and the Southwest.[20]

In early November 1845, after a series of assaults initiated by the Treaty Party against the Cherokee government and those who supported it, the Cherokee council organized a company of "light horse"—police—"to pursue and arrest all fugitives from justice." Certainly, many whites expected bloody reprisals between the Ross and Treaty Party Cherokees, and they believed that the Ross faction planned to massacre those who opposed it. With the whites expecting nothing less than civil war, the army received numerous requests for dragoons to ensure their safety and to keep the peace on the Arkansas frontier and in the Indian Territory. General Arbuckle at Fort Gibson believed that the Ross faction merited the blame for the Cherokee difficulties. On November 15, he wrote to George Lowrey, acting chief, saying, "the Light Horse must be abandoned at once," because he had learned that this police force was intimidating the Treaty Party and Old Settlers. He also demanded that Chief Lowrey arrest the people who had committed murder. Then, without consulting or notifying Cherokee officials, he sent Boone and Company H of the dragoons to the "scene of the disorders."

Soon thereafter, on November 20, 1845, Arbuckle again wrote to Lowrey, from Fort Smith, Arkansas, that he had ordered Boone and his company to remain near Evansville, Arkansas, and notify all the Cherokees displaced by tribal fighting not to cross onto tribal lands in the Indian Territory for the purpose of violence. If they did so, Arbuckle warned, they would forfeit the "protection they now enjoy." Boone, who had been on a leave of absence since October 1, rejoined his company at Camp Washington, Arkansas, on November 4. On November 16, he arrived at Evansville on the Arkansas line.[21]

Although the Cherokees respected Boone, they resented his presence with the dragoons, because they considered Arbuckle's action a violation of their sovereignty and interference in tribal affairs. While Chief Lowrey asserted that the only federal official with whom he would deal was the agent of the Cherokees, Arbuckle paid no attention and expected Boone to keep the peace. Although a general outbreak of violence did not occur, by December General Arbuckle contended that a group of Cherokees under the leadership of Stand Watie of the Treaty Party near Evansville was still causing problems by "killing stock, hauling off corn, and plundering houses of those who have been forced to leave their homes." They were, according to Arbuckle, "a mongrel set of Cherokees, white men with Indian wives, citizens of the United States and one or two mulattoes. . . . They smack of a rebellious spirit and show conclusively that the company have some latent object in view inimical to the peace of the country." Boone, however, saw the situation differently and with less alarm than Arbuckle and reported, "We do not apprehend any act of hostility on their part; they appear determined to abide by the decision of the President of the United States upon their present situation."[22]

Although Boone correctly determined that the Cherokees had no intention of provoking a conflict with the United States, he erred by assuming that they would willingly and easily submit to federal arbitration of their tribal problems. The Cherokee factions adamantly believed they could handle their own political differences and that they could enforce their own laws. They did not need Boone or any other soldiers among them to do so. For them, the alarm that whites were in danger had been caused not by tribal factionalism but by sensational rumors about Cherokee violence arising from the settlers, particularly those in Arkansas.

In response to the general state of unrest along the Arkansas line, Arbuckle sent two additional companies of dragoons to help Boone keep the peace and prevent Stand Watie of the Treaty Party from recruiting followers to help him attack the Cherokee government. Despite the objections to his presence from the Cherokee Nation, Boone easily saw that the tribal conflicts were serious and major bloodshed was a strong possibility, and he remained encamped for several months near Evansville. During that time representatives from the Office of Indian Affairs and the army attempted to negotiate a settlement among the hostile factions. In late winter General Arbuckle reported that the "persuasion of Captain Boone . . . prevented other recruits from joining Stand Watie . . . and organizing for a threatened aggressive movement against the established Cherokee officers."[23]

Certainly, the presence of Boone and the dragoons helped prevent civil war among the Cherokees, and it helped ensure an equitable distribution of annuities among the members of the Cherokee Nation. On January 2, 1846, Boone and Major B. L. E. Bonneville reported to Captain James H. Prentiss, Assistant Adjutant General of the Second Military Department at Fort Smith, "No one charged with crimes by the Cherokee authorities is known to be receiving rations from the United States. Though idle and worthless individuals might escape the closest examination, yet so soon as detected, they would be at once dropped from the provision list." Moreover, Boone compiled a list of the Cherokees who were entitled to receive federal support in the Fort Smith area. After excluding their slaves and counting children under five years of age as being eligible for half rather than full rations, he determined that 325 Cherokees were entitled to full rations and 60 to half rations.[24]

In actuality, General Arbuckle, by sending Boone and the dragoons among the Cherokees, had inhibited the establishment of law and order rather than promoting it. The interference of the army in an internal Cherokee affair slowed the process of Cherokee government, hindered the enforcement of Cherokee laws, and helped portray the Ross faction as the oppressor of the Cherokee Nation. Moreover, Boone could not prevent murder and reprisals among the Cherokees. When some Cherokees fled the violence in Indian Territory, crossing the Arkansas line and making camp near Evansville in Washington County, the white settlers asked Boone to remove the Indians. But he did not have the authority to make them return to their reserve.

Although federal authorities and Cherokee officials did not resolve the matter of factional fighting with a major adjustment of the treaty until August 6, 1846, Boone had played an instrumental role in the execution of federal military and Indian policy on the frontier. He had ridden into a dangerous situation, met with Cherokee leaders, and spoken to them with honesty and candor about the necessity to keep the peace. As a result, he helped maintain order among the Cherokees when the tribe teetered on the verge of civil war. By so doing, he served not only his nation but the Cherokees as well, with dedication and integrity.[25]

After settlement of the Cherokee affair, Boone remained at the dragoon camp near Evansville until October 1846, then he returned to Fort Gibson where he received a six-month leave of absence beginning on October 18. Although this leave would have required him to return to duty in April 1847, he apparently received an extension because he did not report for duty at Fort Leavenworth until June 25. When Congress declared war with Mexico in April 1846, Boone was busy keeping the hostile Cherokee factions apart. Nathan, now sixty-five, wanted to take his company to Mexico, but his age disqualified him and his health also may have begun to fail at this time. In any event, following the death of Major Estace Trenor on February 16, 1847, President James K. Polk officially granted Boone, the senior captain of the regiment, an immediate promotion to Major of the First Dragoons. However, when the end of the Mexican War came on February 2, 1848, with the signing of the Treaty of Guadalupe-Hidalgo, Boone remained at Fort Leavenworth.[26]

After his return to duty following his peace-keeping assignment among the Cherokees, Boone did not take the field again. Instead, garrison life occupied his time. By now, he had accomplished all that he would achieve as a military man. And although Boone knew that he would never have another command in the field because of age as well as failing health, the excitement of the past loomed bright in his mind, and he could not let go of it. All too frequently, he spent much time recalling his early days and telling his stories over and over again, often aided by the warming and mellowing effects of whiskey. One observer at Fort Leavenworth noted, "At present there are a few officers at this post who indulge quite too freely for their own health, or for the comfort of their friends. The most remarkable one in this respect is Colonel B——, of the Dragoons, who can sit up night after night for a week imbibing his toddy, and relating anecdotes by the thousand. The old gentleman's vivacity, wit, and humor are exceedingly entertaining to strangers. Some of his subordinates, however, who have been stationed at the same post with him for several years, say, that after he begins to relate over his anecdotes a few times, they cease to excite any mirth, and become a nuisance."[27]

By 1848, then, Boone had become something of a bore to many of the younger dragoons, especially those who had heard his stories time and again—the flight from the Shawnees with his father in a canoe across the Ohio River; the trip with a new wife from Virginia to Missouri; his run across Missouri in the dead of winter; his confrontation with White Hair in the Osage village; the Sac attack on his rangers in Illinois during the War of 1812; surveying the Neutral Ground; the summer expedition of 1834, when more than a hundred dragoons lost their lives to heat and dysentery; the Ioway reconnaissance; running the Otos out of Missouri; the Salt Plains expedition; the Cherokee affairs.

Boone had experienced much, particularly as a ranger and dragoon. He had been a trapper and long hunter, a surveyor, and a soldier. Indians had shot at him, and he at them. He had known life-threatening cold, hunger that bordered on starvation, exhaustion, and fear. Boone had also experienced the exhilaration of leadership, self-satisfaction upon completing a difficult job, and the peace of mind that public service often provides. He did not, however, experience loneliness. Or, if he did, Boone liked it, just as his father had loved his hunts far from home over weeks and months on end. From the moment that Boone joined the Missouri Rangers in 1832 until he retired in 1848, he spent most of his time away from home. He did not need the day-to-day comforts and companionship of a family, other than that of his fellow rangers and soldiers as they huddled around a campfire or rode across the land executing their orders, doing their duty. Boone wanted and needed nothing more, but he alone understood this, not the young recruits who found him a tiresome bother.

Boone did not bore the young dragoons at Fort Leavenworth for long after returning from his extended leave. On September 9, 1848, he left Fort Leavenworth, never to return to the post or to the army that he loved. Now, at the age of sixty-seven, his health had failed so much that he could no longer serve on duty. The hunts of the distant past, the months of making camps in the cold, rain, and snow, the long marches with the dragoons across burning plains and without adequate food and water now took their toll. Ill, he swung into the saddle of his horse for the last time as an officer in the First Regiment of the Dragoons. Although he received a promotion, based on seniority, to Lieutenant Colonel of the Second Dragoons on July 25, 1850, by President Millard Fillmore, he never served in the army again.[28]

When Boone returned home, he kept about the house. Olive and his children and grandchildren that still lived in the vicinity of Ash Grove in Greene County, Missouri, provided company. Mostly he sat on the cabin porch and offered advice to his slaves about cultivating the corn crop and tending the livestock, but his heart was even less engaged in farming than it had been when he was a young man. As the days faded one into another, Boone's health remained tenuous and a local doctor eventually diagnosed his illness as dropsy, the abnormal buildup of fluids in the body.

In 1850, Lyman Draper, a roving historian who collected reminiscences about frontier life, contacted Boone about visiting him to gain information concerning the life of his father. In mid-December Boone was reported to be in "feeble health and inclined to be dropsical," but he was well enough to meet with Draper at his farm during the autumn of 1851. By that time, Boone had provided written answers for seventeen of thirty-three questions that Draper had sent him. When Draper visited Boone, he wrote down the answers to the remaining questions while Nathan recalled the past. At that time Draper agreed with the observations of German traveler Gottfried Duden, who in the mid-1820s said of Nathan that "only a few hours spent with persons like Boone would suffice to dispel all ideas of crudity which one might entertain [of backwoods people]." At that time, Boone provided Draper with the only detailed information about Daniel that can be considered relatively accurate. He also gave a considerable account of his own life at that time, although his sixty-nine years now began to play tricks on his mind. In late July 1851, Boone was in "bad health," and he confided to a friend that he did not believe he would live "very long." Still, he must have had some strength and energy, because he made this revelation when he was riding about his farm checking his crops and the activities of his slaves.[29]

As Boone's health continued to decline and as the years passed, he realized that he would never return to the army. Still, in mid-January 1853, he reported that he and his family were in "reasonable health," although he told Draper in a letter that "I am much the same as when you was here sometimes better and then again worse." Soon thereafter, however, his health took a turn for the worse, and for a few months he was "very ailing." On July 15, 1853, at the age of seventy-two and after twenty years of service in the army since the Black Hawk War, he resigned his commission in the dragoons.[30]

Boone would live for three more years; by early October 1856, he realized that his life had reached its end and that his health was quickly failing. Much like his father long ago, Boone met his imminent death with cool calculation. On October 12, 1856, he dictated his will, which was later filed with the Greene County Probate Court. In it Boone bequeathed all of his land, slaves, and livestock as well as all other property and accounts to Olive. Boone also provided that she could dispose of this property "as she may choose" at the time of her death. He appointed Olive and his son Benjamin Howard as executors of his estate. Four days later, on October 16, 1856, Nathan Boone died at his home, after being bedridden for thirteen days.[31]

Benjamin Howard, Nathan's youngest son, who lived with his parents in their cabin and operated the farm, stayed at his father's bedside much of the time, just as devoted to Nathan as his father had been to Daniel. Benjamin Howard later wrote that during his father's last days, "he said nothing about dying or at least nothing about future happiness, he only spoke of wanting his will written so that he could provide for mother." After Boone died, Benjamin Howard placed him in a coffin and carried Nathan to the site that his father had selected in the nearby family burial ground, which could be seen from the house. Boone's family crowded around his grave—Benjamin Howard and his wife and children; his sister Mary, who had married Alfred Hosman; his sister Melcina, wife of F. T. Frazier; perhaps Nathan's sons James and John Coburn; and a few others. After the final prayer, nearly everyone walked back to the house, while Benjamin Howard spaded Missouri soil onto his father's coffin. A life had ended, and its legacy passed into the history of the American frontier.[32]

EPILOGUE

BOONE HAD NOT been very attentive to Olive during their fifty-seven years of marriage. In their early years, he had spent much of his time running his trapline and making long hunts in western Missouri. The War of 1812 and his work as a government surveyor also took him away from home for months at a time. But this early home life must have seemed complete and his presence nearly constant to Olive and the children, compared with the time that he spent with them after joining the Missouri Rangers for the Black Hawk War and transferring to the regular army and the dragoons in 1833. Indeed, during the sixteen years after 1832, when he organized a ranger company in St. Charles, until he took his final leave of absence from the army in September 1848, the months that he spent away from home totaled more than a dozen years.

Boone's homecomings were so rare and special that his children remembered them for the rest of their lives. They recalled their father unbuckling his money belt and opening the secret compartments where he kept the gold coins he received as his army pay. His children also remembered the excitement of seeing him ride down the lane that led to their Greene County home and the happiness and relief in their mother's eyes to see that he had come home safely once again. Although Boone's leaves of absence from the army usually lasted several months, he never thought about resigning before his health failed. Nothing at home compelled him to reconsider his lifestyle. Like his father, Nathan was a loner who preferred life in the open spaces to the confinement of a farm. He had no reservations or guilt about leaving, if not abandoning, his family for months at a time. Certainly, he met his basic obligations to his family by providing a home, land, and money, but he met his responsibilities to the army

The youngest child of Daniel and Rebecca Boone in 1781, Nathan lived his entire life on the frontier in Virginia, Kentucky, Missouri, Iowa, and Oklahoma. As a hunter, trapper, surveyor, ranger, and dragoon, Boone spent much of his time away from home although he owned a considerable amount of land and a number of slaves in both St. Charles and Greene Counties in Missouri. *State Historical Society of Missouri, Columbia.*

with far more dedication and success than he did with Olive and the children.[1]

Indeed, the most that he apparently ever did around the house and farm, other than to engage in a few basic repairs and give instructions to his slaves, was to sire children. During the course of their long marriage, Olive bore fourteen children. The records of their births are incomplete, but James, their first child, was born on July 3, 1800. He was followed by Delinda, Jemima, Susan, and Nancy. Then came Olive, Benjamin Howard, John Coburn, Levica, Melcina, Mary, Sarah, Mahala, and Mela, who died as a child. Although the birth dates for most of Boone's children remain unknown, Nancy was born in 1813, and circumstantial evidence places the birth of Benjamin Howard in 1814 and that of John Coburn two years later, while Mary was born on January 22, 1822. Even by frontier standards, Nathan and Olive had a large family, and Olive was either pregnant, nursing a child, or raising young children for upwards of thirty years. If she bore children into her early forties, she would have given birth to her last child sometime

Olive Vanbibber married Nathan Boone in 1799 when she was only sixteen years old. She bore fourteen children and kept the house and family together when Nathan hunted, surveyed, and served in the military. She died in 1858, two years after Nathan. *State Historical Society of Missouri, Columbia.*

during the mid-1820s. In any event, Boone's children probably were born before 1830, so the youngest would have been far more than toddlers when he joined the Missouri Rangers to fight in the Black Hawk War and essentially left home for sixteen years.[2]

Overall Boone's private life is difficult to trace, because he left so few personal papers. In 1830, when he still lived in his fine stone house on the Femme Osage, Boone owned ten slaves. Three boys and two girls were under ten years of age, while the census recorder placed three males in the age category ranging from ten to fourteen. He also recorded one female as between ten and twenty-four years of age and one woman over fifty-five years old. While the two older women probably were the mothers of the eight children, no adult male served the Boone household or farm. With at least two sons still at home, Boone had little need for additional male labor to tend his corn crop and livestock. As a result, he probably kept the black children for capital gains at some future sale. He sold most of his slaves when he moved to Greene County in 1837, and in 1840 he only owned three bondsmen—a male and female somewhere between the ages of ten and twenty-four and a boy under ten years old. These slaves were probably a family.[3]

By 1850, Boone owned fifteen slaves; four were adults who, along with eleven children ranging in ages from two to eighteen, also probably constituted families. These bondsmen helped care for 200 improved and 440 unimproved acres, the latter of which Boone used for grazing 40 sheep, 19 beef cattle, 12 horses, 10 milk cows, 8 oxen, and 40 hogs. On the improved acreage, he produced 2,000 bushels of corn, 560 bushels of oats, and 450 bushels of wheat. Olive and the slave women made 300 pounds of butter from the cream and cleaned 37 pounds of wool for weaving. At that time, Boone's livestock carried a valuation of $1,000 and his implements $250, while his section of land was worth $2,000 or approximately $3.12 per acre. Based on this scale of operation in terms of land, livestock, grain production, and slave ownership, Boone was a prosperous farmer nearly akin to the planter class. Beyond this, the records do not permit a more exact tracing of his home life.[4]

The historical evidence, however, indicates that Melcina's husband, who was a businessman in Ash Grove, and Mary's husband, who farmed south of town, contested Nathan's will. Apparently, they believed that as his sons-in-law who lived close by, they and Boone's daughters were entitled to a greater share of the estate, especially in land and slaves. Benjamin Howard told Lyman Draper that his father's will was "not satisfactory to all," particularly for "two of my brother in laws that is very much displeased." He noted, however, "the balance of the children is well pleased." Eventually, the complaining became too much for Olive and, on November 17, 1856, she renounced Nathan's will and agreed to sell his property except for the land and house. The children could buy whatever they wanted, and she would divide the proceeds among them.[5]

On November 24, 1856, Olive held an auction at the farm. At that time Nathan's eleven slaves were sold for $9,006, with the prices ranging from $300 to $1,257. Olive bought one slave named Rueben for $800, and Mary's husband, Alfred Hosman, bought Cork for $1,202. F. T. Frazier, Melcina's husband, bought Peter for $726. Local residents acquired the other slaves. Boone's other personal property—74 hogs, 26 cows, 25 sheep, 23 horses, and 8 oxen, together with 5,600 bushels of oats, 70 bushels of wheat, and several hundred bushels of corn either shelled or in the crib, plus tools, farm equipment, beds, dresser, tables, clock, washstand and other items—brought $3,928.75. After the sale Olive continued to live with Benjamin Howard at the home place. By that time, she was in "very bad health," and she lived only two more years. On November 12, 1858, she died at the age of seventy-five. Following her death and after a lengthy court fight, the children divided the property and, over time, either sold or lost it.[6]

Moreover, at the time of Boone's death, the country in western Missouri no longer remained part of the frontier. Settlers had claimed much of the land, merchants plied their trade in a host of towns, and Missourians thought not about Indian attacks but about slavery and civil war. By the outbreak of the Civil War, Boone's children had essentially scattered, and few residents of the Ash Grove vicinity—or Americans in general—knew much or anything about Nathan. Yet, Boone and others like him played an important role in resettling the Indians west of the Mississippi as well as keeping the peace along the prairie-plains transition area. Boone did not make Indian or military policy, but he executed many of the policy decisions that contributed to the pacification and settlement of the frontier. Simply put, Boone helped make the army function on the frontier as the War Department and Congress intended. He always served as a dedicated, responsible, and reliable soldier and officer; both military and civilian officials trusted him to get a job done, whether it involved surveying a tribal boundary, leading an expedition to show the power and presence of the army among the Indians, or training dragoons for a fight.

Boone served with the dragoons at a time when federal policy in relation to the settlement of the trans-Mississippi West frontier had not been clearly thought out. Indeed, federal decisions involved little more than provision for moving the eastern tribes west of the Mississippi River, keeping the peace among them, and protecting white settlers and traders who ventured onto the Great Plains. This task proved formidable for an army that always remained under authorized strength and whose training left much to be desired, but Boone played a major role in the execution of that policy. He did so at a time when most easterners considered soldiers to be little more than the dregs of society. Boone, however, did not know about this condescending attitude of many of his countrymen, because he did not have any contact with them.[7]

Although service in the frontier army meant enduring poor living conditions and the monotonous meals of beans, salted pork, and coffee, these hardships were of little consequence to Boone, who had been reared on the frontier and who had spent much of his early life living out of a pack. Moreover, while army pay never matched the incomes that men could make in a host of activities as civilians, it was steady and reliable. His officer pay enabled him to provide for his wife and the younger children, buy land and slaves, and have enough security to meet his needs after retirement.[8]

Certainly, Boone's advancement through the ranks proved gradual, but this reflected army policy rather than lack of ability or achievement on his part. In Boone's army, officers advanced solely based on seniority in their regiments. When Boone served, the army did not have a retirement list that permitted officers to leave with a pension and thus allow for the advancement of junior officers. Congress rejected a retirement system because it would not only be expensive and place a burden on taxpayers but also set a precedent for the civil service. Consequently, officers held onto their ranks until their health forced them to resign or until death removed them from service. This policy both hurt and helped Boone. He held his rank of captain from 1833 until 1847 when a death enabled his promotion to major. Most of his service at the rank of major, however, was spent when he was at home ill with dropsy. Moreover, only another death permitted his promotion to lieutenant colonel in 1850. Yet when he held that rank he never served at a garrison or in the field. Instead, he remained ill at home. Boone maintained his active service in the ranks of major and lieutenant colonel because that status entitled him to receive his salary, even though he was not on duty for six years before he finally resigned from the army in 1853.[9]

The failure of the federal government to provide a retirement policy for the army meant that overage, tired, and ill officers, such as Boone, continued to block the advancement of younger men whose vigor the army desperately needed at its frontier posts. At the time Boone resigned, an officer might spend twenty to thirty years reaching the rank of major; West Point graduates, who made up about 73 percent of the officer corps, bitterly resented the presence of uneducated men, such as Boone, among them. Yet, while the graduates of West Point had the best training in the world as engineers, the army still needed Boone and officers like him, for only they were experienced enough to lead soldiers on grueling campaigns across the frontier and conduct delicate negotiations with Indians. While Boone's health held, then, the army was well served by the wisdom he had gained through experience. Both eastern and immigrant recruits, whether Irish, German, or some other nationality, learned much from him about making their way on the frontier in the army.[10]

Nathan Boone—trapper, hunter, surveyor, ranger, and dragoon—lived much of his life in the harsh environment of the prairie-plains frontier. His life's work contributed to the removal of the tribes to Indian Territory, the early successes in pacifying of the frontier, and the white settlement of the trans-Mississippi West. A genetic and cultural scion of his father, Nathan became the only son of Daniel to achieve national recognition, if not fame, in his own right.

Yet much of Boone's life remains an enigma. As a poorly educated man he left few letters; his reflections to Lyman Draper provide the only substantive, though limited, first-hand account of his life. About his family, much remains unknown. Certainly, he supported the institution of slavery as a necessary labor supply for his agricultural endeavors, but he did not leave a trace of his opinions about the institution. Nor can much be said about his relationship to his wife, children, and friends. His footprints on the past must be traced through the diaries and reports of others. Yet, many footprints remain today. In Iowa, the dragoon trail that Boone helped blaze can still be followed, and a county was named for him. His elegant and well-crafted home near the Femme Osage in St. Charles County is open to the public, and Boone's log house in Greene County still exists, as well. Fort Osage, which he helped found, has been reconstructed on the Missouri. His salt lick remains isolated, but the state of Missouri has made the area a park with a trail for a self-guided tour around the springs Boone used.

Boone, of course, had his strengths and weaknesses like any other man, but his lifelong credits far exceed the debits in terms of service to his country. On November 1, 1856, the editor of the *Weekly Jefferson Inquirer* reflected cogently and accurately about Boone: "His life has been one of usefulness and true devotion to his country, and while we regret his loss as a friend, a citizen, and a patriot, we are thankful that such men did live, and participate in the struggles of our country, at a time when their services were needed." Most men would be grateful to have that said of them when their own lives reach an end.[11]

NOTES

1. The Early Years

1. Notes of Border History—Chiefly Illustrative of the Life of Col. Daniel Boone, Vol. 2, 1851, 150–51, Lyman C. Draper Collection, microfilm, State Historical Society of Missouri, Columbia (hereafter SHS); John Mack Faragher, *Daniel Boone: The Life and Legend of an American Pioneer,* 206.

2. Notes of Border History, 150–51, Lyman C. Draper Collection, SHS; Faragher, *Daniel Boone,* 213; John Bakeless, *Daniel Boone,* 258–60.

3. Faragher, *Daniel Boone,* 206. For log house construction in the Ohio Valley, see Donald A. Hutslar, *The Architecture of Migration: Log Construction in the Ohio Country, 1750–1850.*

4. Notes of Border History, 101–29, Lyman C. Draper Collection, SHS; Faragher, *Daniel Boone,* 146.

5. Notes of Border History, 129–43, Lyman C. Draper Collection, SHS; Faragher, *Daniel Boone,* 215–16.

6. Notes of Border History, 152, Lyman C. Draper Collection, SHS; Faragher, *Daniel Boone,* 216–17; Bakeless, *Daniel Boone,* 288, 291–94.

7. Bakeless, *Daniel Boone,* 295; Faragher, *Daniel Boone,* 154, 217.

8. Bakeless, *Daniel Boone,* 294, 296; Faragher, *Daniel Boone,* 218.

9. Notes of Border History, 152, Lyman C. Draper Collection, SHS; Faragher, *Daniel Boone,* 218–19; Bakeless, *Daniel Boone,* 296–97.

10. Bakeless, *Daniel Boone,* 297; Faragher, *Daniel Boone,* 219.

11. Notes of Border History, 153, Lyman C. Draper Collection, SHS; Faragher, *Daniel Boone,* 219; Bakeless, *Daniel Boone,* 297.

12. Notes of Border History, 154, Lyman C. Draper Collection, SHS; Faragher, *Daniel Boone,* 220.

13. Notes of Border History, 155, Lyman C. Draper Collection, SHS; Bakeless, *Daniel Boone,* 298–99.

14. Notes of Border History, 156, Lyman C. Draper Collection, SHS; Faragher, *Daniel Boone,* 222.

15. Notes of Border History, 157, Lyman C. Draper Collection, SHS; Bakeless, *Daniel Boone,* 304, 306; Faragher, *Daniel Boone,* 222.

16. Notes of Border History, 165–66, Lyman C. Draper Collection, SHS; Faragher, *Daniel Boone,* 223; Bakeless, *Daniel Boone,* 299–300; Hazel A. Spraker, *The Boone Family: A Genealogical History,* 128.

17. Bakeless, *Daniel Boone,* 311.

18. Notes of Border History, 159, Lyman C. Draper Collection, SHS; Bakeless, *Daniel Boone,* 313.

19. Notes of Border History, 159, Lyman C. Draper Collection, SHS.

20. Ibid., 159–60.

21. Ibid., 160.

22. Faragher, *Daniel Boone,* 235–37.

23. Bakeless, *Daniel Boone,* 329–32.

24. Faragher, *Daniel Boone,* 249.

25. Ibid., 250–51.

26. Ibid., 252.

27. Ibid., 254–55.

28. Ibid., 255.

29. Bakeless, *Daniel Boone,* 319; Faragher, *Daniel Boone,* 255–60.

30. Bakeless, *Daniel Boone,* 321.

31. Faragher, *Daniel Boone,* 258.

32. Ibid., 259.

33. Bakeless, *Daniel Boone,* 322; Faragher, *Daniel Boone,* 259.

34. Bakeless, *Daniel Boone,* 322–23; Faragher, *Daniel Boone,* 259–60.

35. Bakeless, *Daniel Boone,* 323.

36. Faragher, *Daniel Boone,* 260.

37. Notes of Border History, 172, Lyman C. Draper Collection, SHS; Bakeless, *Daniel Boone,* 331.

38. Faragher, *Daniel Boone,* 261.

39. Notes of Border History, 18, 172, Lyman C. Draper Collection, SHS.

40. Faragher, *Daniel Boone,* 261.

41. Notes of Border History, 175, Lyman C. Draper Collection, SHS; Bakeless, *Daniel Boone,* 333.

42. Faragher, *Daniel Boone,* 264–65; Bakeless, *Daniel Boone,* 333.

43. Faragher, *Daniel Boone,* 264–65.

44. Notes of Border History, 178, Lyman C. Draper Collection, SHS; Faragher, *Daniel Boone,* 266.

45. Notes of Border History, 178–79, Lyman C. Draper Collection, SHS; Faragher, *Daniel Boone,* 267.

46. Faragher, *Daniel Boone,* 268.

47. Notes of Border History, 178–79, Lyman C. Draper Collection, SHS.

48. Faragher, *Daniel Boone,* 269–71.

49. Notes of Border History, 198–99, Lyman C. Draper Collection, SHS; Faragher, *Daniel Boone,* 271.

50. Notes of Border History, 199–201, 205, Lyman C. Draper Collection, SHS; Faragher, *Daniel Boone,* 272.

51. Notes of Border History, 207, Lyman C. Draper Collection, SHS; Bakeless, *Daniel Boone,* 346; Faragher, *Daniel Boone,* 272.

52. Faragher, *Daniel Boone,* 272; Bakeless, *Daniel Boone,* 347.

53. Notes of Border History, 207–8, Lyman C. Draper Collection, SHS.

54. Faragher, *Daniel Boone,* 273.

55. Notes of Border History, 214, Lyman C. Draper Collection, SHS; Faragher, *Daniel Boone,* 275; Bakeless, *Daniel Boone,* 356.

56. Notes of Border History, 214, Lyman C. Draper Collection, SHS; Faragher, *Daniel Boone,* 273; Bakeless, *Daniel Boone,* 356.

57. Notes of Border History, 214, Lyman C. Draper Collection, SHS; Faragher, *Daniel Boone,* 276.

58. Faragher, *Daniel Boone,* 276–77.

59. Notes of Border History, 215, Lyman C. Draper Collection, SHS.

60. Ibid., 221; Bakeless, *Daniel Boone,* 359; Faragher, *Daniel Boone,* 277–78.

61. Faragher, *Daniel Boone,* 278.

62. Notes of Border History, 18, 175, Lyman C. Draper Collection, SHS; Faragher, *Daniel Boone,* 278; Spraker, *Boone Family,* 126.

63. Faragher, *Daniel Boone,* 278.

64. Ibid., 245.

65. Ibid., 278–79.

66. Ibid.

2. Missouri

1. Notes of Border History, 224, Lyman C. Draper Collection, SHS; Jonas Viles, "Population and Extent of Settlement in Missouri before 1804," 211; John K. Hulston, "Daniel Boone's Sons in Missouri," 364; David D. March, *The History of Missouri,* 83, 108–9, 113.

2. Faragher, *Daniel Boone,* 280.

3. *American State Papers: Public Lands,* 2:472, 552, 872, 3:294, 296, and 8:863; Contract with Robert Hall, January 20, 1800, Boone Family Papers, SHS; Notes of Border History, 224, Lyman C. Draper Collection, SHS; Faragher, *Daniel Boone,* 280.

4. Notes of Border History, 243–44, Lyman C. Draper Collection, SHS.

5. Ibid., 224.

6. Ibid., 227–28.

7. Ibid., 228.

8. Ibid., 70, 229.

9. Ibid., 232.

10. Information for the following several paragraphs comes from Notes of Border History, 233–39, Lyman C. Draper Collection, SHS.

11. Nathan Boone to William Clark, December 13, 1805, Boone Family Papers, SHS.

12. John Joseph Mathews, *The Osages: Children of the Middle Waters,* 7; Willard H. Rollings, *The Osage: An Ethnohistorical Study of Hegemony on the Prairie-Plains,* 5, 16, 19, 20–21, 37–38, 67, 179.

13. Rollings, *Osage,* 17–18.

14. Ibid., 23–29, 42–44; Mathews, *Osages,* 23.

15. Rollings, *Osage,* 45, 47.

16. Ibid., 6–10, 183.

17. William E. Foley, *The Genesis of Missouri: From Wilderness Outpost to Statehood,* 68–70; March, *History of Missouri,* 88; Rollings, *Osage,* 8, 191–92.

18. Rollings, *Osage*, 180–202.

19. Ibid., 182, 184.

20. Ibid., 187, 190.

21. Ibid., 213, 215.

22. Ibid., 181, 202, 210, 215–16.

23. Ibid., 218–19.

24. Ibid., 219–21.

25. Notes of Border History, 239, Lyman C. Draper Collection, SHS; Rollings, *Osage*, 18.

26. Notes of Border History, 239–40, Lyman C. Draper Collection, SHS.

27. Ibid.

28. Marriage rites of Daniel Morgan Boone and Sara Lewis, May 2, 1800, Boone Family Papers, SHS; Spraker, *Boone Family*, 128; Faragher, *Daniel Boone*, 281; Carole Bills, ed., *Nathan Boone: The Neglected Hero*, 51.

29. Notes of Border History, 244, Lyman C. Draper Collection, SHS.

30. Faragher, *Daniel Boone*, 290.

31. Notes of Border History, 244, Lyman C. Draper Collection, SHS; Faragher, *Daniel Boone*, 290.

32. Memorandum of agreement made between Nathan Boone and John Zumwalt, August 15, 1808, Lyman C. Draper Collection, SHS.

33. Ibid.; Notes of Border History, 246, Lyman C. Draper Collection, SHS; Research on Boon's Lick, Lewis Saum Papers, SHS; Clarence Edwin Carter, ed., *The Territorial Papers of the United States*, 13:298.

34. Hulston, "Daniel Boone's Sons," 365–66; Bills, ed., *Nathan Boone*, 5; Kate L. Gregg, "The Boonslick Road in St. Charles County."

35. Malcolm J. Rohrbough, *The Land Office Business: The Settlement and Administration of American Public Lands, 1789–1837*, 41; *Missouri Gazette*, June 5, 1818; Foley, *Genesis of Missouri*, 172; Kate L. Gregg, "The Boonslick Road in St. Charles County, Part II"; March, *History of Missouri*, 165–66; Hulston, "Daniel Boone's Sons," 365; Viles, "Population and Extent of Settlement," 209–10.

36. Rohrbough, *Land Office Business*, 34–35; William D. Pattison, *Beginnings of the American Rectangular Land Survey System, 1784–1800*, 73, 78.

3. The Osage Expedition

1. Carter, ed., *Territorial Papers*, 13:298, 301; Francis Paul Prucha, *American Indian Treaties: The History of a Political Anomaly*, 126; Louis Houck, *A History of Missouri*, 2:227; Foley, *Genesis of Missouri*, 203.

2. Thomas Maitland Marshall, ed., *The Life and Papers of Frederick Bates*, 1:316.

3. Carter, ed., *Territorial Papers*, 13:547.

4. John Glendower Westover, "The Evolution of the Missouri Militia, 1804–1919," 32–33.

5. Ibid., 33, 42, 52, 55–56, 63.

6. Francis Paul Prucha, *The Great Father: The United States Government and the American Indians,* 76.

7. Carter, ed., *Territorial Papers,* 14:185; Prucha, *Great Father,* 76.

8. Carter, ed., *Territorial Papers,* 14:14; Houck, *History of Missouri,* 2:277.

9. Carter, ed., *Territorial Papers,* 14:197–98; Houck, *History of Missouri,* 2:277.

10. *Missouri Gazette,* June 28, 1808.

11. Rollings, *Osage,* 223; Kate L. Gregg, "The History of Fort Osage," 439–40.

12. Houck, *History of Missouri,* 2:277; Rollings, *Osage,* 223.

13. Michael L. Gillespie, *Fort Osage: A History of Its First Occupation* (n.p.: The Author, 1995), 5; Carter, ed., *Territorial Papers,* 14:200.

14. Gregg, "History of Fort Osage," 440–41.

15. Westover, "Evolution of the Missouri Militia," 89–90.

16. *Missouri Gazette,* July 28, 1808.

17. Houck, *History of Missouri,* 2:278; Kate L. Gregg, *Westward with Dragoons: The Journal of William Clark on His Expedition to Establish Fort Osage, August 25 to September 22, 1808,* 21, 52, 55.

18. Gregg, *Westward with Dragoons,* 21–22.

19. Ibid., 22–23, 50.

20. Ibid., 23–25.

21. Ibid., 25–26, 51–52.

22. Information for the next several paragraphs from Gregg, *Westward with Dragoons,* 28–34.

23. Ibid., 58; Rollings, *Osage,* 224.

24. Carter, ed., *Territorial Papers,* 14:227.

25. Gregg, *Westward with Dragoons,* 36.

26. Gillespie, *Fort Osage,* 7.

27. Ibid., 3.

28. Notes of Border History, 289–90, Lyman C. Draper Collection, SHS.

29. Ibid.

30. Gregg, *Westward with Dragoons,* 38.

31. Ibid., 38, 59.

32. Ibid., 38.

33. Carter, ed., *Territorial Papers,* 14:225; Gregg, *Westward with Dragoons,* 39.

34. Gregg, *Westward with Dragoons,* 39–40.

35. Ibid., 39.

36. Ibid., 39–41, 67; Carter, ed., *Territorial Papers,* 14:224.

37. Carter, ed., *Territorial Papers,* 14:209, 224–26; Houck, *History of Missouri,* 2:278–79; Gregg, *Westward with Dragoons,* 41.

38. Houck, *History of Missouri,* 2:279; Gregg, *Westward with Dragoons,* 41–42, 62.

39. Gregg, *Westward with Dragoons,* 46.

40. Ibid., 48.

41. Prucha, *American Indian Treaties,* 126; Rollings, *Osage,* 224; Foley, *Genesis of Missouri,* 205; Carter, ed., *Territorial Papers,* 14:242.

42. Carter, ed., *Territorial Papers,* 14:227; Rollings, *Osage,* 225.

43. *American State Papers: Indian Affairs*, 2:765; Charles H. Kappler, ed., *Indian Affairs: Laws and Treaties*, 96–97; Prucha, *American Indian Treaties*, 127; Foley, *Genesis of Missouri*, 205.

44. Carter, ed., *Territorial Papers*, 14:229.

45. Kapler, ed., *Indian Affairs*, 95; Prucha, *American Indian Treaties*, 128.

46. Carter, ed., *Territorial Papers*, 14:229.

47. Kapler, ed., *Indian Affairs*, 95–98, 110.

48. Mathews, *Osages*, 389; Prucha, *American Indian Treaties*, 128; *American State Papers: Indian Affairs*, 2:764–67; Rollings, *Osage*, 227, 230.

49. Rollings, *Osage*, 231.

50. Receipt, June 16, 1809, Boone Family Papers, SHS.

4. War

1. Louis Houck, *History of Missouri*, 2:98; *Missouri Gazette*, November 23, 1808; Carter, ed., *Territorial Papers*, 14:236.

2. *Missouri Gazette*, February 1, April 5, and April 12, 1809.

3. Ibid., February 1 and April 5, 1809; Foley, *Genesis of Missouri*, 217.

4. *Missouri Gazette*, April 26, 1809.

5. Ibid., June 7 and August 18, 1809.

6. Carter, ed., *Territorial Papers*, 14:412–13; Foley, *Genesis of Missouri*, 216; Houck, *History of Missouri*, 3:99–100.

7. Kate L. Gregg, "The War of 1812 on the Missouri Frontier, Part I," 5–6.

8. Ibid., 6–7.

9. Ibid., 9–10; Foley, *Genesis of Missouri*, 218.

10. David Bissell to Secretary of War, June 28, 1811, Daniel Bissell Papers, Missouri Historical Society, St. Louis (hereafter MHS).

11. Gregg, "War of 1812, Part I," 10–11.

12. Carter, ed., *Territorial Papers*, 14:505.

13. Gregg, "War of 1812, Part I," 11–12; Foley, *Genesis of Missouri*, 220; *Louisiana Gazette*, April 25, 1812; Carter, ed., *Territorial Papers*, 14:505, 518–20.

14. Carter, ed., *Territorial Papers*, 14:519; William Clark to James Monroe, January 1, 1814, William Clark Papers, MHS; William Clark to Joseph Campbell, March 10, 1812, William Clark Papers, MHS.

15. Carter, ed., *Territorial Papers*, 14:520, 522–23; Foley, *Genesis of Missouri*, 220; *Louisiana Gazette*, April 25, 1812.

16. Information for the next several paragraphs from Carter, ed., *Territorial Papers*, 14:529, 531–34.

17. Ibid., 541–42.

18. *Louisiana Gazette*, March 21, 1812.

19. Robert B. Roberts, *Encyclopedia of Historic Forts: The Military, Pioneer, and Trading Posts of the United States*, 458; Gregg, "War of 1812, Part I," 13; Houck, *History of Missouri*, 3:136–37.

20. Roberts, *Encyclopedia of Historic Forts,* 456, 461–62, 464.

21. Gregg, "War of 1812, Part I," 13.

22. *Louisiana Gazette,* May 9, 1812; Foley, *Genesis of Missouri,* 217, 221.

23. Carter, ed., *Territorial Papers,* 14:560–64, 566, 572–73, 582–85; *First Annual Report and Collections of the State Historical Society of Wisconsin* (Madison, 1854), 206.

24. Carter, ed., *Territorial Papers,* 14:565–66.

25. Ibid., 572–73; Foley, *Genesis of Missouri,* 224–25, 227.

26. Carter, ed., *Territorial Papers,* 14:574.

27. Gregg, "War of 1812, Part I," 15–17.

28. Christian Wilt Letterbook, September 6, 1812, and January 12, 1814, MHS; Gregg, "War of 1812, Part I," 19; *Missouri Gazette,* December 12, 1812.

29. *Missouri Gazette,* January 23, 1813; Carter, ed., *Territorial Papers,* 14:642.

30. *Missouri Gazette and Illinois Advertiser,* February 20 and 22, 1813.

31. Ibid., March 6 and 27, and April 24, 1813; Foley, *Genesis of Missouri,* 225.

32. March, *History of Missouri,* 281–83; Kate L. Gregg, "The War of 1812 on the Missouri Frontier, Part II," 191–92; Foley, *Genesis of Missouri,* 227; Carter, ed., *Territorial Papers,* 14:672, 714.

33. Carter, ed., *Territorial Papers,* 14:656; Foley, *Genesis of Missouri,* 228–29.

34. Notes of Border History, 255, Lyman C. Draper Collection, SHS.

35. Gregg, "War of 1812, Part II," 194–95; Foley, *Genesis of Missouri,* 228.

36. March, *History of Missouri,* 285; Gregg, "War of 1812, Part II," 195–96; Notes of Border History, 255–56, Lyman C. Draper Collection, SHS.

37. Notes of Border History, 256–57, Lyman C. Draper Collection, SHS.

38. Ibid., 257.

39. Ibid.

40. Houck, *History of Missouri,* 3:113; Gregg, "War of 1812, Part II," 196.

41. Gregg, "War of 1812, Part II," 196–97.

42. Notes of Border History, 257–58, Lyman C. Draper Collection, SHS; March, *History of Missouri,* 290–91; Gregg, "War of 1812, Part II," 197–98; William T. Hagan, *The Sac and Fox Indians,* 57.

43. Notes of Border History, 257, Lyman C. Draper Collection, SHS; Gregg, "War of 1812, Part II," 198; *First Annual Report and Collections of the State Historical Society of Wisconsin,* 212.

44. Hagan, *Sac and Fox Indians,* 58–59, 63; Gregg, "War of 1812, Part II," 198–99; March, *History of Missouri,* 292; Foley, *Genesis of Missouri,* 229, 231.

45. Gregg, "War of 1812, Part II," 198, 202.

46. *Missouri Gazette and Illinois Advertiser,* May 7, 1814; Houck, *History of Missouri,* 3:115–18; Kate L. Gregg, "The War of 1812 on the Missouri Frontier, Part III," 330–31; Notes of Border History, 259–60, Lyman C. Draper Collection, SHS.

47. Gregg, "War of 1812, Part III," 335; Houck, *History of Missouri*, 3:119–21.

48. Houck, *History of Missouri*, 3:121–22.

49. Ibid., 122–23.

50. Ibid., 123.

51. Gregg, "War of 1812, Part III," 337–38.

52. Ibid., 341.

53. Foley, *Genesis of Missouri*, 232; *Missouri Gazette and Illinois Advertiser*, January 21, 1815.

54. Notes of Border History, 263–64, Lyman C. Draper Collection, SHS.

55. Ibid., 265–67.

56. Houck, *History of Missouri*, 3:130; Gregg, "War of 1812, Part III," 343–44.

57. Francis Paul Prucha, *American Indian Treaties*, 132; Foley, *Genesis of Missouri*, 233.

58. Carter, ed., *Territorial Papers*, 15:14–15; Prucha, *American Indian Treaties*, 132; Foley, *Genesis of Missouri*, 233.

59. Prucha, *American Indian Treaties*, 132–33.

60. William Clark to August Chouteau, May 16, and May 22, 1815, William Clark Papers, MHS; Prucha, *American Indian Treaties*, 133; Hagan, *Sac and Fox Indians*, 79–80; William Clark to Daniel Bissell, July 11, 1815, War of 1812 Collection, MHS; Gregg, "War of 1812, Part III," 344–45.

61. Gregg, "War of 1812, Part III," 345–46.

62. Ibid., 346.

63. Ibid., 347.

64. Ibid.; Prucha, *American Indian Treaties*, 133; Foley, *Genesis of Missouri*, 233; Kapler, ed., *Indian Affairs*, 111, 121.

65. Gregg, "War of 1812, Part III," 347–48; Foley, *Genesis of Missouri*, 233.

66. Kapler, ed., *Indian Affairs*, 127.

67. Foley, *Genesis of Missouri*, 234; Prucha, *American Indian Treaties*, 135.

68. Christian Wilt Letterbook, February 12, 1814, MHS; William Clark to Secretary of War, September 12, 1813, William Clark Papers, MHS.

69. *Niles Weekly Register*, June 17, 1837.

5. Interlude

1. *American State Papers: Public Lands*, 3:293–94, 304; Notes of Border History, 225–27, Lyman C. Draper Collection, SHS; Rolla P. Andrae, *A True, Brief History of Daniel Boone*, 49–51; Bills, ed., *Nathan Boone*, 47; National Register of Historic Places, Inventory Nomination Form, Daniel Boone Home, Department of Natural Resources, Jefferson City, Missouri; Tax list, 1819, Boone Family Papers, SHS; Gottfried Duden, *Report on a Journey to the Western States of North America and a Stay of Several Years along the Missouri during the Years 1824, '25, '26, and 1827*, 79.

2. Gregg, "Boonslick Road in St. Charles County, Part II," 11, 14.

3. *American State Papers: Public Lands*, 6:847; Estate papers of Sharshall Cooper, October 3, 1815, Boone Family Papers, SHS; Estate papers of Enoch Carmack, December 21, 1815, Boone Family Papers, SHS; Public estate sale papers for John B. Galloway, September 12 and 13, 1823, Boone Family Collection, MHS.

4. Duden, *Report on a Journey*, 79; Real estate sale paper, October 2, 1818, Book E, 349, Boone Family Papers, SHS; Carolyn Thomas Foreman, "Nathan Boone: Trapper, Manufacturer, Surveyor, Militiaman, Legislator, Ranger, Dragoon," 326–27.

5. Bond paper, October 9, 1815, Book C, 302, Boone Family Papers, SHS; Loan agreement, Book G, 521, Boone Family Papers, SHS.

6. Duden, *Report on a Journey*, 341–42.

7. Foley, *Genesis of Missouri*, 293.

8. Ibid., 293–94.

9. F. C. Shoemaker, *Missouri's Struggle for Statehood, 1804–1821*, 115–24.

10. Perry G. McCandless, "Thomas Hart Benton, His Source of Political Strength in Missouri from 1815 to 1838," 24–25; Rudolph Eugene Forderhase, "Jacksonianism in Missouri from Predilection to Party, 1820–1836," 6–17.

11. Perry G. McCandless, *A History of Missouri, Volume II, 1820 to 1860*, 8; Shoemaker, *Missouri's Struggle for Statehood*, 66, 68, 136, 151–52; Foley, *Genesis of Missouri*, 294; McCandless, "Thomas Hart Benton," 23.

12. Shoemaker, *Missouri's Struggle for Statehood*, 159, 163–65.

13. *Journal of the Missouri State Convention*, 3; Shoemaker, *Missouri's Struggle for Statehood*, 166; Forderhase, "Jacksonianism in Missouri," 11.

14. *Journal of the Missouri State Convention*, 5; Shoemaker, *Missouri's Struggle for Statehood*, 166–73.

15. *Journal of the Missouri State Convention*, 32; McCandless, "Thomas Hart Benton," 26; Shoemaker, *Missouri's Struggle for Statehood*, 174–92, 249–50.

16. *Journal of the Missouri State Convention*, 17, 28; Shoemaker, *Missouri's Struggle for Statehood*, 200, 210–11.

17. Foley, *Genesis of Missouri*, 296.

18. *Journal of the Missouri State Convention*, 39, 47–48; Shoemaker, *Missouri's Struggle for Statehood*, 196–97, 254.

19. Foley, *Genesis of Missouri*, 296–98; McCandless, "Thomas Hart Benton," 27.

20. Shoemaker, *Missouri's Struggle for Statehood*, 266.

21. Ibid., 268.

22. Information in the next several paragraphs from Faragher, *Daniel Boone*, 315–19.

23. Reuben Gold Thwaites, "The Story of the Black Hawk War," 218–19; Elizabeth B. Rooney, "The Story of the Black Hawk War," 231; Donald Jackson, "The Black Hawk War," 71–72; Joseph I. Lambert, "The Black Hawk War," 442.

24. Julia H. Clark to George Hancock, February 27, 1817, William Clark Papers, MHS; Westover, "Evolution of the Missouri Militia," 72.

25. Hagan, *Sac and Fox Indians*, 86.

26. Ibid., 87–89, 92–93.

27. Ibid., 94–96.

28. Ibid., 97–98.

29. Roger L. Nichols, "The Black Hawk War: Another View," 525; Hagan, *Sac and Fox Indians,* 98–99.

30. Hagan, *Sac and Fox Indians,* 103–5.

31. Ibid., 109; John Hauberg, "The Black Hawk War, 1831–1832," 98–99.

32. Hagan, *Sac and Fox Indians,* 109; Hauberg, "Black Hawk War," 98–99.

33. Hagan, *Sac and Fox Indians,* 111.

34. Ibid., 115–16.

35. Ibid., 116–18.

36. Jacob Van der Zee, "The Neutral Ground," 312.

37. Hagan, *Sac and Fox Indians,* 118; Van der Zee, "Neutral Ground," 313.

38. Van der Zee, "Neutral Ground," 313–15.

39. Hagan, *Sac and Fox Indians,* 120–21, 124.

40. Ibid., 127–29.

41. Ibid., 131.

42. Ibid., 133–34.

43. Ibid., 112; Nichols, "Black Hawk War," 526.

44. Hagan, *Sac and Fox Indians,* 138.

45. Lambert, "Black Hawk War," 446; Van der Zee, "Neutral Ground," 313–15.

46. Van der Zee, "Neutral Ground," 315–16.

47. Ibid., 316; Alonzo Abernethy, "Iowa under Territorial Governments and the Removal of the Indians," 436–39.

48. Van der Zee, "Neutral Ground," 316.

49. Roger L. Nichols, *Black Hawk and the Warrior's Path,* 116.

50. Lambert, "Black Hawk War," 446.

51. Nichols, "Black Hawk War," 528–29; Hagan, *Sac and Fox Indians,* 141–48.

52. Hagan, *Sac and Fox Indians,* 148–53.

53. Hauberg, "Black Hawk War," 92.

54. Otis E. Young, "The United States Mounted Ranger Battalion, 1832–1833," 455–56.

55. Ibid.

56. Ibid.

57. *American State Papers: Military Affairs,* 5:30–31; Hagan, *Sac and Fox Indians,* 169–74.

58. Hagan, *Sac and Fox Indians,* 175–80.

59. Ibid., 180–95.

60. Young, "United States Mounted Ranger Battalion," 458.

61. Hauberg, "Black Hawk War," 122–32; William J. Peterson, "The Terms of Peace," 102–7, 111.

62. Henry Dodge Military Order Book, No. 63, September 23, 1832, 30, State Historical Society of Iowa–Des Moines; Louis Pelzer, *Marches of the Dragoons in the Mississippi Valley,* 72; Francis Paul Prucha, *The Sword of the*

Republic: The United States Army on the Frontier, 1783–1846, 244; Young, "United States Mounted Ranger Battalion," 467.

6. The Dragoon Expedition

1. Louis Pelzer, *Henry Dodge,* 72,
2. Young, "United States Mounted Ranger Battalion," 465–66.
3. Grant Foreman, *Fort Gibson: A Brief History,* 13–14; Statement of the Military Service of Nathan Boone, November 28, 1932, Adjutant General's Office, War Department, Boone Family Papers, SHS.
4. Foreman, *Fort Gibson,* 15–17.
5. Ibid., 18–20.
6. Grant Foreman, "Captain Nathan Boone's Survey Creek-Cherokee Boundary Line," 356; Kapler, ed., *Indian Affairs,* 385–91.
7. Foreman, "Captain Nathan Boone's Survey," 365.
8. Ibid., 357, 365.
9. Grant Foreman, *Pioneer Days in the Early Southwest,* 104, 122.
10. Ibid., 104–5.
11. Ibid.
12. William Salter, ed., "Henry Dodge: Colonel U.S. Dragoons, 1833–1836, Part I," 105; Henry Dodge Military Order Book, No. 63, February 15, 1834, State Historical Society of Iowa–Des Moines.
13. Foreman, *Pioneer Days,* 105.
14. Ibid., 107–8; Young, "United States Mounted Ranger Battalion," 469; Foreman, "Nathan Boone," 328; Statement of the Military Service of Nathan Boone, Boone Family Papers, SHS.
15. Foreman, "Nathan Boone," 328.
16. *American State Papers: Military Affairs,* 6:169–70.
17. Salter, ed., "Henry Dodge, Part I," 102; Hamilton Gardner, "The March of the First Dragoons from Jefferson Barracks to Fort Gibson in 1833–1834," 24.
18. Foreman, "Nathan Boone," 328; *American State Papers: Military Affairs,* 3:245.
19. *Jeffersonian Republican,* October 26, 1833.
20. Gardner, "March of the First Dragoons," 25, 30.
21. Ibid., 30, 33.
22. Pelzer, *Marches of the Dragoons,* 28, 33.
23. Ibid., 34; Foreman, *Pioneer Days,* 120–21; Foreman, "Nathan Boone," 330.
24. Pelzer, *Marches of the Dragoons,* 34–35.
25. Foreman, *Pioneer Days,* 126–27; Pelzer, *Marches of the Dragoons,* 34–35.
26. Wayne T. Walker, "Nathan Boone: The Forgotten Hero," 90; Foreman, *Pioneer Days,* 124, 128–29; George H. Shirk, "Peace on the Plains," 12; Edgar B. Harlan, ed., "Colonel Henry Dodge and His Regiment of Dragoons on the Plains in 1834," 178.

27. Foreman, *Pioneer Days,* 132–33; Pelzer, *Marches of the Dragoons,* 36; Shirk, "Peace on the Plains," 14; Harlan, ed., "Colonel Henry Dodge," 178.

28. Foreman, *Pioneer Days,* 134–35; Pelzer, *Marches of the Dragoons,* 36–37.

29. Shirk, "Peace on the Plains," 18–19; Foreman, *Pioneer Days,* 136–37; Pelzer, *Marches of the Dragoons,* 37–38.

30. Pelzer, *Marches of the Dragoons,* 37–38; Shirk, "Peace on the Plains," 18–20.

31. Shirk, "Peace on the Plains," 22; Foreman, *Pioneer Days,* 138–39; Pelzer, *Marches of the Dragoons,* 38–39.

32. Pelzer, *Marches of the Dragoons,* 31–32.

33. Ibid., 40.

34. Ibid., 40–41.

35. Ibid., 41; Shirk, "Peace on the Plains," 24.

36. Pelzer, *Marches of the Dragoons,* 41–42.

37. Ibid., 42–44.

38. Foreman, *Pioneer Days,* 141; Shirk, "Peace on the Plains," 30; Pelzer, *Marches of the Dragoons,* 43–44.

39. Pelzer, *Marches of the Dragoons,* 44–45.

40. Ibid.

41. Shirk, "Peace on the Plains," 32–33.

42. Foreman, *Pioneer Days,* 145; Pelzer, *Marches of the Dragoons,* 45–46.

43. Pelzer, *Marches of the Dragoons,* 45–46; Foreman, *Pioneer Days,* 146.

44. Foreman, *Pioneer Days,* 147–48; Pelzer, *Marches of the Dragoons,* 47.

45. Foreman, *Pioneer Days,* 148–50.

46. Shirk, "Peace on the Plains," 37; Foreman, *Pioneer Days,* 151; Pelzer, *Marches of the Dragoons,* 46–47.

47. Pelzer, *Marches of the Dragoons,* 46–47.

48. Foreman, *Pioneer Days,* 151; Pelzer, *Marches of the Dragoons,* 46–47.

49. Pelzer, *Marches of the Dragoons,* 46–47; Foreman, *Pioneer Days,* 152.

50. Foreman, *Pioneer Days,* 152; Foreman, *Fort Gibson,* 22–23.

51. Shirk, "Peace on the Plains," 39.

52. Pelzer, *Marches of the Dragoons,* 50; Kapler, ed., *Indian Affairs,* 435; "Fort Des Moines (No. 1), Iowa," 353.

7. Full Stride

1. Louis Pelzer, ed., "A Journal of Marches by the First United States Dragoons, 1834–1835," 361.

2. Mary R. Whitcomb, "Reminiscences of Gen. James C. Parrott," 370.

3. Pelzer, *Marches of the Dragoons,* 51; Jacob Van der Zee, "Forts in the Iowa Country," 180.

4. Salter, ed., "Henry Dodge, Part I," 113–14, 116–17.

5. Elvid Hunt, *History of Fort Leavenworth, 1827–1927,* 61.

6. "Fort Des Moines (No. 1)," 353–54.

7. William Salter, ed., "Henry Dodge: Colonel U.S. Dragoons, 1833–1836, Part II," 251.

8. Pelzer, *Marches of the Dragoons,* 52–53.

9. Ibid., 53.

10. Ibid., 54.

11. Pelzer, ed., "Journal of Marches," 366.

12. Pelzer, *Marches of the Dragoons,* 54–55.

13. Pelzer, ed., "Journal of Marches," 372.

14. Pelzer, *Marches of the Dragoons,* 56.

15. Ibid., 56–57; Whitcomb, "Reminiscences of Gen. James C. Parrott," 369–70.

16. "Fort Des Moines (No. 1)," 357–58; Salter, ed., "Henry Dodge, Part II," 358.

17. Pelzer, ed., "Journal of Marches," 378.

18. Pelzer, *Marches of the Dragoons,* 60.

19. "Fort Des Moines (No. 1)," 357–58; Salter, ed., "Henry Dodge, Part II," 358.

20. Pelzer, *Marches of the Dragoons,* 62; Henry Putney Beers, *The Western Military Frontier, 1815–1846,* 120.

21. Pelzer, *Marches of the Dragoons,* 61; J. C. Parrott, "The First United States Dragoons," 525; Beers, *Western Military Frontier,* 120.

22. Pelzer, *Marches of the Dragoons,* 62; Beers, *Western Military Frontier,* Parrott, "First United States Dragoons," 525.

23. Pelzer, *Marches of the Dragoons,* 250.

24. "Fort Des Moines (No. 1)," 359–60.

25. Nathan Boone to Jesse Vanbibber, September 19, 1836, Boone Family Papers, SHS.

26. Hagan, *Sac and Fox Indians,* 212.

27. Ibid., 213; Beers, *Western Military Frontier,* 120.

28. Foreman, "Nathan Boone," 334.

29. Ibid.; Grant Foreman, *Advancing the Frontier, 1830–1860,* 51.

30. Foreman, "Nathan Boone," 334–35.

31. Ibid.

32. Ibid., 335.

33. Information in this and the next several paragraphs from the *Army and Navy Chronicle,* October 31, 1839.

34. Ibid.; Beers, *Western Military Frontier,* 133–34; Grant Foreman, *The Five Civilized Tribes,* 309–10.

35. *Army and Navy Chronicle,* December 12, 1839.

36. Ibid., and October 31, 1839.

8. The Final Years

1. *Army and Navy Chronicle,* April 16, 1840; *Niles Weekly Register,* May 2, 1840.

2. *Army and Navy Chronicle,* April 16, 1840.

3. Louis Pelzer, ed., "A Frontier Officer's Military Order Book," 260–67.

4. Foreman, *Pioneer Days,* 286, 289.

5. Ibid., 266; Foreman, "Nathan Boone," 338.

6. Foreman, "Nathan Boone," 338; Thomas D. Isern, "Jefferson's Salt Mountain: The Big Salt Plain of the Cimarron River," 161–62.

7. Information in the next several paragraphs from W. Julian Fessler, ed., "Captain Nathan Boone's Journal," 63–64, 68, 70–75, 78, 80–83, 89–90, 93–94.

8. Ibid., 101–2; Pelzer, *Marches of the Dragoons,* 102.

9. Pelzer, *Marches of the Dragoons,* 102–3; Fessler, "Captain Nathan Boone's Journal," 60–63.

10. Fessler, "Captain Nathan Boone's Journal," 60–63; Pelzer, *Marches of the Dragoons,* 104–5.

11. Foreman, *Pioneer Days,* 295; "Texan Diplomatic Correspondence, Part II," 310–12; Foreman, "Nathan Boone," 340.

12. Foreman, *Pioneer Days,* 295.

13. Ibid., 293; Foreman, *Advancing the Frontier,* 220–22; Foreman, "Nathan Boone," 342.

14. Foreman, *Pioneer Days,* 293; Foreman, *Advancing the Frontier,* 223.

15. Foreman, *Advancing the Frontier,* 224.

16. Ibid.; Foreman, "Nathan Boone," 342.

17. Ibid., 343; Foreman, *Five Civilized Tribes,* 322–23.

18. Grace Steele Woodward, *The Cherokees,* 221; Foreman, *Five Civilized Tribes,* 222–23.

19. Foreman, *Five Civilized Tribes,,* 325–26.

20. Ibid., 321–37.

21. Ibid., 339–40, 342–44; William G. McLoughlin, *After the Trail of Tears: The Cherokees' Struggle for Sovereignty, 1839–1880,* 50–51.

22. Foreman, *Five Civilized Tribes,* 342.

23. Ibid., 344.

24. Ibid.; Foreman, "Nathan Boone," 343.

25. Foreman, *Five Civilized Tribes,* 349; Foreman, "Nathan Boone," 344.

26. Statement of the Military Service of Nathan Boone, Boone Family Papers, SHS.

27. Foreman, "Nathan Boone," 345.

28. Statement of the Military Service of Nathan Boone, Boone Family Papers, SHS.

29. B. A. Taney to Lyman C. Draper, December 15, 1850, reel 8 v. 23c, Lyman C. Draper Collection, State Historical Society of Wisconsin; Alice H. Finckh, "Gottfried Duden Views Missouri, 1824–1827, Part I," 342–43.

30. Nathan Boone to Lyman C. Draper, January 14, 1853, reel 8 v. 23c, Lyman C. Draper Collection, State Historical Society of Wisconsin; Statement of the Military Service of Nathan Boone, Boone Family Papers, SHS.

31. Nathan Boone's Will, October 12, 1856, Probate Court Record of Wills, 1834–1871, Greene County Court, Springfield, Missouri, Missouri State Archives, Jefferson City.

32. B. H. Boone to Lyman C. Draper, December 8, 1856, reel 8 v. 23c, Lyman C. Draper Collection, State Historical Society of Wisconsin.

Epilogue

1. Foreman, "Nathan Boone," 345–46.

2. Spraker, *Boone Family*, 126–28, 190–91.

3. Population and Slave Census Schedule, 1830, St. Charles County, Missouri, SHS; Population and Slave Census Schedule, 1840, Greene County, Missouri, SHS.

4. Slave Census Schedule, 1850, Greene County, Missouri, SHS; Agricultural Census Schedule, 1850, Greene County, Missouri, SHS.

5. B. H. Boone to Lyman C. Draper, December 8, 1856, reel 8 v. 23c, Lyman C. Draper Collection, State Historical Society of Wisconsin.

6. Bills, ed., *Nathan Boone*, 66–68.

7. Robert M. Utley, *Frontiersmen in Blue: The United States Army and the Indian, 1848–1865*, 5–6.

8. Ibid., 29–30.

9. Ibid., 31–33.

10. Ibid.

11. *Weekly Jefferson Inquirer*, November 1, 1856.

BIBLIOGRAPHY

Historical Collections

MISSOURI HISTORICAL SOCIETY, ST. LOUIS

Bates Family Papers
Frederick Bates Papers
Daniel Bissell Papers
Boone Family Collection
James Callaway Papers
William Clark Papers
William Hertzog Collins Collection
Voorhis Collection of the William Clark Papers
War of 1812 Collection
Christian Wilt Letterbook

MISSOURI STATE ARCHIVES, JEFFERSON CITY

Probate Court Record of Wills 1834–1871, Greene County Court, Springfield, Missouri

STATE HISTORICAL SOCIETY OF IOWA–DES MOINES

Henry Dodge Military Order Book, No. 63

STATE HISTORICAL SOCIETY OF MISSOURI, COLUMBIA

Agricultural Census Schedule, 1840, 1850, Greene County, Missouri.
Boone Family Papers
William Clark Breckenridge Papers
Lyman C. Draper Collection

Sarah Guitar Papers
Lewis Jones Collection
J. W. Keithy Papers
Bryan Obear Scrapbooks
Lillian Oliver Collection
George Pohlman Collection
Population and Slave Census Schedule, 1830, St. Charles County,
　　Missouri.
Lewis Saum Papers
Slave Census Schedule, 1840, 1850, Greene County, Missouri.
Robert McClure Snyder Collection
St. Charles County Historical Society Scrapbook
Lucille Morris Upton Papers
U.S. Adjutant General Records
Charles Van Ravenswaay Collection
Marie Oliver Watkins Papers
Sarah Lockwood Williams Papers

STATE HISTORICAL SOCIETY OF WISCONSIN

Lyman C. Draper Collection

Newspapers

Army and Navy Chronicle
Columbia Statesman
Jeffersonian Republican (Jefferson City)
Liberty Weekly Tribune
Louisiana Gazette (St. Louis)
Missouri Gazette (St. Louis)
Missouri Gazette and Illinois Advertiser (St. Louis)
Missouri Intelligencer (Columbia)
Missouri Republican (St. Louis)
Niles Weekly Register (Baltimore)
St. Charles Missourian
Weekly Jefferson Inquirer (Jefferson City)

References

Abernethy, Alonzo. "Iowa under Territorial Governments and the Removal of the Indians." *Annals of Iowa* 7 (July 1906): 431–45.

American State Papers: Indian Affairs. Vols. 1–2.

American State Papers: Military Affairs. Vols. 1, 3, 5–6.

American State Papers: Public Lands. Vols. 1–3, 6, 8.

Andrae, Rolla P. *A True, Brief History of Daniel Boone.* Old Monroe, Mo.: Daniel Boone Home, 1985.

Bailey, Garrick A., ed. *The Osage and the Invisible World: From the Works of Francis La Flesche.* Norman: University of Oklahoma Press, 1995.

Bakeless, John. *Daniel Boone.* New York: William Morrow, 1939.

Baker, Olive. "Life and Influence of Danville and Danville Township." *Missouri Historical Review* 7 (July 1913): 200–223.

Barry, Louise. *The Beginning of the West: Annals of the Kansas Gateway to the American West, 1540–1854.* Topeka: Kansas State Historical Society, 1972.

Beers, Henry Putney. *The Western Military Frontier, 1815–1846.* Philadelphia: Porcupine Press, 1975.

Bek, William G. "The Followers of Duden." *Missouri Historical Review* 17 (April 1923): 331–47.

Bills, Carole, ed. *Nathan Boone: The Neglected Hero.* Republic, Mo.: Western Printing, 1984.

Caldwell, Norman W. "Civilian Personnel at the Frontier Military Post (1790–1814)." *Mid-America* 38 (April 1956): 101–19.

———. "The Enlisted Soldier at the Frontier Post, 1790–1814." *Mid-America* 37 (October 1955): 195–204.

———. "The Frontier Army Officer, 1794–1814." *Mid-America* 37 (April 1955): 101–28.

Carter, Clarence Edwin, ed. *The Territorial Papers of the United States.* Vols. 13–15. Washington, D.C.: Government Printing Office, 1948–1949, 1951.

Catlin, George. *North American Indians.* Edinburgh: J. Grant, 1926.

Coles, Harry L. *The War of 1812.* Chicago: University of Chicago Press, 1965.

Davis, Carl L., and LeRoy H. Fischer. "Dragoon Life in Indian Territory, 1833–1846." *Chronicles of Oklahoma* 48 (Spring 1970): 2–24.

Duden, Gottfried. *Report on a Journey to the Western States of North America and a Stay of Several Years along the Missouri during the Years 1824, '25, '26, and 1827.* 1829. Reprint, ed. James W. Goodrich, Columbia: State Historical Society of Missouri, 1980.

Edmunds, David. "Black Hawk." *Timeline* 5 (April–May 1988): 24–27.

Encyclopedia of Missouri. St. Clair Shores, Mich.: Somerset, 1985.

Faragher, John Mack. *Daniel Boone: The Life and Legend of an American Pioneer.* New York: Henry Holt, 1992.

Fessler, W. Julian, ed. "Captain Nathan Boone's Journal." *Chronicles of Oklahoma* 7 (March 1929): 58–105.

Finckh, Alice H. "Gottfried Duden Views Missouri, 1824–1827, Part I." *Missouri Historical Review* 43 (July 1949): 334–43.

Foley, William E. *The Genesis of Missouri: From Wilderness Outpost to Statehood.* Columbia: University of Missouri Press, 1989.

———. "Territorial Politics in Frontier Missouri, 1804–1820." Ph.D. diss., University of Missouri–Columbia, 1967.

Forderhase, Rudolph Eugene. "Jacksonianism in Missouri from Predilection to Party, 1820–1836." Ph.D. diss., University of Missouri–Columbia, 1968.

Foreman, Carolyn Thomas. "Nathan Boone: Trapper, Manufacturer, Surveyor, Militiaman, Legislator, Ranger, Dragoon." *Chronicles of Oklahoma* 19 (December 1941): 322–47.

Foreman, Grant. *Advancing the Frontier, 1830–1860.* Norman: University of Oklahoma Press, 1933.

———. "Captain Nathan Boone's Survey Creek-Cherokee Boundary Line." *Chronicles of Oklahoma* 4 (1926): 356–65.

———. *The Five Civilized Tribes.* Norman: University of Oklahoma Press, 1934.

———. *Fort Gibson: A Brief History.* Norman: University of Oklahoma Press, 1936.

———. *Pioneer Days in the Early Southwest.* Cleveland: Arthur H. Clark, 1926.

Foreman, Grant, ed. "The Journal of Hugh Evans, Covering the First and Second Campaigns of the United States Dragoon

Regiment in 1834 and 1835." *Chronicles of Oklahoma* 3 (September 1925)): 175–215.

"Fort Des Moines (No. 1), Iowa." *Annals of Iowa* 3 (April–July 1898): 351–63.

Gardner, Charles K. *Dictionary of the Army of the United States.* New York: D. Van Nostrand, 1860.

Gardner, Hamilton. "The March of the First Dragoons from Jefferson Barracks to Fort Gibson in 1833–1834." *Chronicles of Oklahoma* 31 (Spring 1953): 22–36.

Godsey, Roy. "The Osage War, 1837." *Missouri Historical Review* 20 (October 1925): 96–100.

Goodwin, Cardinal L. "Early Explorations and Settlements of Missouri and Arkansas, 1803–1822." *Missouri Historical Review* 14 (April–July 1920): 385–424.

Gregg, Kate L. "The Boonslick Road in St. Charles County." *Missouri Historical Review* 27 (July 1933): 307–14.

———. "The Boonslick Road in St. Charles County, Part II." *Missouri Historical Review* 28 (October 1933): 9–16.

———. "Building of the First American Fort West of the Mississippi." *Missouri Historical Review* 30 (July 1936): 345–64.

———. "The History of Fort Osage." *Missouri Historical Review* 34 (July 1940): 439–88.

———. "The War of 1812 on the Missouri Frontier, Part I." *Missouri Historical Review* 33 (October 1938): 3–22.

———. "The War of 1812 on the Missouri Frontier, Part II." *Missouri Historical Review* 33 (January 1939): 184–202.

———. "The War of 1812 on the Missouri Frontier, Part III." *Missouri Historical Quarterly* 33 (April 1939): 326–48.

———. *Westward with Dragoons: The Journal of William Clark on His Expedition to Establish Fort Osage, August 25 to September 22, 1808.* Fulton, Mo.: Ovid Bell Press, 1937.

Hagan, William T. *The Sac and Fox Indians.* Norman: University of Oklahoma Press, 1958.

Harlan, Edgar B., ed. "Colonel Henry Dodge and His Regiment of Dragoons on the Plains in 1834." *Annals of Iowa* 17 (January 1930): 173–97.

Hauberg, John H. "The Black Hawk War, 1831–1832." *Illinois State Historical Society, Transactions, 1932,* 91–134.

Hickey, Donald R. *The War of 1812: A Forgotten Conflict.* Urbana: University of Illinois Press, 1989.

Hildreth, James. *Dragoon Campaigns to the Rocky Mountains.* 1836. Reprint, New York: Arno Press, 1973.

Horsman, Reginald. *The War of 1812.* New York: Alfred A. Knopf, 1969.

Houck, Louis. *A History of Missouri.* Vols. 2, 3. Chicago: R. R. Donnelley and Sons, 1908.

Hulston, John K. "Daniel Boone's Sons in Missouri." *Missouri Historical Review* 41 (July 1947): 361–72.

Hunt, Elvid. *History of Fort Leavenworth, 1827–1927.* Fort Leavenworth, Kans.: General Service Schools Press, 1926.

Hutslar, Donald A. *The Architecture of Migration: Log Construction in the Ohio Country, 1750–1850.* Athens: Ohio University Press, 1986.

Isern, Thomas D. "Jefferson's Salt Mountain: The Big Salt Plain of the Cimarron River." *Chronicles of Oklahoma* 58 (Summer 1980): 160–75.

Jackson, Donald. "The Black Hawk War." *Palimpsest* 43 (February 1962): 65–94.

Journal of the Missouri State Convention. St. Louis, 1820.

Kappler, Charles H., ed. *Indian Affairs: Laws and Treaties.* Vol. 2. Washington, D.C.: Government Printing Office, 1904.

Lambert, Joseph I. "The Black Hawk War." *Journal of the Illinois State Historical Society* 32 (December 1939): 442–73.

Littlefield, Daniel F., Jr., and Lonnie E. Underhill. "Fort Coffee and Frontier Affairs, 1834–1838." *Chronicles of Oklahoma* 54 (Fall 1976): 314–38.

Mahon, John K. *The War of 1812.* Gainesville: University of Florida Press, 1972.

March, David D. *The History of Missouri.* Vol. 1. New York: Lewis, 1967.

Marshall, Thomas Maitland, ed. *The Life and Papers of Frederick Bates.* 2 vols. St. Louis: Missouri Historical Society, 1926.

Mathews, John Joseph. *The Osages: Children of the Middle Waters.* Norman: University of Oklahoma Press, 1961.

McCandless, Perry G. *A History of Missouri, Volume II: 1820 to 1860.* Columbia: University of Missouri Press, 1972.

———. "Thomas Hart Benton, His Source of Political Strength

in Missouri from 1815 to 1838." Ph.D. diss., University of Missouri–Columbia, 1953.

McLoughlin, William G. *After the Trail of Tears: The Cherokees' Struggle for Sovereignty, 1839–1880*. Chapel Hill: University of North Carolina Press, 1993.

National Register of Historic Places, Inventory Nomination Form, Daniel Boone Home, Prepared November 20, 1972. Department of Natural Resources, Jefferson City, Missouri.

Nichols, Roger L. *Black Hawk and the Warrior's Path*. Arlington Heights, Ill.: Harlan Davidson, 1992.

———. "The Black Hawk War: Another View." *Annals of Iowa* 36 (Winter 1963): 525–33.

Parrott, J. C. "The First United States Dragoons." *Iowa Historical Record* 6 (July 1890): 523–26.

Patterson, Nicholas. "The Boon's Lick Country." *Missouri Historical Society Bulletin* 6 (July 1950): 442–71.

Pattison, William D. *Beginnings of the American Rectangular Land Survey System, 1784–1800*. Columbus: Ohio Historical Society, 1970.

Pelzer, Louis. *Henry Dodge*. Iowa City: State Historical Society of Iowa, 1911.

———. *Marches of the Dragoons in the Mississippi Valley*. Iowa City: State Historical Society of Iowa, 1917.

Pelzer, Louis, ed. "A Frontier Officer's Military Order Book." *Mississippi Valley Historical Review* 6 (September 1919): 260–67.

———. "A Journal of Marches by the First United States Dragoons, 1834–1835." *Iowa Journal of History and Politics* 7 (July 1909): 331–78.

Peterson, William J. "The Terms of Peace." *Palimpsest* 43 (February 1962): 95–113.

Prucha, Francis Paul. *American Indian Treaties: The History of a Political Anomaly*. Berkeley and Los Angeles: University of California Press, 1994.

———. "Distribution of Regular Army Troops before the Civil War." *Military Affairs* 16 (Winter 1952): 169–73.

———. *The Great Father: The United States Government and the American Indians*. Vol. 1. Lincoln: University of Nebraska Press, 1984.

————. *The Sword of the Republic: The United States Army on the Frontier, 1783–1846.* Lincoln: University of Nebraska Press, 1986.

Roberts, Robert B. *Encyclopedia of Historic Forts: The Military, Pioneer, and Trading Posts of the United States.* New York: Macmillan, 1988.

Rohrbough, Malcolm J. *The Land Office Business: The Settlement and Administration of American Public Lands, 1789–1837.* New York: Oxford University Press, 1968.

————. *The Trans-Appalachian Frontier: People, Societies, and Institutions, 1775–1850.* New York: Oxford University Press, 1978.

Rollings, Willard H. *The Osage: An Ethnohistorical Study of Hegemony on the Prairie-Plains.* Columbia: University of Missouri Press, 1992.

Rooney, Elizabeth B. "The Story of the Black Hawk War." *Wisconsin Magazine of History* 40 (Summer 1957): 271–83.

Salter, William, ed. "Henry Dodge: Colonel U.S. Dragoons, 1833–1836, Part I." *Iowa Historical Record* 7 (April 1891): 101–19.

————. "Henry Dodge: Colonel U.S. Dragoons, 1833–1836, Part II." *Iowa Historical Record* 8 (April 1892): 251–67.

Shirk, George H. "Peace on the Plains." *Chronicles of Oklahoma* 28 (Spring 1930): 2–41.

Shoemaker, F. C. *Missouri's Struggle for Statehood, 1804–1821.* New York: Russell and Russell, 1969.

Spraker, Hazel A. *The Boone Family: A Genealogical History.* Rutland, Vt.: Tuttle, 1922.

"Texan Diplomatic Correspondence, Part II." *Annual Report of the American Historical Association, 1908.* Pt. 1, vol. 2. Washington, D.C.: Government Printing Office, 1911.

Thwaites, Reuben Gold. *Daniel Boone.* New York: Appleton, 1911.

————. "The Story of the Black Hawk War." *Wisconsin Historical Collection* 12 (1892): 217–65.

Utley, Robert M. *Frontiersmen in Blue: The United States Army and the Indian, 1848–1865.* New York: Macmillan, 1967.

Van der Zee, Jacob. "Forts in the Iowa Country." *Iowa Journal of History and Politics* 12 (April 1914): 163–204.

————. "The Neutral Ground." *Iowa Journal of History and Politics* 13 (July 1915): 311–48.

Viles, Jonas. "Population and Extent of Settlement in Missouri before 1804." *Missouri Historical Review* 5 (July 1911): 189–213.

Walker, Wayne T. "Nathan Boone: The Forgotten Hero." *Journal of the West* 28 (April 1979): 85–94.

Wesley, Edgar Bruce. "Life at a Frontier Post." *Journal of the American Military Institute* 3 (Winter 1939): 203–9.

Westover, John Glendower. "The Evolution of the Missouri Militia, 1804–1919." Ph.D. diss., University of Missouri–Columbia, 1948.

Whitcomb, Mary R. "Reminiscences of Gen. James C. Parrott." *Annals of Iowa* 3 (April–July 1898): 364–83.

Woodward, Grace Steele. *The Cherokees.* Norman: University of Oklahoma Press, 1963.

Young, Otis E. "The United States Mounted Ranger Battalion, 1832–1833." *Mississippi Valley Historical Review* 41 (1954–1955): 453–70.

INDEX